The Wedgwood/Darwin Dynasty

by

Imelda Clift

Imelda Clift
With my best wishes
2008

Published by

MELROSE BOOKS

An Imprint of Melrose Press Limited
St Thomas Place, Ely
Cambridgeshire
CB7 4GG, UK
www.melrosebooks.com

FIRST EDITION

Copyright © Imelda Clift 2008

The Author asserts her moral right to
be identified as the author of this work

Cover designed by Matt Stephens

ISBN 978-1-906050-80-1

Printed and bound in Great Britain by:
Biddles, 24 Rollesby Road, Hardwick Industrial Estate,
King's Lynn. Norfolk PE30 4LS

CONTENTS

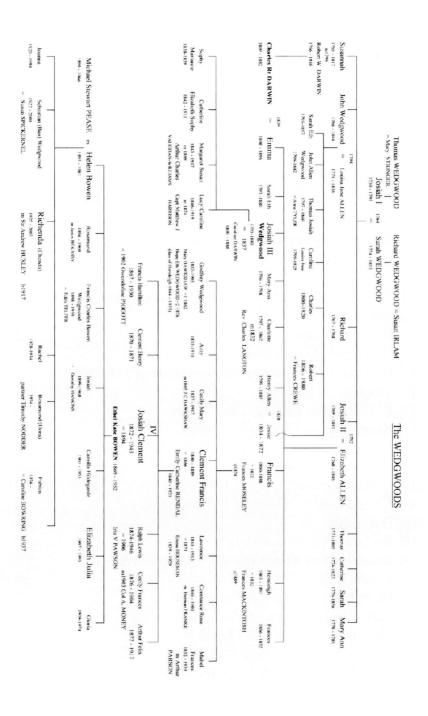

The WEDGWOODS

CONTENTS (cont.)

LIST OF ILLUSTRATIONS

LIST OF ILLUSTRATIONS (cont.)

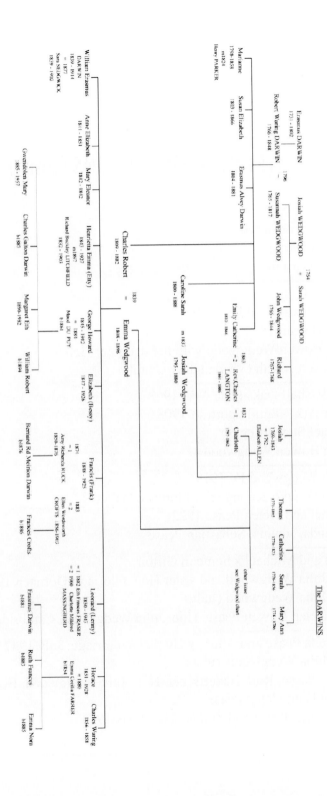

The DARWINS

Foreword
by
RICHENDA, LADY HUXLEY

How refreshing to read about one's ancestors through their family life and not through their works.

My grandfather Josiah IV describes a conversation he had, as a young man, with Gladstone. He – Jos – impudently quoted Napoleon's marshals who, being twitted about their lack of ancestors, replied, 'Nous somme, nous-mêmes des ancêtres!'

Well, yes, quite so: we're all ancestors, and how interesting to read about the ones often left out – the women and their home lives. Imelda Clift has written charmingly about Wedgwood women and throws new light on Wedgwood lives – some very different Wedgwood women.

Sally, wife of Josiah I, immersed in her life with her disabled husband.

Emma, wife of Charles Darwin, splendidly does the same – but holds firmly to her own religion.

Ethel, wife of Josiah IV, had an active, impulsive political husband with whose politics she gladly joined. But then she just as impulsively left him, determined to go her own way after a notorious divorce.

My mother Helen Pease (née Wedgwood) had an active husband with whom she shared a full life of family, politics, local government, home and garden. I used to complain, as a joke, that I was dragged up on sewerage – mostly villages had piped water – the difficulty was getting away the dirty water safely!!

While Julia, unmarried and a comparative invalid and so unlike the others – yet shared their determination to hold to her own beliefs in her own way. Imelda Clift probably knew her better than any of us and from that knowledge has been able to highlight the lives of the other Wedgwood women – a delightful book.

Richenda, Lady Huxley

BIOGRAPHICAL NOTE

Imelda Clift is married and has lived in Cambridge with her husband Donald since 1976. Prior to that time Donald was in the Coldstream Guards and the couple lived either abroad or in Surrey and London. They have four grown-up children: three boys and a girl. Donald is a Londoner and Imelda is from the west of Ireland.

For seven years until 1996 Imelda worked for the *Financial Times* in London as Secretary/PA to the Managing Director at the FT Printing site in the Docklands: before that she was senior secretary to the Managing Director at Heffers Stationers in Cambridge. She worked part-time at the Royal Patriotic Fund Corporation in Queen Anne's Gate, London, from April 1997 to 1998. Since then she has been working on this book.

PREFACE AND ACKNOWLEDGEMENTS

Acknowledgement must first go to the Trustees of the Wedgwood Museum for permission to research the Wedgwood accumulation at the Museum at Barlaston, Stoke-on-Trent, and part of it on loan to Keele University. Grateful thanks to the Curator of the Museum, Gaye Blake Roberts and her staff, who always welcomed me into their very busy office, where their encouragement and enthusiasm (and coffee!) always gave me a boost.

At Keele University Library my sincere thanks go to Martin Phillips (now retired) and Helen Burton, the Archivist, who have been patient and most helpful during my visits to the Archives.

My thanks also to Derek Tatton (now retired) and his staff at the Wedgwood Memorial College, who found me a bed at the College on those nights when I could not face the M6!

I am indebted to various members of the Wedgwood family – particularly the late Richenda, Lady Huxley, the late Dr John Wedgwood in London, and the late Dr Joanna Pease – for their help and enthusiasm at all times, also thanks to Anne Makeig-Jones for sharing past memories with me.

In Switzerland, many thanks to Kim and Andy Leadbeater for translating my interviews with the Hon. Julia Wedgwood's friends in Germany.

Cambridge University Library saved me many hours of research for which I am very grateful.

My research was both a voyage of discovery and a delight in the people I met, many of whom are now my friends. One very knowledgeable man I met in 1998 was Ernest Warrillow who wrote amongst other things, *The History of Etruria*. Ernest and his wife Molly – both almost blind – lived at Horton Hall, Horton, near Leek. His notepaper stated he was 'Lord of the Manor of Horton, Staffs'. An accumulation of his photographs and books is also at Keele University and he graciously gave me permission to quote from his history of Etruria. Ernest died in January 2000 and with many of his friends I attended his funeral in Horton.

In 'Wedgwood country' I visited houses and places which had been part of their lives; Etruria Hall is now a hotel. It actually exists as the central part of the Moat-House and is quite easy to recognise from early depictions. The present owner of Maer Hall, Mr Barry Fradley, showed me around the Hall and when I walked in the grounds I imagined Emma and Charles Darwin strolling there deep in conversation. The Upper House in Barlaston, built by Francis Wedgwood, is now a hotel, different but the same. Its owner, Ms Anne Williams, welcomes me there and I have slept in what used to be Francis's bedroom, not austere as in the days of the Potter's habitation, but now luxurious and very comfortable. The Potteries are now a familiar place, the Wedgwood Museum staff at Barlaston a refuge in times of pessimistic uncertainty, Keele University an ever open door. It is sad when the research is finished and there is no legitimate excuse to chase up to Wedgwood country ...

Cambridge features often in the latter part of this book, which makes research material rather more accessible as I live there. Emma Darwin's second home, 'The Grove' on Huntington Road, is still standing – seemingly unchanged on the outside – behind what is now Fitzwilliam College and is used as accommodation for the College's students. The Hon. Helen Bowen Pease's family is alive and well; Sir Andrew Huxley continues to live in Grantchester and one of Helen's grandchildren lives with his family in her old home at Reynolds Close.

During my research on Helen Bowen Pease, on a more personal level I must acknowledge her daughter Richenda (Lady Huxley). She was always there for me, always willing to look at and advise on what I had written. She also gave me access to numerous letters and family photographs. When Richenda died in April 2003, after a short illness, her loss was felt by many, many people. Later, having attended a memorial service for her and listened to all the tributes and activities she had been engaged in during her life in Cambridge, I am even more grateful that she found time for me.

Inevitably some other people mentioned in this story have passed away since going into print and for this I am sad.

Last but not least my thanks to my husband Donald, my family and dear friends for putting up with the subject of 'The Book' all this time.

INTRODUCTION

Always the first question I am asked is 'Why choose to write about the Wedgwood family?' Then I tell how I met the Hon. Julia Wedgwood – the second youngest daughter of Josiah IV Lord Wedgwood of Barlaston. Julia was the last surviving member of his immediate family. In 1978, when we first met, Julia was seventy-one years of age. I met her amongst another group of friends here in Cambridge and she and I became friends. After my mother died in 1988 Julia – in a spiritual sense – was like a mother to me.

In the early 1990s I decided I wanted to write, but was not sure exactly what to write about, and then I began to think of Julia and her family background. Julia, at that time, was living with her niece, Dr Joanna Pease, in Histon, Cambridge. Joanna was the daughter of Julia's oldest sister, the Hon. Helen Pease.

I did some research using books already in print about Wedgwood in general, but I wanted to concentrate particularly on family life.

This biography begins with the friendship and eventual union between the families of Josiah Wedgwood (1730 – 1795) and Erasmus Darwin (1731 – 1802)

To help make sense of who's who, I have enclosed two relevant family trees.

In 1764 Josiah Wedgwood married his distant cousin Sarah (1734 – 1815). They had eight children. There is a Josiah through all the generations, but this Josiah is the man who put the name Wedgwood on the map and made it famous throughout the world. Sarah was both his loving wife and his helpmate. Their first child, Susannah, married Robert Darwin, son of Erasmus Darwin.

Susannah and Robert had six children, one son being Charles Darwin (1809 – 1882). Charles married his first cousin Emma Wedgwood (1808 – 1896) daughter of Josiah and Sarah's son Josiah II.

As it will be seen on the Wedgwood family tree, cousins marrying cousins does cause some confusion, for instance Emma Darwin's mother-in-law Susannah was also her aunt, Susannah, being Josiah II's sister!

The story continues with the marriage in 1839 between Robert Darwin's son Charles (1809 – 1882) and Emma Wedgwood (1808 – 1896), daughter of Josiah I's son Josiah II.

Also prominent in this story are the following: Josiah (IV) Clement Wedgwood (1872 – 1943) who married his first cousin, Ethel Kate Bowen (1869 – 1952) Ethel's mother, Frances Rendel Bowen and Josiah's mother, Emily Rendel Wedgwood, were sisters. Two daughters of Josiah (IV) and Ethel were Helen (1895 – 1981) and Elizabeth Julia (1907 – 1993).

Helen Bowen Wedgwood was an easy choice for inclusion. Her life was full and fascinating and she was very much a part of the political and social scene in Cambridge. Also Julia Wedgwood was my dear friend and the main inspiration for writing about her and her family.

Then Ethel Bowen Wedgwood played a very important and crucial part in the lives of her husband and children. Her decision to change her whole way of life also changed and influenced the lives of others near to her. Ethel is a necessary part of the whole picture concerning her daughters Helen and Julia.

My biggest problem – some people might see it as an advantage – was the amount of material available on Wedgwood – letters and documents in various archives, as well as present-day members of the family happy to help in my research. When, on the occasion of my first visit to Keele University Library Special Collections & Archives, where the accumulation is on loan from the Wedgwood Museum at Barlaston, I requested certain papers, the sight of Archivist Martin Phillips wheeling in a trolley full of boxes and files almost caused my courage to desert me!

This book is based largely on correspondence covering a period of almost three hundred years. The letters are all from primary sources. They have been sifted carefully and quoted directly from *so much* correspondence, because they express the thoughts of their writers more eloquently than any words I could write.

All these people became real when I held their actual letters in my hand, becoming familiar with their writing styles as I followed their everyday lives. I cried when they lost their children, felt outraged when, in Sarah's case, she was rarely mentioned in books written about her husband, hated the bad influence certain people had on Sarah's son Tom.

Emma's diaries were a personal insight into her everyday life and eventually I could sometimes read between the lines.

At all times I have tried to avoid making assumptions or making statements without proof and have endeavoured to portray a true picture of these Wedgwood families.

IC

PART I:

WEDGWOOD/DARWIN DYNASTY

Chapter 1

RELATIVE VALUES

Sarah Wedgwood grew up in the peaceful countryside of Spen Green, Cheshire. She was the only daughter of Richard Wedgwood. Her father was the eldest brother of wealthy potters Thomas and John Wedgwood, of the Big House, Burslem, Stoke. Richard, unlike his brothers, began as a cheese supplier but became a successful merchant and banker, owning 75 acres at Spen Green. Sarah received a good education, above average for a girl at that time. Her home life was happy and secure and this was reflected in her attitude. In 1760, when she was twenty-six, her mother died. Sarah took charge of their home. She was practical, intelligent, and enjoyed her new responsibilities. As an only daughter she was wealthy and if her brother John, two years older, should die before her, she would inherit her father's entire estate.

For Sarah, social gatherings were usually within the extensive Wedgwood circle of relations. In the mid-18th century, out of 42 potworks at Burslem, six belonged to the Wedgwood family.

One distant cousin, Josiah, was known to Sarah and they became better acquainted in the late 1750s when he fell ill and she visited him. After that, she saw him during her visits to the Big House at Burslem, home of her uncles, where Josiah was a neighbouring potter at the Ivy House. Sarah always enjoyed visiting her uncles. Her long hair flying out behind her, she would ride pillion on her father's horse when Richard frequently visited his brothers. She and Josiah continued to see each other – he would ride his horse Taffy the ten miles to Spen Green. Soon the couple realised how they felt about each other and wished to marry. Sarah had grown up pale and slim with reddish hair and blue eyes – not beautiful, but her air of self-assurance was attractive. Her sense of humour and strong feeling of family tradition were also endearing.

By 1763 Josiah was only in his thirties, but was already a successful businessman. Apart from a right knee crippled by smallpox when young, he was in his prime – self-confidence and ambition were his greatest strengths. He wasn't handsome but had a robust, vital air, not too tall, stockily built, a nose a little too big but eyes that seemed to be forever looking towards far horizons. Born in July 1730, he was the youngest of the thirteen children of Thomas and Mary Wedgwood. They lived near a pot works by the churchyard at Burslem. The works had belonged to Thomas's father, and his father before him.

During Josiah's courtship he continued to improve his position as a potter. He rented, from Sarah's uncles, working premises for £10 per annum, plus a small adjacent cottage, Ivy House. He employed his second cousin, Thomas Wedgwood, as his manager.

Richard Wedgwood saw the strong attraction between his beloved daughter and Josiah but felt Sarah could have made a better match – the fact that she would be rich one day heightened his awareness of Josiah's lack of capital. As an heiress, on marriage her estate would go to her husband. Sarah was sure of her love for Josiah and his feelings for her, but understood her father's reluctance to let her go. She followed Josiah's career with great attention and teased her father about their shared characteristics. He had to agree.

Richard admired Josiah for his strength of purpose and for establishing himself as an independent potter, but was he a worthy suitor? Finally, after close inspection of Josiah's business, he saw that the couple were determined to get married. He met Josiah and requested certain formalities and provisos before giving his consent.

In 1762 Josiah had befriended a successful businessman, Thomas Bentley. They corresponded frequently and on 9th January 1764 Josiah wrote about Sarah – he sounded impatient:

My Dear Friend,
I had acknowledged the receipt of your very kind Letter
before now, but hoped by waiting a post or two to be able
either to tell you of my happiness, or at least the time
I expected to be made so. But 'O Grief of Griefs' that

pleasure is still deni'd me, & I cannot bear to keep my friend in suspence any longer, though I own myself somewhat ashamed and greatly mortified, to be still kept at bay from those exalted pleasures you have often told me (& I am very willing to believe) attend the Married state. ... I have gone through a long series of bargain making – of settlemts Reversions, Provisions &c:&c: Gone through it did I say. Wo^d to Hymen I had, No I am still in the Attorneys hands from which I hope it is no harm to pray 'good L^d. deliver me'. Miss W. & I are perfectly agreed, & could settle the whole affair in 3 lines and so many minutes, but our Pappa, over carefull of his daughters interest wo^d by some demands which I cannot comply with, go near to separate us, if we were not better determined. On Friday next Mr W. & I are to meet in great form, with each of us our Attorney, which I hope will be conclusive, you shall then hear farther from

Your obliged & very affectionate fr^d

Josiah Wedgwood[1]

Two weeks later on 23rd January he again wrote to Thomas:

... All matters being amicably settled betwixt my Pappa (Elect) & myself, I yesterday prevailed upon my dear Girl to name the day, the blissful day! When she will reward all my faithfull services, & take me in her Arms! To her Nuptial bed! To – Pleasures which I am yet ignorant of, and you, my dear friend, can much better conceive than I shall ever be able to express. In three words, we are to be married on Wednesday next... [2]

Top: *Engraving of the Ivy House Works in Burslem, from Eliza Meteyard's work on the life of Josiah Wedgwood, published in 1965.*

Above Left: *Portrait, oil on canvas, of Josiah Wedgwood I, founder of the Wedgwood Company (1730 − 1795), painted in late 1782 by Sir Joshua Reynolds.*

Above: *Sarah Wedgwood, wife of the founder of the Wedgwood Company, Josiah I (1730 − 95), oil on canvas, painted by Sir Joshua Reynolds circa 1782/83.*

Left: *Oil on canvas, portrait of Thomas Bentley, after an original by John Francis Rigaud.*

Photos courtesy of the Wedgwood Museum Trust, Barlaston, Staffordshire

Chapter 2

NEW LIFE – LUNAR GROUP

Sarah and Josiah were married on 25th January 1764 at Astbury in Cheshire, and Richard Wedgwood, whom Josiah forever afterwards addressed as 'Father', gave a grand party to celebrate the union. Afterwards Josiah wrote to Bentley and referred to himself and his new bride as '*two married Lovers, happy as this world can make them*'.

Sarah chose wisely in Josiah – she too was intelligent with a lively mind and an eagerness to become part of a future that promised to be exciting and innovative. Josiah not only had a wonderful vision of the future but also the gift of inspiring those around him. Sarah knew she and Josiah were at the beginning of a great journey, but even in her wildest dreams could never have foreseen that this new dynasty in the late 18th century would make 'Wedgwood' a household name for centuries to come.

Sarah's first home with Josiah was the Ivy House, covered in greenery, modest and much smaller than Spen Green. Where before she had been surrounded by fields and quiet surroundings, she was now amidst kilns and smoking chimneys. The house was near the middle of Burslem. A small enclosed garden at the front overlooked Green Bank, a green in name only, now an open space where children played among clay and broken pot shards.

But she was in love, and happy to exchange her father's large house for her very own home with her husband. Among her belongings from Spen Green, she brought her spinning wheel, at which she was adept. The workplace remained the same, the pottery industry continued in its familiar way and Sarah was still within an environment she knew and with which she was comfortable. She settled into her new role with anticipation and pleasure.

By 1764 the war between France and Spain had just ended. At that time families in circumstances similar to Josiah Wedgwood were classed as the new commercial aristocracy. England's government recognised them as a major and important contributor to the economy. At this period, particularly in the Midlands the industrial revolution was gathering pace. The majority of work once done in the home was transferred to the factory with its power-driven machinery. Many workers moved from their rural way of life to an urban environment. This change in the manufacture of goods continued to grow over the next 70 years.

The inventiveness of men of that time, their wish to improve what was already there and in many instances their ambition to become more prosperous, were all instrumental in fuelling the industrial revolution. These men all fed each other's enthusiasms and ambitions, but more rewarding – they shared their knowledge.

Many of them became friends, and dined at each other's houses, sometimes accompanied by their wives. Sarah was a willing partner in all of this. As a woman in the mid-18th century, she was unusually intelligent, had a good knowledge of business and actually worked in her husband's interests and must have stood out as an independent individual. She was a willing secretary, she knew what was happening in his business, he shared his problems with her, his successes, his failures, his decisions. She did not simply act as hostess when her husband's colleagues visited them, but participated in discussions – and her contributions were respected. These meetings introduced Sarah to great thinkers. Here are brief notes on early members of the Lunar Group:

Matthew Boulton, a sociable, gregarious man, was the instigator of one such get-together early in 1765 that led to the forging of lifelong friendships. His home, Soho House (and Works) in Birmingham, was always a welcome venue. He had water power but experimented continually with steam. The meetings usually took place when the moon was full – to give people some light on their way home. Hence the group was called the Lunar Group and later the Lunar Circle.

Although informal in its structure and procedures, it became a most informative and important centre of knowledge and influence.

Dr Erasmus Darwin, grandfather of Charles, was a leading member of the Lunar Group, became a lifelong friend of Josiah, and also his family doctor. A large, ungainly man with an embarrassing stammer, he nevertheless had a charming manner and made friends easily. He was brilliant, with a free-thinking and inventive mind, not only a scientist and a popular and successful physician but also with a great love of literature. He wrote prose but his first love was poetry, for which he gained countrywide acclaim.

Josiah Wedgwood, with his varied interests, was a valuable Group member. Apart from his work for better transport conditions, he was a scientific potter and an astute businessman.

Richard Lovell Edgeworth, only son of wealthy Anglo-Irish parents, was interested in the movement of wheel carriages by steam.

Thomas Day was a thinker rather than a doer. He wrote eloquently on politics, morality and education.

James Watt, the inventor, steam power being his main objective. In 1767 he visited Mathew Boulton's engineering works and they agreed that Watt would experiment on steam engines at the Soho factory.

Dr W Small was a Professor of Natural Philosophy.

Dr Joseph Priestley was a chemist and mathematician.

James Keir was a soldier and friend of Erasmus Darwin. Having met members of the Society he left the Army and became part of the Group.

Shortly after his marriage Josiah wrote to his older brother John, who worked for him in London:

> *Sally* [Sarah's nickname] *is my chief helpmate in this as well as other things, and that she may not be hurried by having too many Irons in the fire, as the phrase is, I have ordered the spinning wheel into the Lumber room. She hath learned my characters, at least to write them, but can scarcely read them at present.*[1]

Elizabeth Meteyard has written about Josiah's reliance on his wife:

> *[he] ... consults her invariably sound judgment, as he finds it to be, in matters of form, ornament & combined results, and here dismisses to the lumber room the spinning wheel which has accompanied her from Spen Green, for he is*

soon aware that more intellectual vocations befit her.[2]

Thomas Bentley had become an integral part of Josiah's business, a man who, after Sarah, would become his closest friend and confidant. In Thomas, Sarah also found a staunch and true friend with whom she worked in harmony over the years. When Thomas and Josiah first met in Liverpool, he was a successful general merchant. Born on New Year's Day 1730, Thomas had had a good education, and was an intellectual, as were his circle of friends, whom he was happy to share with Josiah. In 1759, Thomas's wife died in childbirth. Her sister Elizabeth became his housekeeper. Thomas and Josiah complemented each other in their attitude to life – where Josiah was go-ahead, enthusiastic and an entrepreneur, Thomas was cautious, with a clear business mind, and rarely impulsive.

During their successful business partnership from 1768 to 1780, Josiah and Thomas, because they were seldom in the same place at the same time, conducted their business through numerous letters. The greatest source of insight into Sarah's life with Josiah comes from these letters.

Chapter 3

CHILDREN – NEW FACTORY SITE – TRAGEDY OF A BROTHER AND SON

A first child, Susannah, was born to Sarah and Josiah in January 1765, a year after their wedding. Josiah invited his brother John to her christening and wrote of their new baby, who already had a pet name:

> *Sukey is a fine, sprightly lass, and will bear a good deal of dandleing, and you can sing – lulaby Baby – whilst I rock the cradle, but I shall hardly find time for nursing as we have another Turnpike broke out amongst us here betwixt Leek and Newcastle and they have – vi et Armis –* [1]

Josiah was referring to his involvement in the quest for better transport. He became a leading campaigner for good roads and canals. Around Burslem there were approximately 150 separate potteries, finding work for nearly 7000 people. Essentials were supplied by travelling hucksters and packmen on horseback, but in bad weather the roads were almost impassable because of mud and pot-holes.

Also in January Josiah wrote to Thomas on his current role:

> *I scarcely know without a good deal of recollection whether I am a Landed Gentleman, an Engineer or a Potter, for indeed I am all three and many other characters by turn.* [2]

The following year their son John arrived. When he was two, Sarah and Josiah decided to have their children inoculated against smallpox. Inoculation was very new in 1767 and they were both apprehensive, but Dr Darwin was in favour and they trusted his advice. Afterwards, in a letter to Thomas Josiah expressed their doubts:

> *I thank you for your kind solicitude for our Children, they are now past the worst, and I hope out of danger from that terrible disorder the smallpox.*
>
> *They both had convulsions at the first appearance of the eruptions, and have had a pretty smart pox as our Doctor terms it. I believe they have had no dangerous symptoms, but have been so very ill that I confess I repented what we had done, and I much question whether we should have courage to repeat the experiment, if we had any more subjects for it.[3]*

Life was good. Sarah now had two young children, her husband's business was increasingly successful and in 1765, after Queen Charlotte had ordered a complete tea service, Josiah had his bills and letterheads proudly printed with 'Josiah Wedgwood, Potter to Her Majesty'. He and Sarah enjoyed both the prestige and the subsequent new business.

Josiah looked around for a larger site on which to build a new factory, while Sarah knew a larger house was needed. After much searching Josiah bought for approximately £3,000 an estate of some 350 acres a few miles outside Burslem.

There was enough room to build a factory and a new home for his family, plus a house for Thomas Bentley. Josiah also had plans to build accommodation for his workers.

Work began on the factory in 1767 and took two years to complete. The new home for Sarah and their family was under way and Sarah was involved in all the plans. Although Thomas Bentley was busy with the new factory, Sarah also often sought his advice when arranging both her home and gardens. Josiah, in a letter to Thomas, said:

> *... she will not fix upon a spot for either house or Gardens, no nor even the stables till you have viewed and given your opinion of the premises.[4]*

Josiah recognised the importance of including women as valuable customers for his wares and always welcomed Sarah's ideas. In his letter to Thomas in 1767, when contemplating buying larger premises in London he wrote:

> ... when you will have the advantage of your good sister's thoughts upon the subjects as you go through them, which is no inconsiderable advantage. I speak from experience in Female taste, without which I should have made but a poor figure amongst my Potts, not one of which of any consequence, is finished without the Approbation of my Sally. I have given your love to her which she received very kindly, and in return hath sent you a watch, by way of a love token I suppose ...[5]

The summer of 1767 was tinged with tragedy when Josiah's brother John, aged forty-six, was drowned in London. One night in June when he was walking home, having dined at the Swan restaurant in Westminster, he accidentally fell into the Thames at a spot where the lighting was poor. Josiah was unable to attend his funeral, as Sarah was expecting their third child and he was reluctant to leave her. Richard, a second son was born on 2nd July, but his life was to prove all too brief.

Josiah's infected knee continued to cause him pain and finally he decided to have that leg amputated below the knee, a courageous choice at a time when surgery was in its infancy. On 28th May 1768, ever after referred to by Josiah as St Amputation Day – two surgeons sedated him with laudanum and performed the operation. His good friend Thomas Bentley was in attendance. Josiah 'would not be assisted, or have the operation hidden from his view; but seated in his chair, bore the unavoidable pain without a shrink or a groan ...'.[6]

For the remainder of his life he wore a wooden leg. Thomas remained with the couple afterwards to assist with the business and to support Sarah. Later, after Thomas had departed, Josiah wrote to him:

> ... At present I am well even beyond my most sanguine expectations, my leg is allmost healed, the wound is not quite 2 inches by one & half, I measured it with the compasses this morning when I dressed it. Yes, when I dressed it, for I have turned my Surgeon adrift and Sally

and I are sole managers now, only we give him leave to peep at it now and then, when he lifts up his hands and eyes, and will scarcely believe it to be the wound he dressed before ...[7]

Again on 20th June he wrote:

... have been to the Workhouse, and have had 2 airings in the Chaise – have left off my Laudanum and do better without it. The skin on the upper part of the wound is healed and got down to the bone, which I tell you to confute all those who deny the present to be an age of Miracles[8]

Tragically no miracle was forthcoming when the young couple's second son Richard caught a gastric infection, from which he died in June. Sarah's father came to stay, to help during Josiah's convalescence and to comfort his daughter. Sarah showed great strength of character in attending to Josiah, still weak after the amputation, while grieving for her lost son. She continued to deal with her husband's letters and tried to keep his everyday life free of problems. He made a good recovery and towards the end of 1768 Sarah, Josiah and his sister, Catherine Willet, went to London and visited the theatre.

Eliza Meteyard described the situation in the capital at that time. The new warehouse was on a corner of Newport Street and St Martin's Lane, including accommodation for Josiah and his family. A book-keeper/warehouseman and a housekeeper also lived there.

It is pleasant to catch glimpses of the preparations made for the Ladies comfort. New grates are put in some of the rooms; new beds and fenders are bought; a glass bookcase is set up in the drawing room; and a wealth of comfortable bedding comes up by waggon from Staffordshire. The little party travel leisurely in their own chariot accompanied by a maid-servant, and meet with the usual disagreeables in the winter season – bad roads and poor horses. But they make amends for all these things when they reach Newport Street. Bright fires glow. There are tea-parties, supper and rubbers at whist. ... There are gentlemen too in abundance; and Mr Wedgwood is the merriest among them, except when he is called away ...[9]

There are very few of Sarah's personal letters remaining but here is part of one she wrote to Thomas Bentley, who had gone to Burslem while they were away:

Thank you Dr Sir for my kind letter (Dr Sir says Mrs Willet that's more than I dare say) however I say again Thank you Dr Sir for saying such fine things of my Lad & I will thank you again for conveying that Smile to me I have seen it ever since & you do not cannot know how much good it has done me. Mrs Willett too let her say what she will is better for it for we have all things in common ... [Josiah] is rambled to the Parliament house to hear the debates ab^t the Preston election & when he will return nobody knows. We have variety of weather wet mornings & fine Afternoons which makes the Streets so dirty it prevents our rambling so much as we wish either by Moon or Sun however we omitt very few Oppertunitys & I can assure you are right busy on Saturday night Mr W & I were at Drury Lane to see Jane Shore & the Masquerade & were very much entertain'd they play much better than at the Other house. ... I know not when this way of life will end but certainly it cannot last always & indeed I do not wish it may... .

Mr Wedgwood joins me in Complem^{ts} to yourself and all enquiring Friends.

I am Sir Y^r much Obliged & Affectionate Friend

S WEDGWOOD[10]

A warm, gossipy letter to a friend, with a hint of flirtation when she mentions Thomas's 'smile'.

Sarah must have been glad to see the finish of 1768, when they could look ahead to the new factory, and, more exciting, their new home. Josiah had decided to name the works 'Etruria' and their new home 'Etruria Hall'.

Chapter 4

ETRURIA – NEW FACTORY – NEW HOME

By June of 1769 the main portion of the works was nearing completion and Josiah, Sarah (who was again pregnant) with their two children and friends, went to the works on 13th June to celebrate. Etruria was surrounded by high walls, except where bounded by the canal, and covered about seven acres of the old Ridge House estate, and it was felt that work was far enough advanced for an opening ceremony. Josiah sat before the pot-thrower's board while Thomas turned the wheel and Josiah threw six vases with a black basalt body, about 10 inches high and 5½ inches at the widest part.

> *They were fired at the close of July and in November were sent to London where they were painted in matt encaustic colours in the purest Etruscan style by David Rhodes. ... Within the fillet in the lower portion of the vases are inscribed the words "Artes Etruriae Renascuntur" (The Arts of Etruria are Re-born), whilst on the vases are the following words "June XIII M.DCC.LXIX".*[1]

Referring to these vases in a letter to Bentley on 19th November 1769, Josiah says:

> *The six Etruscan Vases ..., three handled, sent to you a fortnight since, were those we threw and turned the first at Etruria, and should be finished as high as you please, but not sold, they being first fruits of Etruria...*[2]

16

MRS. WEDGWOOD.   JOSIAH WEDGWOOD.

[FROM FLAXMAN'S MEDALLIONS.]

Top: *Wedgwood plaque, with a view showing Etruria Hall circa 1773, with the Trent & Mersey Canal in the foreground.*

Above Left: *Josiah Wedgwood, his wife Sarah and their family painted in the grounds of Etruria Hall in the Summer of 1780 by George Stubbs. Oil on wood panel.*

Above: *Oval Wedgwood plaque, portrait of Erasmus Darwin by George Stubbs, date 1783.*

Photos courtesy of the Wedgwood Museum Trust, Barlaston, Staffordshire

Left: *Sarah and Josiah I Medallions by Flaxman*

The house planned for Thomas Bentley was completed before Etruria Hall and became known as Bank House. Thomas never found it convenient to live there, however, as he needed to be in London, where the partners had a showroom in Charles Street, off Grosvenor Square. He moved from Liverpool in 1769 to London and bought a large house in Little Cheyne Row, Chelsea. Meanwhile Josiah's sister Catherine and her husband the Reverend William Willet moved into Bank House, which had also been used previously by Josiah and Sarah briefly while waiting for Etruria Hall to be completed.

A third son, Josiah II, was born to Sarah and Josiah in August 1769.

By November the Hall was ready and despite the absence of her husband on business, Sarah, en famille, moved to their new home. Josiah wrote to Bentley on 11th November:

> *... We were three days upon the road, though we lost no time and travelled a little by moonlight each evening, but at the last stage – Etruria – I was rewarded for all the risque and pains I had undergone in a tedious, long and dirty journey.*
>
> *I found my Sally and family at Etruria! just come there to take possession of the Etruscan plains, and sleep upon them for the first night. Was not all this very clever now of my own dear Girls contriving. She expected her Joss on the very evening he arrived had got the disagreeable business of removing all over, and I would not have been another night from home for the Indies.*
>
> *Tonight we are to sup 120 of your workmen in the Town Hall* [3]

The house itself, to match the personalities of both Josiah and Sarah, was without frills. It was not the house of an aristocrat, but solid and substantial, to suit a businessman with a family. This did not come cheaply – in the initial stages of building Etruria, Josiah complained that his architect, Joseph Pickford of Derby, had doubled his original estimate.

Samuel Warrillow wrote of the Hall:

The principal rooms of the Hall were large, lofty and tastefully decorated with terra cotta bas reliefs, and stained glass was used to advantage. From the windows of the great salon Etruria woods could be seen and the beautiful valley, stretching from Hartshill to Longport. In the salon there was a splendid collection of vases, medallions, cabinets of ware, gems and objects d'art...

The Library at Etruria Hall was a haven of peace stocked from floor to ceiling with books. The fireplaces in these rooms were in excellent taste, some designed by Adam, and often set with jasper plaques...[4]

Capability Brown was credited with landscaping the grounds around Etruria Hall (he and Josiah were acquainted), but it is more likely that William Emes did the landscaping. He is mentioned in accounts as having received £117.19.2 for work on the estate. The area around the Hall was enhanced to look like a park. Nine hundred trees were brought from Brompton Nursery in London, conservatories were built and a lake was formed.[5]

Sarah's view from her drawing room windows improved with the years, as trees and flowers grew in abundance. The Hall, built on a slight incline, was reached by a long drive. A smooth expanse of lawn swept down to the wide canal, with many saplings already established all around.

As promised the village for the workers and their families took shape at the upper end of the Works. One long street (with smaller offshoots) ran from the canal bridge towards the foot of the Etruria woods, with accommodation for some 200 Wedgwood employees. In time the village grew, to have its own church, schools, a wharf, the Etruscan bone mills and other buildings such as inns, a post office and huckster's shops. Wells gave a good supply of clear water. The houses had earth floors, well lit rooms of a decent size with windows of green glass.

Chapter 5

SARAH'S ILLNESS

Late in 1769 Sarah's greatest concern was Josiah's failing sight. He consulted the surgeon Mr James Bent, who diagnosed liver disease. Sarah again had to attend to Josiah and his correspondence. In a letter to Bentley on 6th December, Sarah wrote:

> *The complaint in Mr Wedgwood's eyes which he mentioned to you in London growing worse he has consulted Mr Bent who advises him to use them as little as possible and not to write by Candle light at all, for which reason he knows you will excuse his not writing. Mr Bent has ordered him to take some pukes; he has already taken one and thinks he is something better and is to take another tonight...* [1]

Shortly afterwards her father, Richard, became ill so Sarah, with baby Josiah, went back to her old home at Spen Green to be with him. During her absence Josiah became very depressed and pessimistic about both his eyesight and his health in general. He felt the danger of losing his sight greater than the loss of his leg. As soon as Richard improved, Josiah hurried to Spen Green to collect Sarah and baby Josiah. On their return home he wrote to Thomas Bentley on 22nd January 1770:

> *I left Spen Green yesterday and this time have brought my wife and child along with me — Etruria now becomes*

to brighten up, and looks like itself again, 5 long weeks
of absence have hung heavily upon me, but her aid was
much wanted to nurse and comfort an aged and worthy
parent; and I was well pleased that she was able to pay
this debt of duty and affection to him. [2]

For the rest of his life Josiah, in times of stress, suffered headaches, blurred vision and spots before his eyes.

Sarah's fifth child arrived one evening in May 1771, while Josiah was not at home. He wrote afterwards to Bentley:

...we had a Midwife attending here, but she is sent away
without her errand, and all things remain as they were.
My Wife as pert as a maggot & talks of holding out
another month P.S. ... This is chiefly to tell stories of my
Wife – Would you think, my dear friend, she could have
served me so slippery a trick? After my waiting here so
long to receive a certain present, that she should bring it
forth in my absence, when I had only turned my back of
home for a few minutes without thinking anything of the
matter. I left her at near 8 last night, to go for an hour to
our Club, quite well as usual. Came home before 10, and
just as I came into the house, little Tom (for so they call
him) came into the world, and a very fine lad they tell
me he is. A month old at least. And all are well as can be
expected ...[3]

Sarah suffered from rheumatism, which seemed to be more severe in winter. During 1772 socialising was curtailed, as the rheumatism became very severe. Eliza Meteyard maintained that Sarah became rheumatic from living in the damp of a new house. Despite his business commitments, Josiah was preoccupied with his wife's condition and found difficulty in concentrating on anything else. He was also about to open a showroom in Bath, but he had to stay in Burslem most of that year.

The many letters Josiah wrote about Sarah's health convey his deep concern for her welfare. Dr Eramus Darwin was in regular attendance at the Hall. Josiah wrote to Bentley in March 1772:

We had Dr Darwin with her yesterday. He says he is afraid her disorder will be stubborn, they have bled her twice and are now going to blister her. She is very ill, not the least help for herself. Her wrists, Shoulders, neck, Hips, knees, Ancles, & feet are all violently affected, & she is as complete a Cripple as you can easily imagine. Dr Darwin has ordered her to Buxton, to bathe there as soon as she is able, & I am nail'd down here as fast as a Rock ...[4]

On 6th April he wrote again:

Mrs Wedgwood is better, she can now walk to her bed & the fever has left her. I have mention'd going to Bath with her instead of Buxton Mr Bent is on my side & Dr Darwin rather against me, so that the matter is doubtful at present...[5]

Josiah was eager to take Sarah to Bath to take the waters, but it was the end of May before she felt up to the journey. The waters were supposed to help cure diseases of the skin, gout, rheumatism and infertility. Sarah just wanted to stop the pain.

Bath at that time was in its heyday. Fashionable society people went there at the height of summer to see and be seen. The Pump Room, a beautifully proportioned and very grand room, was a favourite place for people to relax, gossip and socialise. If Sarah had been feeling well, she too would have enjoyed the whole atmosphere, but she was not interested in Bath's social scene.

Josiah wrote to Bentley frequently about Sarah's condition. After two weeks in Bath he wrote again:

... the lameness continues so long in her knees & feet without any amendment that I cannot help being much concern'd least it should fix in those parts, especially her knees, as they seem the most affected, & make a crackling noise like dry'd parchment when-ever she bends them ...[6]

While they were away Thomas Bentley, a widower for more than a decade, decided to marry again. Sarah and Josiah were unable to be with him on his wedding day, but in July Sarah felt well enough to travel, so they left Bath for London to visit Thomas and his new wife, Mary, the daughter of a Derby engineer, Thomas Stamford, and fifteen years younger than Thomas.

Sarah became pregnant again some time in August. Josiah was concerned for her and when she felt unwell he put it down to her condition and wrote to Bentley voicing his fear of a miscarriage.

Later in August he wrote:

> ... I am very sorry to acquaint you that the flattering hopes I had conceived of her speedy recovery are all vanish'd. Her sickness & Vomiting, with all the unfavorable symptoms are return'd, & as Doctr. Darwin, who attended her yesterday, apprehends an inflamation of the Liver, & she is so extremely weak and emaciated I am really alarm'd for her safety, & in great distress. — But I must beg of you not to take any notice of this in your letters to me, only in generals of her not recovering so fast as we hoped for &c. [7]

Sarah miscarried in September. She was seriously ill and Dr Darwin warned Josiah that her recovery would be extremely slow. Josiah wrote to Bentley on 7th September:

> My Dear Friend, Mrs Wedgwood has had an extreme bad night, and miscarried this morning. Her situation is attended with much danger. Mr Bent says her case is the most singular one he has ever known & nothing but the greatest attention in nursing & keeping every thing quiet about her can save her life. I will write again in the morning ....

He continued on the 8th:

> Doctr Darwin, who has been here all night gives us more hopes of Mrs W—s recovery this morning than he could last night. She has had a very comfortable night, slept very well, & her Stomach retains the little food she takes into it. The Circumstances attending her miscarriage

reduc'd her so extremely low that we were all under the greatest apprehensions for her, but the Doctr gives us more hopes this morning, though he says her recovery will be extremely slow, & depend much upon some dropsical symptoms leaving her in a few days which Persons in her late situation are sometimes liable to.

I hope my Dear Friend will excuse me entering into any particular details of business whilst my mind is in this state of Anxiety & distress for the safety of my Dear Girl ... [8]

While Sarah was convalescing Josiah decided what she should eat and drink, and although her nurses were horrified, his remedy – including ripe plums and cider – seemed to work. In his next letter to his friend he wrote:

But well as we think her compared with her situation a few days since, you never saw such a changling, nothing but skin & bone, pale as her cap, & does not seem to have a drop of blood in (her) body. Her lips to day begin to incline towards a blush of red, & as she relishes what she eats I hope to give you a better account of her soon.

Doctr Darwin has left me to act as Physicion in his absense but I believe I shall not gain much credit in my office amongst the female Nurses here, as I have prescribed what they durst not think of for my Patient.

When nothing would stay upon her stomach I gave her fruit, ripe plumbs &c as often as she would eat them, & she has never vomited since. — For the wind, I have given her Cyder that blows the cork up to the Cieling. She relishes it vastly & it does her good. I hope to continue these good accts. to you ... [9]

Towards the end of September and into October Sarah began to regain her strength, but early in November she was again ill and on 2nd November Josiah wrote to Bentley:

An Ugly fever hangs upon her, with a sort of Ague fitte at uncertain periods which Mr Bent says are very bad symptoms & he thinks the only thing that can save her wod. be going to Italy or the south of France... [10]

On Dr Darwin's advice, Sarah was moved to his house at Lichfield where he could give her more attention and Josiah sounded much more cheerful when he wrote to Bentley from Lichfield on 9th November:

... My wife has not had any of her shivering fits since Wednesday last, & as she gets strength very fast in their absence, I am very willing to flatter myself that she will have no more

I shall return home tomorrow & leave Mrs W. with her Doct.r for a week or ten days, & hope the change of place, air & company will have a good effect – In her absense I am to make the revolution in our household, & if I can make so much time, take a trip into Lancashire to see our Children there ... [11]

Sarah remained at Lichfield for three weeks, returning home in time for Christmas with her family. Bentley had invited Josiah and Sarah to spend Christmas with himself and his new wife, Mary, in London, but Josiah, in his letter to him on 21st December, declined:

... thank you for your kind invitation of Mrs W & myself to keep our Xmass with you at Chelsea. My wife is not well enough to take such a journey at present, neither could she leave her little folks who are coming home to spend their Xmas Holidays with her. [12]

However, during the Christmas holiday Sarah had a relapse. Writing to Bentley Josiah said on 26th December:

I sho.d have wrote to my Dear Friend by Thursday mornings Post but my poor Girl was taken so ill that I could not employ a moment's attention to anything else. A sudden sickness and giddiness seized her betwixt nine and ten o'Clock, which was immediately followed by faintings, attended with cold sweats, and her legs and arms and face as cold as clay. In this terrible situation she continued for many hours when we thought every moment would be her last. When she could be sensible of anything she complained of most severe cold, which baffled all our endeavours with hot flanels, hot bricks, chafeing &c to remove 'till about 3 in the afternoon, when her natural heat began to return and her sickness began to abate a little, and from that time she has had no returns of it, and we are very willing to flatter ourselves with the pleasing hopes of her recovery, though that must be a work of time; she is again reduced to such an extreme weak state, and will be confined mostly to her bed for some time.

I sent for her favourite Esculapius [Dr Darwin] who came here last night and he is just now left us. He says if we can preserve her through the cold weather to April she will do very well, and make a perfect recovery in the summer. For this purpose he advises me to bring her to Lichfield as soon as she is able to travel so far with safety, the Air there being milder than with us, and from thence to take her to Bath for the Winter which he thinks will now be of great service to her. ... I would not have been from home on Thursday morning for a Kingdom, for the fate of my poor Sally was then several times so nicely balanced that a very little foolish treatment, a trifle, might have decided against her. This will make me very cautious of leaving her 'till her health is better established, and I shall from time to time advise you how that good work goes forward with us... [13]

More promising news came in his letter of 28th December:

I have the pleasure of telling my Dear fr.d that Mrs Wedgwood continues to recover tho' very slowly, she has sat up a little yesterday & to day, & I hope if we have no more relapses she may still be restor'd again to her family & friends, but it must be a work of time for she is extremely reduc'd by this last attack both in her strength & spirits... [14]

At the close of 1772 Sarah was feeling vulnerable and unsure of her future health. Previously she had been a strong woman, physically and mentally, but now those strengths had wavered. She was thirty when she married Josiah: it was not unusual in those days to marry late rather than early. By 1772, now aged thirty-eight, she had had six pregnancies, having miscarried the last one, and had also lost one child, Richard, in 1768. In her environment in an English community in the mid-18th century the social and local expectations of a middle class wife's role were very plain to Sarah. She did not criticise or question the frequency of the children conceived in her marriage to Josiah, who loved her and whom she always loved. Family planning was unknown and Marie Stopes' first birth control clinic in London in 1921 was in the far distant future.

But Sarah was tired. She needed a rest.

Chapter 6

FAMILY AFFAIRS

Early the following year Sarah remained delicate, and Josiah wrote to Bentley in January:

> ... I want to see you much on many accounts I cannot write, & want to say a thousand things to you, but my poor Girl cannot be left at present, & is not able yet to travel any at all from home. She has only been out once for half an hour since her last terrible relapse, & though she does I hope upon the whole grow better, it is so very slowly that I have little hopes of her being able to take any long journey, & have not yet any notion when I shall dare to leave her... [1]

In February Josiah did go to London for discussions with Bentley. On his return to Etruria he wrote to him on 1st March:

> ... only my Poor Girl, who was confin'd to her room & very weak & poorly, but in pretty good spirits, & chearfull as usual. (wish I could stop the account here, without proceeding to tell my Dear Friend that she has this morning had a most severe return of her complaint, & God knows what will be the consequence. She is reduced to the lowest degree imaginable, & how to treat her I do not know. Cordials may increase the complaint & yet one would imagine they were absolutely necessary for she has the appearance of a Person

bled to death, & indeed that is nearly her case. ... I almost despair of any medicines being of use to her, & I tremble for the effects of these frequent relapses ...[2]

By Spring Sarah's health improved. This was a relief to Josiah, who had found it difficult to be interested in work while his wife was so ill. He returned to dealing with his business. In 1773, Empress Catherine of Russia commissioned Wedgwood and Bentley to supply a complete creamware service for fifty people, with a painting of different scenes of Britain on each of the 952 pieces. the Empress also requested a frog painted green within a shield on each piece. The frog was a reference to the palace of Kekerekeksinen (meaning 'frog marsh') where the service was required. The Empress would rename the palace Chesme Palace in 1780.

This was a major commission, involving a lot of work. The service was completed by 1774 and cost in the region of £3,000. Before the service was shipped to Russia it was exhibited in London where it was greatly admired. After some time at Chesme Palace the service then went to the English Palace at Peterhof, before finally in 1910 being placed in a permanent display at the Hermitage Museum in Leningrad – now St. Petersburg.

Sarah was again pregnant in 1774 and their sixth child, Catherine, was born on 30th November. Josiah felt the birth had been uncomplicated and wrote to Bentley that same day:

... will rejoice with me in Mrs Wedgwood's safe delivery, and the welcome addition to our Family of a fine, healthy and perfect Child.

My dear Girl gave me, as usual, a very short notice of the approaching critical moment. At past four this morning she gave me a gentle notice to leave her bed and call the Midwife; and a quarter before five news was brought me that I had another Daughter, and all was well.

Mrs W. continues in a good way, and I hope to see her below again in a few days; for it is becoming fashionable here for the Ladies in the straw to become well and leave it as soon as they are able; and even a Lady of Fashion may be seen in her Carriage again, without shame, in ten days, or a fortnight after delivery... [3]

Sarah, however, took some time to get over this latest pregnancy. She felt depressed and uncertain about her health. Her father Richard was also concerned for her and urged her to take more care of herself. Since Sarah's marriage Richard had lived a quiet life in the farmhouse at Spen Green, but was very much a part of his daughter's life and he and Josiah were always good friends.

Sarah's brother John had taken over Richard's business as a cheese merchant. He had never married and had led a hectic and over-indulgent life. When he was forty-two, he became very ill. Dr Darwin attended him, but he could not cure him and he died in November 1774. After his son's death Richard moved to Etruria Hall where he remained until he died in 1780.

In the new year of 1775, Sarah was feeling better and started to enjoy their social life with friends. Josiah had to visit London in March and one letter Sarah wrote to him on 14th March said:

I wrote to my Dear Jos on Saturday but on receiving his agreeable and flattering letter, I sent for it back again, which I now wish I had not done, my Dear Jos would see by a former letter what were my sentiments, notwithstanding which, I should have been very happy to have seen him, and I still hope, it will not now be very long. ... Girandoles [Candelabras] – *I do not know where they should be placed in our Drawing room, indeed I think it is rather too full furnished already and I think a pair of Vase Candlesticks on the chimney and a pair of silver ones on the Table quite enough for that room. However, I only mention these as you desired my opinion and would wish you to do what you think is proper in it.*

We have no Whole Wax Candles we have large pieces which in Wax will do tho not in Tallow but if you please may buy a pound or two.

Thank you for offering to buy me anything. I do not know that I want anything either for my self or Family unless you chose to make us a present of a Box of Oranges which we shall be glad of your company to help to eat and I shall be glad of a pound or two of Almond powder.

I must give over or be too late for the Post we are all very well and join in love & Duty. Adieu my Dear Friend and believe me ever Yours S Wedgwood[4]

Chapter 7

CHILDREN'S EDUCATION – MARY ANN ILL

Josiah and Sarah's children were growing up. They had always looked on Thomas Bentley as an uncle and he treated them as such. Mary Bentley was shy, but friendly and hospitable. Her health was not good and she regretted not being able to give Thomas the children he would have liked. She and Sarah were friends and enjoyed visiting each other. The childless Thomas treasured this insight into Josiah's family life, which he had always shared. He would send to the family, either by wagon or coach, presents, perhaps a doll for Sukey and other toys for the younger children – in the summer of 1775 he sent a large playhouse, which could easily be put up or taken down on the lawn outside the Hall. Dr Darwin's boys, who often stayed at the Hall, also came over from Lichfield to enjoy this new addition.

Thomas went to Paris in 1776 for seven weeks, supposedly for a holiday, although he brought back many decorative ideas for his work. That year he bought a substantial house in London on the main road between Hammersmith and Turnham Green. Josiah wrote to him after he moved:

> ... Mrs Wedgwood joins me in thanking you for your kindly invitation to ... (pray give it a name if it has none!) and we shall not need of a second. Do not be in haste to set your newest garden. I will come and help you dig and weed and sow and gather, and we will be joint gardeners as well as just potters ... besides I could teach you to bowl, and love riding on horseback – to think less, and play more,

all of which will be of great service to you and of some to myself... [1]

The children's education was of great concern to Josiah and Sarah. John was away at school in Bolton, while Jos, aged eight, and five-year-old Tom joined him there early in 1777, where they all remained for the next two years. It had been arranged that Sukey would stay with the Bentleys in London while she attended a school known as Blacklands from 1775. Having arrived back at Etruria after leaving Sukey, Josiah wrote to Thomas:

You have made Mrs Wedgwood and myself extremely happy by your very kind and friendly letter, and the good history it contains of our dear Girl's behaviour upon our departure. It was womanly, affectionate & such as we hoped for from her. We make some little allowances for the kind partiality of her journalist, & the company we had the satisfaction to leave her in, who would support her mind, & administer relief with that delicacy & propriety which would naturally guard her manner of expressing the grief she must feel upon so trying an occasion. – However we know our dear Sukey to be a good and affectionate Girl, & hope, nay, are perswaded she will deserve this character as well from her Father & Mother Bentley, as she has done from her Father & Mother Wedgwood; & under this perswasion we with the greater confidence beg you to take her under your care & protection & to bestow a small place in your affections upon her as she merits it by an affectionate attention, & obedience to you.

... Do not talk of thanks to us – When! Or how! Shall we be out of debt? Never – so we can only continue our acknowledgments, & be grateful & affectionate to our lives end... [2]

At Blacklands, Sukey's studies improved greatly. She was a moody girl and not very strong. She resembled her father and shared some of his characteristics – indeed, she had always been his favourite child. She remained in London for three years, then she returned home because of illness. Josiah blamed Sukey's delicate condition on the school system. In July of 1778 he wrote to Bentley:

> *Sukey is now very well, and is pretty strong, which I attribute very much to rideing on horseback. We sally forth, half a dozen of us, by 6 or 7 o'clock in a morning, and return to breakfast with appetites scarcely to be satisfied. Then we are very busy in our hay and have just made a new garden. Sometimes we try experiments, then read, and draw a little, that altogether we are very busy folks, and the holidays will be over much sooner than we could wish them to be. Poor Sukey is quite out of patience with her old Spinet and often asks me when her new one will come.* [3]

Fortunately the new harpsichord arrived from Newcastle the following week.

Despite her unpredictable health Sarah was again pregnant and in September 1776 she gave birth to a third daughter, Sarah. Then in August 1778 they had their last child, a fourth daughter, Mary Ann. On 19th August 1778 Josiah wrote to Bentley:

> *... , yesterday evening she presented me with another fine girl and with as little trouble to her-self and family as could be expected. She sent for the midwife whilst we were bowling (after making tea for us as usual in the afternoon) without so much as acquainting me with the matter – Slipt upstairs just before supper, and we had not risen from table before the joyfull tidings of a safe delivery, and all well was brought to us, and as soon as the young visitor was dressed she joined the company in the dining room. The mother eat her supper, went to sleep, and all are in a very fine way this morning, but from a sort of decorum established amongst the sex, originally intended, no doubt, to impose upon us poor men, and make us believe what sufferings they underwent for us and our bantlings...* [4]

But sadly Mary Ann was not a 'fine girl' and it soon became apparent that she was mentally handicapped. Because of the baby's delicate condition, Sarah could not accompany Josiah on his travels as often as she would have liked. At fourteen months Mary Ann was having severe health problems, and in his letter to Bentley in November, Josiah reported:

> ... *Our little girl, Mary Ann, breeds her teeth very hardly, and unfortunately several of them are pushing forward at the same time. This brought on convulsions which lasted thirteen hours without intermission the first attack, which was on Friday morning, and when this left her we found she had lost the use of her arm and leg on one side. She had a slight return for about half an hour the last night, but is better again today.*
>
> *Doctor Darwin was here on Friday with my father and ordered our little girl to be electrified two or three times a day on the side affected, and to be continued for some weeks. We are willing to flatter ourselves that she has received some benefit from electricity already, as she begins to move her arm and leg a little, and this will encourage us to proceed in the same course. The Doctor gives us great hopes of our poor little girl's limbs being restored, even without the assistance of the electric shocks, but apprehends they will hasten the cure and thereby prevent the diseased limbs being shorter than the others which must be the case if they continue long in their present inactive state. We have lanced her gums and keep them open, as teeth do not yet appear, by means of the sharp end of an ivory modelling tool. I am the electrician upon this occasion which must confine me at home for some time...* [5]

In a continuing report on 23rd November he said:

> ... *We thought our little girl much better yesterday. She is lively and playfull, more so than we had observed since her illness, but this morning she is fallen off again and has some return of spasms in her face. We have just now*

bathed her in warm water, which has evidently relieved her and she can smile and play a little again. Whilst she continues subject to these spasms we dare not electrify her, or use much friction, or anything to irritate, but endeavor to make and keep her easy and quiet. When these convulsive remains leave her, we are not without hopes that the use of her limbs may be restored, though at present she does not attempt to make the least use of them, but makes use of her mouth in a hundred little instances to assist her other hand in the management of her playthings... [6]

The treatment sounds horrific, but Sarah and Josiah, with help and advice from Dr Darwin, simply did what they thought was best for their baby girl. Her sisters and brothers loved and cared for Mary Ann until she finally died in 1786, aged only eight. She left a large gap in the lives of all of them.

Chapter 8

ETRUSCAN SCHOOL

1779 was a pivotal year for Josiah and Sarah's children. Until then, the older boys had been attending a Unitarian school in Bolton and by the end of that year Josiah had decided that his sons would be better off, both in health and education, if they stayed at home and had tutors. The last straw was in October 1779, when young Josiah was ill at school. Josiah and Sarah went to collect him. Having arrived, Josiah wrote to Bentley from Bolton on 3rd October:

> *On my return from Bishton I found a letter from Mr Holland acquainting us that one of our boys (Joss) had been poorly for some days, which they supposed proceeded from some little indigestion, but as the complaint had not yielded to a few days' rest, gruel, and kitchen physic, they thought it better to acquaint us. Upon this intelligence my wife and self set off for this place the next morning and found our little fellow very poorly. I called in Docter Taylor, who tells me he does not apprehend any danger but thinks the country air, with gentle exercise and a recess from his buseness will be very necessary for him. A puke and some opening physic has had a good effect, but there is still a considerable fever upon him. We shall take him with us back to Etruria as soon as he is able to travel, but am afraid that will not be of some days yet... [1]*

In a letter from Etruria to Bentley dated 9th October, Josiah reported on their return journey:

> ... *We were three days on the road, as our poor fellow could not bear traveling expeditiously. The air and exercise has been of service to him, but he has still a considerable degree of heat and fever upon him. We have brought his brother Tom along with him who is far from being well. I believe the truth is, that they have more business, confinement, and phlogisticated air than their machinery can dispense with, and how to remedy this evil, and give them such an education as the fashion of the times requires, I am utterly at a loss to determine...* [2]

Josiah had now firmed up on his plans for educating his children at home. He wanted an all-round education, both in mind and body. He felt that with his supervision they would have the chance to look at their individual lives and get an idea of what future occupation might appeal to them. He listened to advice from his friends Dr Darwin and Thomas Bentley – and followed some of it.

Setting up a classroom at the Hall was something new but Sarah welcomed the opportunity to improve the education of her children. It was good also to have them near her. At that time Sukey was fourteen, John thirteen, Jos ten, Tom eight, Catherine five and Sarah, still a baby, three. And so the Etruscan School came into being.

In October 1779, in his letter to Bentley Josiah told him how pleased he and Sarah were in the young woman they had engaged as maid and teacher to their young daughters. In a later letter he mentions that the little girls have English lessons with their nurse in the school, which was a room near the nursery and at intervals Susan, apart from her exercise, would play music.

He wrote again on 23rd November:

> ... *Before breakfast we read English together in the news paper, or any book we happen to have in the course of reading. We're now reading Ferber's travels, with the globe and maps before us. After breakfast they go and write an hour with Mr Swift and with this small portion of time, and writing their French exercises and entering some*

experiments which they make along with me, all which I insist upon being written in a fair legible hand, they have improved more in writing in these few weeks here than they did in the last twelve months at Bolton. After writing if the weather permits they ride or drive their hoop, or jump a cord or use any exercise they please for an hour and the remainder of the day is filled up with two French lessons, and Mr Swift attends them here an hour in the evening for accounts, in which their sister joins with them: and we have agreed to add four Latin lessons a week to the above business, for which Mr Byerley and Mr Lomas have kindly offered their assistance. This last is intended only to prevent their losing what they have already learnt, 'till I have decided upon this part of their learning... [3]

Doctor Darwin thought that the boys should learn French rather than a dead language, such as Latin, so John and Josiah Jnr went to Lichfield for a month to learn French with Robert Darwin. Their teacher was a Mr Potet and Josiah employed him afterwards for a year at Etruria Hall. Also in 1781, Josiah took on a scientific adviser, Alexander Chisholm, to teach science to the children, plus arithmetic and geometry. The young pupils were certainly kept busy, with a full curriculum.

It is not clear how long the school existed: John went back to Mr Holland in Bolton for a short time, and in 1782 he became a boarder at Dr Enfield's Warrington Academy. In February of that year, young Josiah went off to school in Edinburgh.

Chapter 9

GEORGE STUBBS – DEATH OF THOMAS BENTLEY

George Stubbs, the artist famed for his studies of racehorses, was an acquaintance of Josiah's. It was arranged that Stubbs would paint a portrait of the Wedgwoods and in August 1780 he took up residence at the Hall and started work. Great interest was taken by the family as they watched their likenesses gradually appear on the canvas. Josiah was impatient to see the finished picture but Stubbs would not be hurried. Josiah wrote to Bentley in August:

> *... We make but little progress with the family piece at present but Mr S Talks of laying to in good earnest soon.*
> *... Our three little lasses and their coach are just put into colors, and the characters of the children are hit off very well. I have given him one sitting, and this is all we have done with the picture. The stable is preparing, and the horses are to sit this week...*

Later he wrote:

> *... Our picture goes on very slowly, but we may report some progress and I think the likenesses promise to be strong, but I do not know what to say upon this subject because the likeness in those that approach towards being finished grows weaker as the painting increases. Mr Stubbs says*

the likeness will come in and go off many times before finishing, so I can say nothing to this matter at present, only that the first sketches were very strong likenesses, and the after touches have hitherto made them less so, but I daresay he will bring them about again before he takes his final leave of the picture... [1]

That autumn Sarah and Josiah entertained many friends at the Hall. Stubbs enjoyed the extra company and some of Josiah's guests commissioned him to do further portraits. He also painted Sarah's father, Richard.

In what was to be one of the last letters he would write to his friend, Josiah wrote to Bentley:

Yesterday morning we had three parties at the same time. Lady Caroline Egerton, two of Lord Waldegrave's daughters, and Lady Ann ..., Lord Huntingdon, Mr and Mrs Sneyd, and another lady composed a second party, and Mrs Thomas Gilbert, with two Miss Crawfords her visitors, who by the bye sing and play upon the Piano Forte like angels, Mr and Mrs Sneyd of Belmont, and two daughters, with my wife and six sons and daughters, made up a third party ... my wife was very good, and exerted herself wonderfully upon the occasion. We paid a visit to Cotton on Sunday, which we had promised I believe three summers, and brought the last mentioned party with us on Tuesday in the committee boat. They are with us still, but leave us sometime to day. ... I wish our dear friends at Turnham Green could have been of our party for three or four days past, particularly upon the water on Tuesday. The weather was very fine, and the scenery we passed through extremely beautifull to say nothing of the Piano Forte and three or four melodious and willing voices which accompanied us... [2]

The final letter Josiah wrote to his partner and friend is recorded as 12th November 1780. Thomas had been unwell in June and Josiah suggested he came to Etruria, *'and I will willingly go with you to Buxton, Matlock or any other place ...'* but there is no mention of his health in following letters. However on 25th November their mutual friend, the publisher, Ralph Griffiths of Turnham Green, wrote to Josiah:

> ... *Our poor friend yet breathes, but, alas, it is such breathing as promises but a short continuance. Almost every hope seems to have forsaken us! I dread the thought of what will be the contents of my next!*

Thomas died the next day. Josiah had hurried to Turnham Green and arrived just after his death. Thomas was just fifty, and although he had never been as fit as Josiah and had sometimes been depressed, he had not suffered any serious illnesses, and his death was an unexpected loss. In a letter to Bentley on 2nd May 1778, Josiah had said:

> *I find the oldest men – Philosophers, nay even Christians and the firmest believers – cling as fast to this wicked world as younger folks. ... Well – since it is, and will be so, let us my dear friend enjoy and diffuse amongst our friends every real happiness within our reach, and not torment ourselves with needless anxieties, nor waste an hour of the very small portion of time allotted us here – I know these are your sentiments, and I will endeavour more and more to make them those of*

> *Your ever affectionate friend Jos Wedgwood*[3]

A letter written to a true and warm friend whom he knew would understand what he was trying to say.

Thomas Bentley's death left a great emptiness in Josiah's life and in the lives of his family. He had been such an integral part of their lives, an uncle to their children, a dear friend and partner to Josiah and for Sarah a close and loving friend. With his death the greatest source of information about Josiah and Sarah's everyday life ceased. Now the only glimpse of Sarah is through letters between her children and herself, and these are rare.

The month after Bentley's death, George Stubbs finished his portrait of the Wedgwood family. This picture has since become the most well known and oft-reproduced of the many pictures of Josiah and his family. The original now hangs in the Wedgwood Museum at Barlaston, Stoke-on-Trent.

The portrait depicts Josiah looking slightly indifferent, probably bored by having to sit still. Sarah and the children look elegant and at ease on their estate, with a glimpse of gentle countryside through the trees. On the right, behind Josiah, but far enough away not to be intrusive, smoking chimneys appear on the horizon. This picture gives an idea of Sarah's fashion sense for formal occasions. In everyday life she did not suit frills and flounces and her clothes reflected this.

The 18th century ladies wore dresses with skirts so wide they needed plenty of room to negotiate doors or stairs. The width was achieved by means of whalebone or rods of osier (willow shoots). Josiah's plans for his showrooms in London, with his usual foresight, took ladies' wide skirts into account and he made sure the display rooms were large. Some dresses were closed at the front while others had an inverted V, allowing the petticoat to be seen.

Décolleté continued to be the favourite style of bodice and a modesty piece of material would be either inserted to conceal the lower part of the décolletage or draped around the shoulders.

In George Stubbs' family portrait, Sarah's elegant white and gold dress does not appear to have a bustle: she looks slender, her hand, outstretched to her children, shows her sleeve length and it appears to match the lace of her hat, which suits her hairstyle.

John Flaxman, sculptor and illustrator, one of Josiah's best known artists, engraved a medallion of Sarah in which her hair is beautifully portrayed. L Jewitt describes hair fashions at that time, and Sarah's in particular:

> *In the latter half of the 19th century ladies hair fashions were so elaborate and intricate that once arranged they would have to stay that way for some weeks. The process of building up the immense structure was a tedious and expensive one, and the head had to be preserved with great care. So much care, indeed, was sometimes taken, that ladies provided themselves with a net-bag, which enveloped the whole head, including the face, and fastened round the neck. These they put on when they went to what was supposed to be rest, but which, in reality, must have*

been torture, and were propped and bolstered up with the utmost care to prevent the structure being damaged...

Mrs Wedgwood's hair and head-dress, it will be seen by the accompanying engraving, were, in comparison with the monstrosities then in vogue, particularly simple, graceful and elegant. The Toupee is formed of the hair brushed up from the forehead: close curls fit to the side of the head, and a loose one beneath the ear. On the top of the head the back-hair is brought up and plaited, and graceful folds of gauze are lightly and negligently arranged.[4]

Some time later Joshua Reynolds painted portraits of both Josiah and Sarah. Josiah had aged since his friend's death and looked older than his fifty-two years. Sarah seemed sombre and slightly austere.

Since Thomas's death, Josiah's nephew Tom Byerley had taken over more responsibility for the business. Tom had sown his wild oats and travelled abroad until 1777 when he returned home and rejoined his uncle in the pottery business. Now in the early 1780s Josiah and Sarah saw him as a trusted friend and relied on him increasingly. With Bentley gone, Josiah had to spend more time at the London showrooms and eventually he sent Tom Byerley to live there.

In 1782 Josiah communicated to the Royal Society an account of *'an attempt to make a Thermometer for measuring the higher degrees of Heat, from a red-heat up to the strongest that vessels made of clay can support'[5]* and in 1783 Josiah was admitted as a Fellow of the Royal Society in recognition of his invention of the pyrometer.

Chapter 10

FRIENDSHIPS

Erasmus Darwin had also had a long friendship with Thomas Bentley and he too mourned his loss with Josiah and Sarah. Erasmus was always a staunch friend to both of them. Josiah felt that the doctor had, in all probability, saved Sarah's life during her serious illnesses in 1772 and 1773 and for that alone he was indebted to his friend.

Erasmus had married Mary Howard in 1758, and they had five children, of whom two died in infancy. After a long illness Mary died in 1770. Their first son, Charles, studied medicine at Edinburgh University. Whilst doing an operation he cut his finger and died after the wound became infected. Erasmus never got over his loss. His second son, also called Erasmus, was a disappointment to his father. He had no ambition and eventually committed suicide. Robert, the third son, in a way made up for his father's heartbreak with his other sons. Like his father, Robert trained to be a doctor.

Erasmus enjoyed female company. One of his favourites was Anna Seward, whom he had known since she was a child. Anna, the daughter of the Revd Thomas Seward, Canon of Lichfield, was an intellectual who gathered around her men and women of like interests. Later known as the Swan of Lichfield, Anna was greatly attracted to Erasmus and although he also enjoyed her friendship, he could not return her strong feelings. She was piqued when she realized he was not serious about their relationship.

Eventually Eramus met and fell in love with a beautiful widow, Mrs Elizabeth Chandos-Pole. Her husband died in 1780, leaving her with three children. She and Erasmus married, but she did not like Lichfield and they moved to Derby. In the nine years of their marriage they had seven children, of whom three boys and three girls survived infancy. The girls in the early 19th century were renowned for their beauty.

Josiah Wedgwood and Erasmus Darwin were characters almost larger than life. They could between them achieve most of the things they wanted, be they business ventures or social conquests.

On 13th March 1784, Erasmus wrote to Josiah:

> *Mrs Darwin says she hears your whole family are going to town in a body like a caravan going to Mecca, & we therefore hope you will make Derby a resting-place & recruit yourselves & your camels for a few days, after having travell'd over the burning sands of Cheadle & Uttoxeter ...[1]*

The young Wedgwoods were always happy to visit the Darwins.

Josiah and Sarah took it for granted that their business would be carried on by their sons. The boys were, like their parents, Unitarians. Their lives up to now (the year 1787) had been comfortable. They were used to socialising with scientific and educated men. John, who had left Edinburgh University at the end of 1785, helped with the work of the firm both in London and at Etruria. After a year Josiah sent him to the Continent to further his career.

Tom and Josiah II finished at Edinburgh in 1787 and they returned home in July of that year. After a summer holiday they were expected to work at Etruria. Young Josiah wrote to his mother, while she and his father were away from home:

> *Dear Mother,*
> *I have just received your kind letter & will observe your instructions. We are both of us very well pleased that we are to stay at home which is very pleasant now, especially as there has fallen rain last night & today. The crop of hay is very poor & some part of it very bad, quite burnt. I mean above the bowling green, which is in pretty good order. I have been at Newcastle & Fenton & our friends at both places are very well...[2]*

Josiah had long had an ambition, a dream, and that was to make a perfect copy of the Barberini Vase, later known as the Portland Vase. It belonged to the Duchess of Portland and in 1790 the Duke of Portland – her son – lent it to Josiah. Josiah's reproduction, which took four years to perfect, was certified as a correct and faithful imitation. He said it was his greatest achievement.

Sarah's daughters, Catherine and Susannah, were growing up and Susannah, now twenty, wished to banish her pet name of Sukey and be known as Susan. She was particularly musical and loved to play the spinet. Most of her leisure time was spent with the Darwins at Derby where, as all were aware, Robert was the big attraction. She was a great favourite of Erasmus and she gave him music lessons whenever she went to stay.

Josiah gradually began to loosen his overall hold on the daily running of the business. His health was not great, his eyesight was poor and this probably contributed to his frequent headaches. When possible he and Sarah travelled to places where he felt the air would improve his health.

Josiah's partner and cousin Thomas Wedgwood died suddenly in 1788 and afterwards Josiah, having reassessed the set-up within the works, decided to take his three sons John, Josiah II and Thomas, and his nephew Thomas Byerley into partnership, Byerley being allotted one-eighth as his share in the partnership. John finally had to confess to his parents that he was not happy in the work. Finally in 1792 Josiah bought him a junior partnership in the London and Middlesex Bank. During 1793, young Josiah took over the shares of his brothers John and Tom.

Tom was unlike either of his older brothers. He was happy to have his head in a book or spend time in the laboratory with Alexander Chisholm. He often suffered from headaches, which led to depression which sometimes lasted for several days. Doctors thought his illness involved his digestive system. But he was very handsome, with a gentle disposition which endeared him to everyone. He was relieved when Jos took over his shares in the family business, as he wanted to be free to do other things.

Sarah and Josiah took advantage of more free time. Physically Josiah had slowed down but mentally he was as alert as ever. He loved books – Sarah said he was buying too many books for his library and should not buy any more until he built another house, or first read some of those books he already had. He and Sarah enjoyed their gardens and were always involved and interested in any improvements to the grounds around the Hall. Their children also loved being part of any time spent in the gardens. The parents always enjoyed welcoming their many friends to their home. Elizabeth Meteyard, referring to their lifestyle, said:

> *... on the harpsichord the newest music, on the shelves the newest books. Each day at 3 o'clock the dinner table was laid for unexpected as well as expected guests, for it was never known who might arrive before or after the meal.[3]*

They travelled with their daughters to some of their favourite places in England and Wales, sometimes for pleasure, sometimes for their health. Sarah was never completely free of rheumatism and Susan also suffered from the same complaint. In the summer of 1791 Sarah, Josiah and Susan went to Weymouth and in October Josiah wrote to his friend R L Edgeworth in Ireland:

> *Mrs Wedgwood, my daughters & self were* [at Bristol hot wells] *in Augt. last, but only as birds of passage on our way to Weymouth, where we bathed for 2 or 3 weeks; But it has not prevented the setting in of winter bringing a severe rheumatic complaint upon Susan, who is now confined by it; & Mrs W has not been so well this autumn as usual, but is now getting better ...[4]*

Chapter 11

JOY AND SORROW – JOSIAH DIES

In December 1792, the first of Sarah's and Josiah's sons, Josiah II, married Elizabeth (Bessy) Allen, the eldest of the nine daughters of John Bartlett Allen, of Cresselly. The Allens were an old family of Pembrokeshire, descended from William Cecil – Queen Elizabeth's Chief Secretary of State and 1st Baron Burghley. The marriage was a social step up for Jos, and his parents were well pleased with his choice. The newly wed Jos wrote to his father from Devonshire Place, London, in January 1793:

> *I have just received your very kind letter containing £3000 for which I return my hearty thanks. I have deposited it with John who will employ it as he thinks most for my advantage. Bessy desires me to thank you for your expressions of regard for her. We shall not stay longer in town than what I first proposed & we will then avail ourselves of your hospitable invitation. Bessy requests my mother will accept her best thanks for the watch which she has presented her with ...[1]*

Immediately after their marriage Jos and Bessy lived with his brother John for three months in London, after which they moved to Little Etruria, the house built initially for Thomas Bentley.

In September the following year John wrote to his parents asking permission to marry Louisa Jane 'Jenny' Allen, sister of Jos's new wife Elizabeth Allen. His choice of a bride was again happily received by his parents, as will be seen in a letter written to him by his father:

> *My dear John,*
> *... I have shewn your letter to your mother and asked*
> *her opinion upon the subject and find that we are happy*
> *enough to agree in our sentiments respecting the choice*
> *you have made of a companion for life. It is no doubt a*
> *subject of the first importance to you both, and you will*
> *do well to consider each others tempers and dispositions,*
> *whether they are such as are likely to make you mutually*
> *happy in each other, for I need not tell you it must be*
> *mutual or not at all in the married state. Your friends*
> *here, not only your mother and myself but your brothers*
> *and sisters, wish with sincerity and earnestness for your*
> *welfare and happiness, particularly upon your entrance*
> *upon so interesting a connection, and I am sure you will*
> *do us the justice to believe that the real happiness of the*
> *parties weighs more with us than any other consideration*
> *whatever, and we have so exquisite a sample before us*
> *from the same family of everything that is desirable and*
> *lovely in the female character, and hearing besides so*
> *excellent a character of the lady of your choice, we do*
> *not hesitate to give our free and most cordial assent with*
> *our sincerest wishes and prayers for your long continued*
> *enjoyment of all the comfort and happiness your intended*
> *union can bestow ...[2]*

John and Jenny were married the following year and lived in London. Eventually John moved his family to Cote House, near Bristol. His new home was a popular meeting place for his sisters and brothers, and Tom in particular was a frequent visitor. Gardening was John's passion and he was very proud that he chaired a meeting where the Royal Horticultural Society came into being.

Towards the end of 1794, Josiah began to feel uncomfortable about his health. His right jaw ached, and he also felt pain in his non-existent leg. He was short of breath and most activities weakened him. He knew that at sixty-five he was not the strong, agile man he used to be, but had hoped he had a few more years to enjoy his and Sarah's retirement.

Left: *Portrait, oil on canvas, of Josiah Wedgwood II, son of Josiah I, painted by William Owen. Date early 19th century.*

Below Left: *Oil on canvas, Bessy Allen, wife of Josiah II, early 19th century, painted by George Romney.*

Photos courtesy of the Wedgwood Museum Trust, Barlaston, Staffordshire

Below Right: *Thomas Wedgwood* (author's collection)

In the latter half of that year he and Sarah went first to Blackpool and then on to Buxton. For a time the change of air helped, but only briefly. They returned home. Josiah's jaw became swollen and unbearably painful. The family thought it must be toothache, and Mr Bent was called – but he was shocked to discover that the now inflamed jaw and throat were gangrenous. Dr Darwin and two other surgeons attended but they knew it was too late. Laudanum was supplied to ease the pain, as Sarah and their daughters nursed Josiah.

On the evening of 2nd January 1795, Josiah was in great pain and his doctor, Erasmus Darwin, treated him with laudanum. Josiah must have known that his end was near. On that evening he told Sarah and Susan not to disturb him, as he hoped to sleep soundly through the night. Next morning, when it was discovered that his bedroom door was locked from the inside, Greaves, the carpenter, was asked to get a ladder and climb in through Josiah's window and open his bedroom door. Josiah was found dead in his bed.

Afterwards Thomas Byerley wrote from Etruria to Samuel Boardman, one-time partner of Thomas Bentley in Liverpool:

> *I have the extreme unhappiness to announce to you the decease of our revered and ever to be lamented Mr Wedgwood. This mournful event happened on Saturday last after an illness of about three week – in which he was perfectly sensible till near the fatal and melancholy period, and to the great consolation of his friends was without much pain the last two or three days of existence...*
>
> *My poor uncle had the comfort in this his last illness to be attended only by his children, who nursed him with an anxious care and constancy that has not been surpassed.*
>
> *This long watchfulness and anxiety of mind has been too much for the tender frame of Miss Wedgwood* [Susan] *who has been in a poor state of health for some time, and she has suffered extremely, but is now much better – The rest of the family are as well as can be expected ...[3]*

Josiah Wedgwood was an entrepreneur – vital to his success was his excellent acumen in production, in marketing, in his knowledge of people. He had integrity in all his dealings. His ability to acquire his materials in England, his highly skilled workforce, his great reputation for quality in whatever he manufactured, all resulted in big sales at home and ever increasing exports. One of his greatest strengths was the support and love of his wife, who shared his ambitions and achievements.

Josiah's estate, which consisted of approximately 380 acres, was worth half a million pounds. His last Will read:

> *... I give and bequeath unto my dear and affectionate Wife, Sarah Wedgwood, all that messuage or dwelling-house situate at or near Etruria aforesaid, with the buidings, gardens, and appurtenances thereto belonging, late in the holding of Mr Thomas Wedgwood; and also all that field or piece of land in which the same stands, containing eight acres or thereabouts; and also all that close, piece, or parcel of land lying contiguous to the said dwelling-house, called the Horse Pasture, containing by estimation twelve acres or thereabouts; and also all that piece or parcel of land situate at Etruria aforesaid, heretofore purchased by me from Mr Hugh Booth; To have and to hold the said messuage or dwelling-house, pieces or parcels of land, here-ditaments and premises, with their and every of their appurtenances, unto my said Wife, Sarah Wedgwood and her assigns, for and during the term of her natural life. ... Also I give and bequeath the sum of Three thousand pounds unto my said Wife, to be paid to her within twelve months next after my decease. ... Also I give and bequeath the sum of Ten thousand pounds unto my Executors ... upon trust that they, my said Executors, do and shall place the said sum of Ten thousand pounds out upon some good and sufficient public or private security or securitys, at interest, to be approved of nevertheless by my said wife, and do and shall pay to, or permit and suffer my said Wife to receive and take the interest, dividends, and produce of the said sum of Ten Thousand pounds, as the same shall from time to time become due to and for her own use and benefit for and during the term of her natural life.*

Josiah also left Sarah the contents of their house.
To each of his three daughters he left £25,000.
To his sons – Thomas £29,000,
          John £30,000,
          Josiah a proportionate sum and, with the exception of the shares held by Thomas Byerley, the whole of his business, including Etruria Hall.[4]

Chapter 12

SUSAN MARRIES ROBERT DARWIN
SARAH LEAVES ETRURIA HALL

Sarah, a widow at sixty-one, now faced a future without her beloved Josiah. No more being at the centre of an exciting life, no more being part of discussions about what to do next, where to go, who to see. The reality of her loss was hard to bear, and gradually she became less outgoing and more taciturn. She continued to live at Etruria Hall for a number of years. Her daughters Catherine (Kitty) who was twenty-one, Sarah (Sally) who was nineteen, Susan aged thirty – until marriage – and Tom aged twenty-four, lived there with her.

Alexander Chisholm, their former tutor, also lived at Etruria, in the gatehouse. Josiah bequeathed '*one annuity or yearly sum of Twenty pounds unto Mr Alexander Chisholm, for and during the term of his natural life; recommending it to my Son Josiah Wedgwood to give him any further assistance that he may stand in need of, to make the remainder of his life easy and comfortable ...*'.

After his father's death, Josiah II continued to work at Etruria with his cousin Thomas Byerley, who for many years was the working head of the business. Jos was only twenty-six, just three years married, when he inherited the immense responsibilities of the family, the business and a vast estate. His father never knew that Jos, from choice, would not have wished for the burden of the Etruria Works and all that entailed, but he had found himself in the position of being the only son who actually stayed and worked with his father. He was – in Josiah's eyes – the likely choice to succeed him. He enjoyed all the benefits of his inheritance but felt he did not fit the role of a businessman. He preferred to see himself as a country squire. During the next four months, gradually he left the running of the factory to Thomas Byerley. He found a new home for his family at Tarrant Gonville, in Dorset, where he could live the life of a country gentleman, far removed from the smoke of the Potteries. He hunted and shot and took part in country business. Improving his breed of sheep was one of his many interests.

Josiah thought he could supervise the work at Etruria by visiting two or three times a year, but in time it was obvious that this was not satisfactory, and not fair to his employees. He knew he would have to go back.

Apart from the loss of her husband and the absence of her son with his young family, Sarah also had to see Susan leaving home, as after their year of mourning, she married Robert Darwin. The newly-weds went to live at their new home, The Mount, overlooking the Severn at Shrewsbury. Robert was now a doctor. It had always been understood while Susan and Robert were growing up that they would be married one day, the only regret was that her father was not there to see it. Susan had always been her father's favourite and they had been close. Most of her life Susan had been preoccupied with her health, and like her mother 'took the waters' at places such as Bath or Buxton. After her father's death she too became ill. She continued to be 'delicate' after marriage, although she and Robert went on to have six children.

Robert was not only a well respected doctor but also a successful businessman and was comfortably off. There was a strong feeling of friendship between him and the Wedgwood brothers, but especially with Josiah II. In company Robert and Susan appeared sociable and outgoing, but the family remembered them as being introvert and even inarticulate at home.

By 1799, it was decided that Sarah and family would leave the Hall and find somewhere suitable near Jos in the south. Sarah was reluctant to leave, but realised the practicalities of such a move. Tom was rarely at home – he travelled abroad and when in England liked to stay with his other brothers or with friends. He was now getting ready to go travelling again, this time to the West Indies. Before leaving, a new temporary home was found for Sarah and the girls. This was a country house, Staplegrove, near Taunton in Somerset and nearer to Jos. The future plan was that Tom would buy a suitable home for his mother, himself and his sisters somewhere near.

Prior to leaving the Potteries, where she had lived all her life, Sarah wrote to Jos:

> *I thank you very sincerely my dear Jos for your letter of the 3 inst., and for all the trouble you have had about a house for us, and I am sure we shall all be very glad to be in your neighbourhood, and old Michaelmas will suit us better than new, as we cannot be there before the middle of October...*
>
> *I was sorry to find Tom could not bear Exmouth and shall be very happy to hear how he is. I expect the girls in a day or two they talk of spending a day at Clifton which will rest the horses.*
>
> *The Dr* [Erasmus Darwin] *returned yesterday from Derby where he had been to meet his 2 Uncles and his Aunt whom he had not seen of 14 years, he says 2 of them look younger and better than when he saw them, the other had a stroke of the Palsy some years ago and has not perfectly recovered they are all older than the Dr ... I am very happy to hear such good acct of the health and improvement of my dear children give my best love to them all & to Tom accept the same yourself and believe me ever*
>
> *Yours most sincerely*
>
> *S Wedgwood*
> *remember me kindly to Miss Dennis*
> *All friends here send love thanks for your acct of your building I think you have done wonders.*[1]

Sarah sounded confident and pleased that her son was concerned for her welfare. She was businesslike in her discussion of family affairs. It is also obvious that Jos had taken over matters that were once his father's preserve. And in the future he always seemed to be the person his family turned to for help or advice.

Sarah and her daughters went to visit Jos at Tarrant Gunville. A letter in March 1800, from Sally and Kitty to their brother Tom, admired Gunville.

My mother was but indifferent when she began her journey here, but travelling has recruited her as it usually does, and she is now brisk ...[2]

Tom writing to Jos in May 1800:

The good account of my mother has given me the purest pleasure – don't omit to tell her so – she is the best mother that ever lived ...[3]

Tom was abroad only a short time and on his return, as planned, he found Eastbury Estate, which was adjacent to Jos's estate. He, his mother and two sisters settled into their new home. Thomas Byerley and his family moved into Etruria Hall, which Josiah had arranged to lease to him.

Tom had suffered since childhood from headaches and a delicate stomach and – probably as a result – he suffered from depression. He tried all sorts of odd remedies, but the depressions could last for weeks. He was a perpetual traveller, driven by the hope that he would find a cure in other countries and climates.

He was the most handsome of the boys, more scientifically minded than his brothers. He was emotional, unselfish yet over-sensitive, and relied heavily on the support of his family.

He was introspective and self-analytical, which made life serious for him. His friends were mostly from the world of literature and science, among them the poets Samuel Taylor Coleridge and William Wordsworth, Thomas Poole and Humphry Davy the chemists, the social critics Charles and Mary Lamb, Basil Montague, novelist William Godwin, poet Robert Southey, and Dr Thomas Beddoes, who was also his doctor.

Tom was also a skilful draughtsman and in the emerging world of photography he was '*the first, so far as was known then, to gain a semi-permanent impression of an article on white paper or white leather impregnated with silver nitrate – the basis of all photographic sensitive material up to that time*'.[4]

Chapter 13

COTE HOUSE – COLERIDGE CONNECTION

Tom's brother John's home in Wales, Cote House, was popular for social gatherings, both of Wedgwoods and Allens, and it was here that Samuel Coleridge – through their mutual friend Thomas Poole – became acquainted with the Wedgwoods.

In November 1802, Tom wrote to Poole to say he was on his way to Cote House where, with his sister, he was due to meet Coleridge:

> *We then proceed to South Wales, where I shall shoot for a fortnight or so, having sent a man and seven dogs before me.*[1]

They planned to be at Cresselly in December. Cresselly was the country house of John Bartlett Allen, father of Tom's two sisters-in-law, Jane and Elizabeth. The house in Pembrokeshire was a few miles from Tenby. En route Tom and Samuel stopped at an inn, the Blue Boar, at St Clear, Carmarthen. Coleridge wrote to his wife on 16th November:

> *My Dear Love,*
> *The inn, the Blue Boar, is the most comfortable little public house I was ever in, Miss S Wedgwood left us this morning for Cresselly ... fifteen miles from this place.*[2]

A few days after this letter they arrived at Cresselly, where they remained for about a month. Apart from the Wedgwoods, the company at Cresselly consisted of daughters Jessie Allen aged twenty-five, beautiful and intelligent – she afterwards married Jean-Charles de Sismondi, the historian; Emma, a very sociable and affectionate young woman, and the youngest daughter Fanny aged twenty-one.

Coleridge admired Sally and mentioned her in a letter to his wife on 4th December 1802:

> *I am very comfortable here. Sally Wedgwood is really the most perfectly good woman I ever knew...* [3]

Sally was also impressed by Coleridge and when he and Tom left Cresselly she wrote to him in Cumberland:

> *I feel very much obliged to you for your interesting account of your journey & am very glad to find that you both arrived safely at Keswick after so many dangers, I think the weather must be much colder with you than it is here as poor Tom has suffered so much from it, he had better return here as soon as he can, we have had snow only one day & no very severe weather...*
>
> *We are all very glad to hear your good account of Mrs Coleridge & your little ones, I congratulate you on having a girl though I believe you do not feel this piece of good fortune as you ought, the Allens are sorry the little new comer is not a boy as they wished very much that it should be called Cresselly. My reason for being glad is equally selfish. I rejoice because I think you will now be inclined to write a very interesting book that you told us you had been thinking of on the character of women – I hope your little girl will be a greater beauty than you expect, it would be very hard upon her to have no beauty when her brothers have so much.*
>
> *We (I mean the three girls & myself) are very much gratified by your kind remembrance of us, & much pleased to find that you think with pleasure of the time you spent with us, we shall long continue to celebrate those three weeks as uncommonly happy ones, & we feel as we ought gratitude mixed with feelings of kindness when we think of you. We have regretted very much that we could never*

find a convenient time for the lectures on poetry that you kindly promised us, as we particularly wished to know something on that subject. We all charge you not to forget to send the remainder of the Lady Christobel when you have finished it, your promise to me I feel secure about as it is recorded in your pocket book…

Will you tell Tom with my love that if he does not make a party in the north for Trewerne & has courage enough to try it soon I should be very glad to meet him & stay sometime with him there but I am afraid as I am no shooter that that will do no good. I do hope to hear a better account of him soon.

The girls desire me to remember them most kindly to you & to say that they heartily wish it may not be long before they have again the pleasure of seeing you. … They beg you will give their love to Tom & say how sorry they are that he has any doubt about coming to Trewerne, they are very unwilling to give him up as a neighbor, & wish he would leave the north & come here till his cottage is ready.[4]

Coleridge's life was then at a crossroads. As usual he was short of money and was thinking of becoming a Unitarian minister. Josiah II and Tom came to his rescue. They jointly set up an annuity for Coleridge, each contributing £75, with no conditions. Coleridge was reluctant to accept such generosity, but eventually was persuaded and gave up the idea of being a minister.

It was known among their circle of friends that Coleridge used opium regularly. Tom was also introduced to this drug and used it in an attempt to overcome his despondency and poor health.

Unlike her sister, Kitty did not have any admiration for Coleridge. Later in 1803 when he was again invited as Tom's guest, she wrote to Tom:

… I don't know whether we shall ever agree in our sentiments respecting this gentleman, but I hope if we do not that we may agree to differ. I certainly felt no scruples of conscience in joining the attack at Cresselly. I have never seen enough of him to overcome the first

*disagreeable impression of his accent and exterior.
I confess too that in what I have seen and heard of
Mr Coleridge there is in my opinion too great a parade
of superior feelings; and an excessive goodness and
sensibility is put too forward, which gives an appearance,
at least, of conceit, and excites suspicion that it is acting;
as real sensibility never endeavours to excite notice.*

*... You see I have not much to say, but 'tis the impression
I have of his thinking himself much better than the world
in general that inclines one to look more closely into his
own life and conduct; and as his judgments of others are
not inclined to the favourable side, he does not from his
own conduct claim lenity...* [5]

The prospect of a lengthy war with France loomed in mid-1803.
When hostilities broke out, Tom was in Paris. He returned immediately
to London. He was worried about his mother and sisters at Eastbury
and his brother's family at Gunville – only a few miles from the
Dorset coast. There were fears of a French invasion. At that time Jos
was High Sheriff of the county. He was also concerned about his
family *'but his old mother is averse to moving and Bess is unwilling
to send the children away'*.[6]

In October 1803 Tom wrote to Jos:

*It seems to be the general opinion that the French
will land somewhere or other. Now your family is on
the coast have you anticipated deliberately all the
circumstances immediately arising from a landing in
your neighbourhood? I am afraid there would be a great
deal of stress, great difficulty of removal. Your horses
would be pressed for service. Might it not be wise, in
so awful a moment of danger, for your family and my
mother's to retire to the centre and most secure part
of the island? Or at any rate, to make immediate and
complete arrangements for removal, such as packing
valuables, etc. and perhaps to occupy Cote House for the
next critical month. For as Pitt said at Margate:– Expect
the French every dark night. Don't suppose that I write in*

a moment of excessive alarm; I have heard the subject a good deal canvassed lately... [7]

Kitty wrote to Tom from Eastbury in October, also worried about the possibility of a French landing:

... What I most fear is that in very bad weather we should really be obliged to go, and my mother would perhaps suffer from want of accommodation on the road; besides the hurry and confusion of the scene – or even travelling in very cold weather is a great risk for her. She is not in the least alarmed, and I believe would dislike the thought of removing; but we shall certainly consider whether we had not better. Jos will not be here in case of danger and it would be one anziety the less for him ...[8]

Tom wrote again to Jos on 18th October:

I don't know what to say about their continuing in Dorsetshire. I am afraid my mother's want of apprehension of danger is derived from a very inadequate consideration of it. Now, as Kitty says, a forced march in mid-winter happening when she may be indisposed might be very distressing. I should think Cote House tolerably secure... [9]

Sarah was eventually persuaded because she and her daughters moved to Cote House where Tom joined them in November. His fears of an invasion were unfounded.

Chapter 14

END OF AN ERA – NEW HORIZONS

Sarah and her daughters continued to live at Eastbury Park. Jos, his wife Bessy and their children were nearby. Tom still liked to travel but always eventually returned to his family.

Early in the 1780s, Tom sold his estate to Jos, and in 1803, with a loan from his brother-in-law, Jos acquired an estate of 1000 acres at Maer, nine miles from Etruria. At the same time he purchased Parkfields – a comfortable house in its own grounds on the outskirts of Barlaston – for his mother and sisters should they wish to move there. He thought of using Maer Hall as a second home when he visited Etruria.

Sarah never ceased to worry about Tom's poor health. He was fragile and always needed tender loving care, which his family lavished on him. He seemed to get strength and some peace when in Gunville with Jos and Bessy. Bessy was a kind and generous woman, who knew how close the two brothers were: she too was always there for Tom when he was ill. Between 1800 and his death in 1805, during his many journeys either abroad or visiting friends and relatives, Tom wrote profusely to Jos. He tried to spare his mother from knowing how desperate and unhappy he was and at the top of one letter dated 10th January 1803 he put:

> *Read this to yourself – and extract what you judge proper for the feelings of my mother ...'*

He continues:

I take 20 drops of Laudunum with my dinner.[1]

Opium did not improve his health; he tried to overcome the habit but could not. In many of his letters he sounded suicidal. In March 1803 in barely legible hand writing he wrote to Jos from the Lake District:

> *The uniform failure of every successive effort has given me an utter distaste for the scene around me – I now live on opium and tea and my nerves are increasingly on the thrill – but I can't not support myself without them. ... The Kindest regards to TP* [Thomas Poole] *tell him how I am situated – and how sorry I am – Beg him to write to Stowey and get me a lump of English opium if possible and have it sent by Taunton coach to me at the Luffs – as soon as possible – I have a strange feeling about coming to Gunville – like the last bite of the apple, I feel that its selfish and regret's are so mixed...* [2]

In 1804 their spendthrift brother John had to confess that he was in a financial mess and after discussion – and financial help from Jos, his sisters and Robert Darwin – it was decided that John would sell Cote House, rejoin the family pottery business and move back to Staffordshire. His wife Jane, with their seven children, joined him and they went to live at Etruria Hall. At this time Thomas Byerley was happy to move to London.

In July 1805 Tom's condition grew much worse. Here is a letter written by Bessy to her sister Emma Allen, dated 12th July 1805, with an account of his death:

> *... I was writing to you on Wednesday morning, when all the agreeable feelings with which I sat down to the employment, were cruelly dampt by the sad intelligence that poor Tom was so ill that there was no hope of his recovery.*
>
> *He had not been worse than usual, and we thought him rather better, from the custom he had taken up of going out every day with Jos in the gig; but on Monday I think he got a little chilled, which brought on much*

internal pain, and left him weak. On Tuesday night Joe parted with him with an engagement as usual to go and breakfast at Wood Gates, but at midnight he rang his bell, and told his servant to give him something, for he was very weak, but not ill. He told him also to come in in two hours' time, and see how he was, and to call Jos at 5. The servant did so, and found him as he thought sleeping, but in fact he was then without any sign of sense except that he still breathed. When Jos came he also thought him sleeping, and sat down an hour and half beside him, before he discovered that he was not; when he did he became alarmed and sent for Dr. Crawford, who immediately said he was dying. He continued in that state, his head quietly reposing on his arm, till seven in the evening, when he expired without seeming to have suffered the least pain. What a day for poor Jos, watching him dying for 12 hours...

We have prevailed on his mother and sisters to come down here, till they go to Staffordshire, which they now mean to do as soon as they can. On Tuesday will be the funeral, and we wish them to go before that, as we are so near the Church. He is to be buried in the Vault belonging to this place. He has left his fortune equally between all his brothers and sisters, and he has left a discretionary fund in Jos's hands to supply the generous purposes that his death would otherwise have cut short, to assist a great number who have often felt his bounty before. He has also left a memorandum with Jos that Edward Drewe is to have £20, Caroline £20 as a remembrance from him, and each of their daughters a hundred a piece. This Caroline does not yet know, as I did not hear it till to-day; but I am more gratified at it than I can express, as I know it will give Caroline so much pleasure to have been remembered by him. Indeed the more I think of him the more his character rises in my opinion; he really was too good for this world. Such a crowd of feelings and remembrances fill my mind while I am recalling all his past kindnesses to me and mine, and to all his acquaintance, that I feel myself quite unfit to make his panegyric, but I trust my children will ever remember him with veneration as an honour to the family to which he belonged... [3]

Tom had spent all his adult life travelling in search of peace and good health but never found it. Sarah and all the family took a long time to come to terms with their loss.

Meanwhile, Jos became resigned to moving back to his roots in Staffordshire. He was concerned that the business, with John as the main family representative at Etruria, was not doing too well and he knew he owed his relatives his full support.

By 1807 the problem of John Wedgwood's continued extravagant lifestyle was growing. He and his wife Jane entertained lavishly, beyond their income. Jos wanted to dissolve John's partnership in the firm without causing family discord. He presented John with the full picture of his debts, pointing out the difficulties the business had with exports. John finally agreed and took his family first to Southend and later to Baring Place in Exeter to be near Jane's and Bessy's widowed sister, Caroline Drew.

During 1807, Jos had sold his properties in the South. The new Wedgwood family home, Maer Hall, awaited them. It was a large Elizabethan house and Jos, with his wife Bessy and eight children, returned to Staffordshire in 1808.

The hall had extensive gardens with a lake in the centre and woods all around. Rhododendrons sheltered the long drive. On a hill over the small road across from the stables stood the church and cemetery.

The estate had facilities to suit all ages. There was shooting, fishing, skating on the lake in the winter, riding and, of course, walking. Maer became the favourite family place of the Wedgwoods and Darwins. Jos, later accompanied by his son Josiah III (Joe) rode to and from the works each day.

Sarah was feeling her age and realised that this house move would be her last. She was seventy-six in 1810 and her health was failing. She was glad to have the company of Sally and Kitty. Although the girls had had marriage proposals over the years, neither found a suitor they wished to marry. They were both comfortably off, and during their lifetimes gave much of their inheritance to charities.

Now the Wedgwood families were in the Potteries en masse, close to their relatives and good friends the Darwins. Robert and Susan were only 25 miles away in Shrewsbury. Sarah and her daughters did not take long to adapt to their new life at Parkfields, near Barlaston. It was good to be back where they felt they belonged. Jos had mixed feelings. He was a solid character, honest and conscientious, and took his responsibilities seriously. He knew he would always have to oversee financial matters for his mother, brothers and sisters. Bessy, like Sarah before her, was a great support to her husband and helped him to the best of her abilities.

Jos – still on an economy drive – decided to end his contribution to the Coleridge annuity and wrote to him in November 1812 giving loss of business as the reason. His late brother Tom's contribution continued. Jos also decided he would again lease Etruria Hall, but for about three years he and his family again lived there: this cut down the expense of living at Maer. By 1816, when commerce and trade abroad became buoyant again, he felt optimistic about the future and moved back to Maer Hall – this time for good.

Jos made it a habit to dine with his mother and sisters once or twice each week. Sarah had been living quietly at Parkfields. She enjoyed Jos's visits, especially when he talked of his work at Etruria. She knew when to let go, to listen but not interfere and to acknowledge that change in the workplace was inevitable. She was never very demonstrative, but her daughters knew she was pleased to have them living with her. She enjoyed seeing old friends when they would reminisce about the past and endeavour to foretell the future. It is unfortunate that, unlike her children and her husband, she did not keep many letters, which she undoubtedly received. In 1814, she was eighty years of age. Her health deteriorated and in January the following year she died. She was buried in the parish church of Stoke-on-Trent near her husband. Her will, made four years previously, read as follows:

> *To my Exors 1400£, upon trust to apply them to the use of my son John Wedgwood for life, and then to his wife Louisa Jane, and then to divide the legacy among the children of John Wedgwood.*
>
> *To my son Josiah Wedgwood and to my daughters Susannah Darwin, Catherine Wedgwood and Sarah Wedgwood 1400£ each.*

To my niece Ann Holland	*10 guineas*
To my niece Jane Turner	*5 guineas*
To my niece Mary Byerley	*5 guineas*
To Elizabeth Moore	*40£ and my clothes*
To George Jones	*10£*
To my niece Sarah Byerley	*20£ a year for life*
To Mrs Elizabeth Steele	*6 guineas a year for life*
To Mrs Elizabeth Eiver	*6 guineas a year for life*
To Mrs Ann Stevenson	*6 guineas a year for life*

Executors:– my daughters Catherine Wedgwood and Sarah Wedgwood.

Witness:– Thomas Malkin[4]

Sarah's eldest daughter, Susan, who had married Robert Darwin and with whom she had six children, had never been strong. Like her mother, she suffered from arthritis from an early age. Two years after her mother died she became seriously ill. Susan and her family were particularly close to her brother Josiah II, his wife Bessy and their children. They visited each other's houses and Josiah and Robert Darwin were colleagues, both personally and in business. When Robert saw how ill Susan was – he had diagnosed peritonitis – he immediately sent for her sisters Kitty and Sally. In a letter Kitty wrote to her brother Jos from The Mount just before Susan died she said:

> *The Doctor has not the slightest hope & her suffering is terrible. The pain indeed is gone that was her first illness, but she has such severe vomitings and sickness that he says he does not think her suffering much lessened ... this evening she is worse, & he is very wretched. ... He was afraid our seeing her would agitate her & she does not know we are here. Marianne & Caroline [Susan's daughters] are always with her & keep up pretty well. ... The Doctor has just been to tell us he does not think she will pass the night...* [5]

She died the next day – she was fifty-two.

At the time of Susan's death her oldest daughter Marianne was nineteen and Caroline seventeen: their younger sisters were Susan, who was fourteen, and Emily Catherine, aged seven. They had two brothers: Erasmus, aged thirteen, and Charles Robert, aged eight. Charles' two elder sisters took care of him. In later years Charles, who went on to write *The Origin of Species* – still controversial to the present day – had to admit he could not remember much about his mother.

After Susan's death The Mount was a gloomy place, so the children spent more time at Maer with their first cousins. The brotherly feelings between Josiah II and Robert Darwin were strengthened even further after Susan died.

Chapter 15

MAER HALL – JOSIAH II AND FAMILY

Bessy and Jos settled back into their life at Maer Hall with their growing family. There was sadness in the household when one daughter, Mary Anne, born in 1796, died aged two. Their first child, Sarah Elizabeth, was born in 1793; Josiah III (Joe) in 1795; Charlotte in 1797; Henry Allen (Harry) in 1799; Francis (Frank) in 1800; Hensleigh in 1803; Fanny in 1806 and Emma in 1808.

Bessy and Jos had had a special system for bringing up their children. Jos felt that parents should always be truthful and he believed that sincerity in either the parent or the tutor was the cornerstone of education. The results of their parents' guidance produced children who, from an early age, showed independence and in later years a strong belief in their own strength and integrity.

At the Hall there was always a great feeling of freedom. Doors and windows were open and welcoming. Jos had inherited his parents' books and with his own collection there was an adequate library. The comfortable ambience of their home was a welcome place for good company and interesting conversation.

Joe, like his father before him, would not have chosen a career as a potter, but, again like his father, he was the oldest son and Jos needed him to learn the business. Harry trained to be a barrister. Frank happily joined his father as a potter. The two younger daughters, Fanny and Emma, were very close and did everything together. The family's nickname for them was the Dovelies. The girls had different temperaments, however: where Fanny was calm and unhurried. Emma was vivacious and had a lively manner.

As a young girl, Emma was uncomplicated and confident. She knew French, Italian and German, she was a skilled needlewoman, loved to dance, and enjoyed sports such as archery, riding and skating. Her greatest love was music: she was excellent at reading music and had lessons from Chopin for a short time. Most days of her life she found time to play, if only for a few minutes. Emma was pretty with large grey eyes, a high forehead and a happy demeanour. Although she was untidy in her everyday life, her mind was organised and methodical. All the girls had long hair, as was the fashion. Charlotte's fair hair reached her knees, while Emma's hair was a chestnut colour and very thick. She had a natural aptitude for hairdressing and later, on special occasions, did Charlotte and Elizabeth's hair in elaborate styles.

While they were growing up, Jos took his daughters abroad many times. This was partly educational and partly for pleasure. When Emma was ten, Jos and Bessy took the four girls to Paris with Frank and Hensleigh. They were abroad for several months. During their stay Jos and Bessy, with Elizabeth and Charlotte, went to Switzerland, particularly to place the boys with a Mr Cheneviere at Geneva. Harry had been there previously.

Emma would never forget her first visit to Paris, and how foreign it looked. She and Fanny were left at a boarding school in Paris while their parents were absent. The girls missed their family. They were delighted when in September they all returned to Maer. The girls' aunt Jessie (Bessy's sister) had married an Italian, Jean-Charles Leonard de Sismondi, an Italian economist and historian, and their home was in Geneva. They did not have a family of their own but welcomed relatives whenever they cared to visit them. Having dear Aunt Jessie in Geneva was an added incentive for the Wedgwoods to visit the Continent.

Bessy's sister, Emma Allen, wrote to her niece, Elizabeth Wedgwood, while staying at Maer Hall:

> *I marvel at the strength of the girls' spirits as much as I do at the perfection of their tempers. I feel now very sure that not only not a cross word ever passes between them, but that an irratable feeling never arises. Fanny to be sure is calmness itself, but the vivacity of Emma's feelings, without perfectly knowing her, would make me expect that Fanny's reproofs, which she often gives with an elder sister air, would ruffle her a little, but I have never seen*

that expressive face take the shadow of an angry look,
and I do think her love for Fanny is the prettiest thing
I ever saw...

At that time Emma was eleven. Her aunt also describes a typical day:

... get up every morning by candlelight, breakfast at 7.30,
by 10 the Bible and then reading Italian with both girls.
Much to do till 1 o'clock, then find an hour for music
when we come in at 3 or half after. There was an ... extra
half an hour for music between dinner and tea.[1]

Bessy took Fanny and Emma, then aged sixteen and fourteen respectively, up to London to go to school at Greville House on Paddington Green, where they stayed for one year. The teaching at this school was disappointing, and the only excitement for Emma was when she had to play the piano for Mrs Fitzherbert, a friend of King George IV. Afterwards their education was supervised by their sisters Elizabeth and Charlotte. A Sunday school had been established in the laundry room at Maer where the two older sisters taught some 60 children from the estate and surrounding houses. When she left school Emma also taught there. When Bessy thought the time was right for Emma at sixteen to be confirmed, as she was away from home she wrote a letter to her daughter Elizabeth:

As the confirmation will soon take place I think it will be
right in Emma to be confirmed, and therefore I hope she
will feel no objection. You and Fanny had better go with
Emma and if your aunt Sarah's horses and carriage are
disengaged, I advise you to ask her to lend them to you,
that you may make the most respectable appearance you
can ...

She then suggested that Emma should read something about confirmation:

... but do not let her be alarmed at that, it will be but little
and the subject is simple ... perhaps one ought not to

*press it, any more than as an opinion that it is better done
than omitted, as it is better to conform to the ceremonies
of our Church than to omit them, and one does not know
that in omitting them we are not liable to sin ...*[2]

The children's aunts, nicknamed Kitty and Sally Wedgwood, still
lived at Parkfields, but Kitty had been ill with a stomach tumour and in
the spring of 1823 she and Sally moved to The Mount, where Robert
Darwin could look after her. After a painful four months, Kitty died,
aged forty-nine. Sally was now alone and was content to remain at
Parkfields with two servants and her housekeeper, but Jos worried about
her and had a small house built for her on Maer Heath, near Maer Hall.
The house was named Camphill and she moved there early in 1827.

Emma and Fanny in particular took advantage of their aunt
Jessie's hospitality. They loved Switzerland, but when they visited
Italy the poverty depressed young Emma and they hurried back to
Geneva. Jessie was a favourite aunt and always kept up a lengthy
correspondence with her sisters and nieces in England. Having
someone like Jessie in Geneva, where she and Sismondi moved in
high society was a wonderful opportunity for young girls such as
Emma and Fanny.

Bessy was beginning to slow down. In 1824 she was sixty years
old. She divided her time riding her donkey Peggy around the peaceful
grounds of Maer, while her daughters walked beside her. During that
year, when Jos and Bessy accompanied the girls abroad, Bessy went
only as far as Geneva.

In 1826, when aunt Jessie was visiting the family in England, Bessy
decided to send Fanny and Emma back with her to Geneva for a few
months. She knew she would miss her 'babies', but thought being
abroad would broaden their education and improve their languages.

The girls were now twenty and eighteen respectively. Although
excited at going to stay with their aunt Jessie they were also afraid
that they would miss Christmas at home. To her sister Elizabeth,
Emma wrote:

*This week has been very quiet except Monday, when
there was a Ball in the Theatre in commemoration of the
restoration of the Republic, where everybody may come
that pays 6Fr. We were to dance with whoever asked us ...*[3]

Present also was the Prince of Denmark, who invited them to a ball at his house in the country. He was then eighteen years old and Emma said he danced nearly always with a Mrs Lambton, with whom his name was linked at that time. She decided she could not warm to Frenchmen however.

Aunt Jessie wrote frequently to Bessy to reassure her that the girls were enjoying themselves. At the end of January 1827, she said:

> *... I hope the girls had dancing enough on Saturday, they could hardly stand when they came in. They are remarkably well, and look so blooming that I receive endless compliments on their fraicheur. ... There is a pretty gaiety about Emma, always ready to answer to any liveliness and sometimes to throw it out herself, that will cheer everybody that lives with or approaches her. There is some disposition to silence in Fanny, which I am glad to see Sismondi perseveringly combat, and I think no one can be so persevering as he is. He says always he thinks Emma the prettiest, but he acts as if he thought Fanny was, he says there is something particularly pleasing to his taste in her countenance. I am very glad of it; the world soon shows which is really the prettiest, and when two go so much together, it is difficult that the one not preferred should not be mortified. Fanny looks remarkably well in a ballroom; she holds herself well, is most radiant in her person and brilliant in her colouring; so that it is never known we perceive the difference. How I do wish they were my own children, from whom I should never be separated...* [4]

Their brother Frank was go to Geneva to bring them home but Emma wrote to her mother on 25th March:

> *... Aunt Jessie was thinking of our making a little tour with Frank. I know we should enjoy it very much, but we have already had so much pleasure and been so long from home, that if you and Papa had rather we came home sooner, we shall be perfectly satisfied. I assure you I do not wish anything about it. And you are always so*

ready to give us pleasure that I am sure you will, if you have not some good objection or wish... [5]

Emma was surprised to learn her parents were not expecting them until July. In April, she wrote again to her mother:

I shall be very sorry to leave aunt Jessie whenever it happens, but then I shall be so glad to come home and see you all that I don't mean to trouble my head about anything, but let things take their course according to aunt Jessie's maxim. Sometimes I take a violent longing to go home, but it goes off in 5 minutes ... [6]

Although Emma and Fanny enjoyed the Swiss social life, they missed their family at Maer. Emma's homesickness came through in her letter to her mother. Their stay in Geneva was a most enjoyable time, the social life was fun and being abroad was enlightening. Most of all they loved being with aunt Jessie and her husband.

Eventually, in May, their father and their first cousins, Caroline and Charles Darwin, went to fetch them. Charles went only as far as Paris, the only time he visited the Continent. Charles had a very high regard for his uncle Jos and loved to visit Maer. In his *Life and Letters Vol 1* he said:

My visits to Maer during these two or three succeeding years were quite delightful. ... Life there was perfectly free; the country was very pleasant for walking or riding, and in the evening there was much very agreeable conversation, not so personal as it generally is in large family parties, together with music. In the summer the whole family used often to sit on the steps of the old portico, with the flower garden in front, and with the steep wooded bank opposite the house reflected in the lake. ... I was also attached to and greatly revered my Uncle Jos; he was silent and reserved, so as to be a rather awful man; but he sometimes talked openly with me. He was the very type of an upright man with the clearest of judgment ... [7]

Jos was very fond of his Darwin nephews and nieces, Caroline in particular reminded him very much of her mother Susan – Jos's sister. Charles was a special favourite and he often turned to his Uncle Jos for advice. When he was invited to join HMS *Beagle*, as a naturalist on its surveying voyage round the world under the command of Captain Robert Fitzroy, his father was not happy to give his consent, but Jos persuaded Robert to allow him to go. They sailed in December 1831.

Back home, life at Maer was happy and carefree. Emma, now a young woman, enjoyed the many social gatherings. In a letter to Jessie, Emma's mother Bessy wrote in October 1828:

> ... *Emma is going down with Miss Morgan to pay a visit to the Miss Aclands at Clifton. Her manners are in her favour & she is more popular than any of my girls. Her manners to men are very much to my taste, for they are easy and undesigning without coquetry...* [8]

House parties were usually where young people met each other. Emma's brother Josiah III – who preferred to be called Joe – was slow in choosing a bride. At thirty-six he was still single.

By 1827 both of Jos's sons, Joe and Frank, were in partnership with him in the family business, Jos retaining half of the shares and his sons a quarter each. Business was improving and Jos acquired a pair of carriage horses. Bessy, now sixty-four, loved her new carriage, which made it so much easier for her to get around.

Henry (Harry) married his first cousin Jessie in 1830 – his uncle John's youngest daughter. They lived at Etruria Hall where in 1831 Jessie's parents, John and Jane, joined them, together with Jessie's elder sister, Elizabeth, now aged thirty-six. However, they stayed only a short while because romance intervened: Emma's brother Frank met Frances Mosley at a ball and fell instantly in love and they soon married. Jos insisted Frank went to live at the Hall, as was fitting for the man who was mostly involved in running the pottery empire. John, the spendthrift brother, and his family moved to a house called Seabridge near Maer.

A year after Harry's marriage Hensleigh married his first cousin, Fanny Mackintosh. Fanny was the daughter of Sir James Mackintosh and the late Kitty Allen, Bessy's sister. Emma's sister Charlotte, married the Revd Charles Langton in 1832. She had met him at Hensleigh's wedding the previous year.

Suddenly there were fewer people at Maer Hall. Emma and Fanny, the 'Dovelies' were, as always, inseparable – but it was not to last. During 1832 a cholera epidemic struck the Midlands. Many people became infected, and Fanny was one of them. Emma helped to nurse her, but Fanny never recovered and died before the end of that year. Emma felt she had lost part of herself. After Fanny's death, Emma wrote:

> *At 9 came on the fatal attack and in 5 minutes we lost our gentle, sweet Fanny, the most without selfishness of anybody I ever saw, and her loss has left a blank which will never be filled up. Oh, Lord, help me to become more like her, and grant that I may join her with Thee never to part again. I trust that my Fanny's sweet image will never pass from my mind. Let me always keep it in my mind as a motive for holiness. What exquisite happiness it will be to be with her again, to tell her how I loved her who has been joined with me in almost every enjoyment of my life.*[9]

That same year, Jos, who had always been interested in politics, stood as the Stoke-on-Trent candidate for the first reformed parliament and was elected by a comfortable majority. His family were very proud of him and Bessy also felt this was a step up in their children's social status. '*A worldly feeling I must confess but one I find myself not able to contend with*,' she wrote to her sister Jessie.

The following year, after the heartbreak of the previous one, the birth of three new babies within the family was a comfort. Hensleigh and Fanny had a daughter, Julia (nicknamed Snow because she was born during a snowstorm); Frank and his wife – known as Fanny Frank – had a son, Godfrey, and in 1834 Harry and Jessie had a daughter, Louisa.

Bessy, with Emma and Elizabeth, went to visit Hensleigh and Fanny and their new baby. But while in London, Bessy had an epileptic fit and fell, seriously injuring her spine. She was eventually moved back to Maer but could never walk again without assistance and her life became much quieter. At Maer, Elizabeth and Emma looked after their mother.

During these years Emma received several proposals of marriage but she did not feel sufficiently attracted to any suitor to marry.

John's wife, Jane, became ill and while visiting Robert Darwin at The Mount her health deteriorated. Robert gave her his best attention but she did not recover and died there in 1836. John was completely lost without Jane, but their daughter Elizabeth, who had been their constant companion, looked after him and eventually they went to live with his other daughter Jessie and her husband Harry at Seabridge.

Chapter 16

CHARLES DARWIN – EMMA WEDGWOOD

Having set off in 1831, Charles Darwin arrived back from his voyage on HMS *Beagle* in October 1836. The following month he went to Maer. Emma wrote to her brother Hensleigh's wife Fanny, in London:

> *We enjoyed Charles visit uncommonly. We had been very handsome in inviting all the outlyers of the family to meet him, and the late morning the chaise from Tern Hill did not come, and we persuaded them to stay, and had just made ourselves comfortable and planned a walk when the chaise arrived. However, we got them to let us send it off, though Caroline felt it to be rather naughty, and we had a very nice snug day of them to ourselves. Charles talked away most pleasantly all the time; we plied him with questions without mercy. Harry and Frank made the most of him and enjoyed him thoroughly...* [1]

After Charles had visited all his family and friends he returned to Cambridge. He took lodging in Fitzwilliam Street, with a manservant to look after him, and resumed his research. After three months he moved to London where he got lodgings in Great Marlborough Street. He lived there for the following two years. Now at twenty-seven he was very happy in his chosen career.

Charles had been born in 1809 into a loving family, and although his mother died when he was only nine, his sisters, particularly Caroline, cared for him well. His father Robert was not only a successful Shrewsbury doctor, but also a well-to-do banker, living at The Mount. Charles' first school was St Chad's, then in 1818 he went to Dr Sam Butler's public school in Shrewsbury. He was bored because his favourite subject, science, was not in the curriculum. He left in 1825.

His father was worried that Charles might fritter away his life on self-indulgent pleasures – he loved to go fishing, hiking, or hill walking, especially North Wales, and adored shooting. One of his favourite pastimes was to visit his uncle Jos at Maer, where there was lots of both fishing and shooting. Robert hoped that Charles would follow in his footsteps and study medicine. With this in mind he sent him to Edinburgh University in October 1825. After two years there Robert had to accept that his son would never be a doctor, so he suggested he become a clergyman and sent him to Christ's College in Cambridge in February 1828. Charles, who was to become the great proponent of evolution, *did* study divinity and at that time accepted the Bible's teaching.

A second cousin, William Darwin Fox, was also up at Cambridge then and they became lifelong friends. William introduced Charles to entomology. Another person who influenced his studies in Cambridge also recommended him for his fateful voyage on the *Beagle*: John Stevens Henslow, professor of botany at the university.

Charles gained his BA and in August of that year, when his father still had hopes of his becoming a clergyman, Charles asked permission to join Captain Robert Fitzroy's crew as the ship's naturalist on the *Beagle*, due to sail to South America before the end of the year. Robert refused but said '*if you can find any man of common sense, who advises you to go, I will give my consent.*' Charles, feeling sure his uncle Jos would back him, went across to Maer to talk about it. Jos supported him and wrote at length to Robert with reasons why he should give his permission. Meanwhile Charles also wrote to his father from Maer on 31st August:

> ... *I have given Uncle Jos, what I fervently trust is an acurate and full list of your objections and he is kind enough to give his opinion on all. The list and his answers will be enclosed, but may I beg of you one favour, it will be doing me the greatest kindness if you will send me a*

decided answer – Yes or No – If the latter I should be
most ungrateful if I did not implicitly yield to your better
judgment and to the kindest indulgence which you have
shown me all through my life, – and you may rely upon it
I will never mention the subject again; ... I do not know
what to say about Uncle Jos' kindness, I never can forget
how he interests himself about me... [2]

Robert gave in, and for the next five years Charles did what he loved best. He had a wonderful opportunity to study geology and natural history – everything he observed made him want to find its origin. When he returned to England in 1836 he was a confident and experienced naturalist.

At the beginning of 1837 Emma, with her brother Joe, went to Edinburgh for about two months to stay with their cousin, Lady Gifford. On their return, Joe – now aged forty-two – became engaged to his first cousin, Caroline Darwin, five years younger than him. They had known each other all their lives. The family, especially his mother Bessy, were overjoyed, as it wasn't so much a surprise, more a puzzle as to why it took them so long to decide. On 1st July 1837 Emma wrote to her sister Elizabeth:

On Friday I went directly after breakfast on the pony to
tell aunt Sarah the good news, and took a nice little note
of Jos's to her, which was rapturous enough to please her
very much. ... It is delightful to see how much attached
he is to her. Whenever I have talked to him alone he has
burst out, in a way as if could not contain himself, about
her exquisite charm... . [3]

Caroline Darwin's family were also pleased about yet another union between the two families. Charles, in London, writing to his friend, W D Fox, on 7th July:

... I returned last night from a flying visit of eight days to
Shrewsbury; & I have now got a piece of news to tell you,
... Caroline is going to be married to Jos Wedgwood. ...
I do not know whether you recollect him, he is the
eldest son. He is a very quiet grave man, with very

much to respect & like in him, but I wish he would put himself forward more. He has a most wonderful deal of information, & is a very superior person; but he has not made the most of himself. I am very glad of the marriage for Caroline's sake, as I think she will be a very happy person, especially if she has children, for I never saw a human being so fond of little crying wretches, as she is. But I am an ungrateful dog to speak this way, for she was a mother to me during the early part of my life... [4]

The social circle at this time in London, involving Darwins, Wedgwoods and Allens, included the Lyells, Thomas and Jane Carlyle, Maria Edgworth, author and daughter of Richard Lovel Edgeworth and the novelist Elizabeth Gaskell.

Hensleigh and Fanny Wedgwood enjoyed a busy social life in London; their home was a popular rendevous for their many friends and relations. Erasmus Darwin, Charles' brother, known as Ras, unmarried and five years older than his brother, was an elegant 'man about town' and a frequent visitor. He had a house nearby. Ras greatly admired Fanny and was always happy to act as her escort when Hensleigh was not free. The novelist Harriet Martineau was attracted to Ras and they were often seen together. The family did not approve of this friendship and Charles, in a letter to his sister Susan in April 1838 wrote:

... Erasmus has been with her [Harriet] noon, morning, and night ... if her character was not as secure, as a mountain in the polar regions she certainly would lose it ... Lyell called there the other day & there was a beautiful rose on the table, & she coolly showed it to him & said 'Erasmus Darwin gave me that'... [5]

Ras's father, Robert, disliked Harriet both as a person and for her writing. He was concerned that he might become too attached to her. But Ras never did marry.

Emma, in 1838, was now thirty and unmarried. Either with her parents or a member of her family, she would occasionally visit relatives. Bessy and Jos also welcomed friends to stay at Maer, sometimes for a few days, sometimes for longer. All the family were sociable and enjoyed having house parties.

Bessy, before her back injury, always looked forward to social outings where there was music and dancing, and her daughters were happy to accompany her. They were well aware that at such gatherings they could encounter the man they would like to marry.

Emma went to Paris in the summer of 1838 with her brother Harry and his wife Jessie plus her cousin Catherine Darwin. As usual they stayed with the Sismondis. On their return there was a gathering of the clans at Hensleigh's house in London. Emma and Catherine, Ras, Charles, and Thomas and Jane Carlyle all came to dinner. Emma and Charles had more time to get to know one another in surroundings other than at Maer, and were more relaxed with each other. They had always liked each other, now they realised how compatible they were.

Charles, now living alone in London, started to think of marriage. He took the question very seriously and that summer he drew up a list of pros and cons. If married he would have a wife as a companion, perhaps children. She would care for him, their family and their home. Against marriage, his first thought was that being single he would have freedom of choice in both people and places, no problem with in-laws, and not have the expense and worry of a home and bringing up children. Having thought of all these things, he wrote: *'Only picture to yourself a nice soft wife on a sofa with good fire & books & music perhaps – compare this vision with the dingy reality of Grt Marlbro' St.'*[6] He decided marriage was best, and the sooner the better. It sounds a cold and calculating conclusion, but it was practical too.

Whenever he had the opportunity, Charles travelled north to Shrewsbury and invariably went across to visit his uncle Jos and aunt Bessy and the rest of the Wedgwoods. Emma was eligible, near his own age and someone with whom he was at ease. And he decided she fitted his secret list of requirements as a wife.

Towards the end of 1838, Charles began to think of asking Emma to marry him. She had also become more aware of him as a possible suitor but was unsure of his feelings. Finally, on 11th November, Charles left London for Maer, having decided to propose. Emma was happy to accept and after discussion with her family, it was decided the marriage would take place early in the new year.

The records of Charles' life before Emma show that only one woman appeared to have had any great attraction for him and that was

Fanny Owen of Woodhouse. The Owens were friends of the Darwin family. Before embarking on HMS *Beagle* he and Fanny were friends and corresponded for a time, but while he was still abroad he learned that she had married a Mr R M Biddulph.

Emma wrote to her aunt Jessie to tell her the good news on 15th November. In this letter it now became apparent that she had been attracted to Charles for some time and that their respective families had already seen the signs of a possible match.

> *Nothing is pleasanter than writing good news, and I am sure you will be pleased with what I have to tell you. When you asked me about Charles Darwin, I did not tell you half the good I thought of him for fear you should suspect something, and though I knew how much I liked him, I was not the least sure of his feelings, as he is so affectionate, and so fond of Maer and all of us, and demonstrative in his manners, that I did not think it meant anything, and the week I spent in London on my return from Paris, I felt sure he did not care about me, only that he was very unwell at the time.*
>
> *He came to see us in the month of August, was in very high spirits and I was very happy in his company, and had the feeling that if he saw more of me, he would really like me. He came down again last Thursday with aunt Fanny, and on Sunday he spoke to me, which was quite a surprise, as I thought we might go on in the sort of friendship we were in for years, and very likely nothing come of it after all. I was too much bewildered all day to feel my happiness and there was a large party in the house, so we did not tell anybody except Papa and Elizabeth and Catherine. Dear Papa, I wish you could have seen his tears of joy, for he has always had a great regard for Charles, and Charles looks up to him with the greatest reverence and affection. I believe we both looked dismal (as he had a bad headache) for when aunt Fanny and Jessie [Wedgwood] went to bed they were wondering what was the matter and almost thought something quite the revese had happened. Fanny Hensleigh was 'cuter, and knew quite well what had happened. I went into their*

rooms at night, and we had a large party talking it over till very late...

Catherine was delighted, indeed I was so glad to find that all of them had been wishing for it and settling it. It is a match that every soul has been making for us, so we could not have helped it if we had not liked it ourselves.

... I must now tell you what I think of him, first premising that Eliz. thinks pretty nearly the same, as my opinion may not go for much with you. It is a match that every soul has been making for us, so we could not have helped it if we had not liked it ourselves. ... He is the most open, transparent man I ever saw, and every word expresses his real thoughts. ... He is particularly affectionate & very nice to his father and sisters, and perfectly sweet tempered, and possesses some minor qualities that add particularly to one's happiness, such as not being fastidious, and being humane to animals. We shall live in London, where he is fully occupied with being Secretary to the Geological Society. ... Mamma takes it very comfortably and amuses herself a good deal with planning about houses, trousseaux and wedding-cake. ... I bless the railroad every day of my life, and Charles is so fond of Maer that I am sure he will always be ready to steam down whenever he can, so that we shall always be within reach of home. ... The real crook in my lot I have withheld from you, but I must own it to you sooner or later. It is that he has a great dislike to going to the play, so that I am afraid we shall have some domestic dissensions on that head. On the other hand he stands concerts very well... [7]

Remembering how Sarah and Josiah I had hoped for a union between Susan and Robert Darwin, it is now apparent that the two families are irrevocably intertwined, and the relationships become intricate. Charles's mother, Susan Darwin, was the sister of Emma's father (Jos II). Now, when Charles married Emma, Jos II would be both his uncle and his father-in-law. In his letter to Robert about the forthcoming marriage, Josiah II refers to himself as 'uncle father'. Very confusing!

Charles' father, Robert, wrote to Josiah II on 13th November from Shrewsbury:

Dear Wedgwood
Emma having accepted Charles gives me as great happiness as Jos having married Caroline, and I cannot say more.

On that marriage Bessy said she should not have had more pleasure if it had been Victoria, and you may assure her I feel as grateful to her for Emma, as if it had been Martineau herself that Charles had obtained. Pray give my Love to Elizabeth, I fear I ought to condole with her, as the loss will be very great.

ever dear Wedgwood your affectionate Brother

R W Darwin[8]

Emma's father replied:

My dear Doctor
A good cheerful & affectionate daughter is the greatest blessing a man can have after a good wife – if I could have given such a wife to Charles without parting with a daughter there would be no drawback from my entire satisfaction in bestowing Emma upon him – You lately gave up a daughter – it is my turn now – At our time of life our happiness must be in a great measure reflected from our families, and I think there are few fathers who have on the whole more cause to be grateful with the conduct & present circumstances & future prospects of our families – I would have parted with Emma to no one for whom I could so love & so entirely feel as a father & I am happy in believing that Charles entertains the kindest feelings for his uncle father.

I propose to do for Emma what I did for Charlotte & for three of my sons – give a bond for £5000 & to allow her £400 a year as long as my income will supply it which I have no reason for thinking will not be as long as I live. Give my love to your fireside and believe me
Affectionately yours

Josiah Wedgwood

A note from Emma was added to her father's letter as follows:

My dear Uncle
I have begged a bit of Papa's letter to thank you from my heart for the delightful way in which you have received me into your family & to thank my dear Marianne & Susan for their affectionate notes which gave me the greatest pleasure. One of the things that give me most happiness is Charles's thorough affection & value for Papa. I am my dear Uncle yours affectionately Emma W.

   You will be glad to hear that Mamma has quite got over her disappointment about Miss Martineau & amuses herself a good deal in planning about houses, cake & c.[9]

The family often teased Robert about his dislike of Harriet.

Chapter 17

LOVE LETTERS – LONDON
HOUSE HUNTING

Having proposed and been accepted by Emma, Charles went to his family at Shrewsbury and from there wrote to her to express how he felt and also to discuss where they should live. He worried in case Emma would find life with him quiet after Maer:

> *My own dear Emma,*
> *Marianne & Susan will have told you what joy and happiness the news gave all here ... there never was anybody so lucky as I have been, or so good as you. Indeed I can assure you, many times since leaving Maer I have thought how little I expressed, how much I owe to you; and as often as I think this I vow to try to make myself good enough somewhat to deserve you.*
>
> *I hope you have taken deep thought about the sundry knotty points you will have to decide on. We must have a great deal of talk together when I come back on Saturday ... do have a fire in the Library ... it is such a good place to have some quiet talks together. My chief fear is that you will find after living all your life with such large & agreeable parties, as Maer only can boast of, our quiet evenings dull. ... I am so selfish, that I feel to have you to myself, is having you so much more completely, that I am not to be trusted. Like a child that has something it loves*

beyond measure, I long to dwell on the words my own dear Emma...

... I have written to Erasmus, & I am well sure he will most heartily congratulate. My father echos & re-echoes Uncle Jos's words 'you have drawn a prize!' Certainly no man could by possibility receive a more cordial welcome, than I did from everyone at Maer on Monday morning. ... My life has been very happy & very fortunate and many of my pleasantest remembrances are mingled up with scenes at Maer, & now it is crowned...

I kiss the hands with all humbleness and gratitude, which have so filled up for me the cup of happiness – It is my most earnest wish I may make myself worthy of you.[1]

Charles reluctantly returned to London and during their brief separation many loving letters sped between the happy couple. Their letters were full of happiness for the future and enthusiastic about setting up home together in London. All through Charles' married life with Emma and their family he showed such a loving, caring side to his character that contrasted with the man whose work was so scientific and serious.

From the beginning of their courtship, Emma's letters reveal how she was always concerned about Charles' health and worried that he might be overdoing things. He too would have realised how sympathetic and understanding she was and he would have been confident of her future strength and kindness.

Emma always knew that she and Charles had very different beliefs. She had traditional Christian views and although Charles had never really been religious: now as an adult he had serious doubts. Emma hoped that they would always be frank with each other and that there would be no misunderstandings between them. Her letter in mid-November is optimistic for their future and although she was keen to know his thoughts she was reluctant to hear him voice them. She wrote:

... When I am with you I think all melancholy thoughts keep out of my head but since you are gone some sad ones have forced themselves in, of fear that our opinions on the most important subject should differ widely. My

reason tells me that honest & conscientious doubts cannot be a sin, but I feel it would be a painful void between us. I thank you from my heart for your openness with me & I should dread the feeling that you were concealing your opinions from the fear of giving me pain. It is perhaps foolish of me to say this much but my own dear Charley we now do belong to each other & I cannot help being open with you. Will you do me a favour? Yes, I am sure you will, it is to read our Saviour's farewell discourse to his disciples which begins at the end of the 13th Chapter of John. It is so full of love to them & devotion & every beautiful feeling. It is the part of the New Testament I love best.

This is a whim of mine it would give me great pleasure, though I can hardly tell why I don't wish you to give me your opinion about it.[2]

In her next letter to Charles she says she is pleased that he had read Jesus' discourse to his disciples. She goes on to discuss their new home in London:

My dear Charles,
Your letter has just come in & as I am sitting with Mamma instead of going to church I shall find it much pleasanter to have a little talk with you than to listen to Allen's Temperance sermon. Thank you dear Charles for complying with my fancy. To see you in earnest on the subject will be my greatest comfort & that I am sure you are. I believe I agree with every word you say, & it pleased me that you sh^d have felt inclined to enter a little more on the subject…

I think nothing could be nicer than the south side of the Regent's Park & quite near enough to Cov. Gardens if it is not too dear. Tavistock Square sounds grand. I have no doubt I shall bring my mind down to care properly for these sublunary matters in a short time…

Monday. On Friday Caroline & Jos came, she looking so well that I fully expect that she would perform the journey quite well & it is a pleasure to think of her as

*being safe at Shrewsbury. She was very charming &
affectionate to me. I am in very good heart about her she
looks so well & in such good spirits. ... Suppose you take
a look at some houses in the back lanes about the Regents
Park: Hensleigh thinks they are nice ones. What do you
think of Bayswater & Kensington gardenways? ...*

*I don't expect you to answer my letters as quickly as
I answer yours. I have nothing else to do you know but
waste my tediousness upon you, so don't think of writing
when you are busy or tired & if a letter does not arrive
when I am rather expecting one I shall read an old one
over again instead. When you see Miss Martineau thank
her for her little books which I have read & liked much &
they will be very useful to me...* [3]

Charles wrote on 27th November:

My dear Emma,
*... I positively can do nothing, & have done nothing this
whole week but think of you & our future life ... you may
then, well imagine how I enjoy seeing your handwriting.
I should have written yesterday but waited for your letter:
pray do not talk of my waiting till I have time for writing
or inclination to do so ... it is a very high enjoyment to
me, as I cannot talk to you, feel your presence, by having
your own dear hand within mine.*

*And now for the great question of houses. Erasmus
& myself have taken several very long walks; & the
difficulties are really frightful. Houses are very scarce &
the landlords are all gone mad. They ask such prices ...
I feel sure, that a central house would be best for both
of us, for two or three years ... I am tied to London, for
rather more than that period; & whilst this is the case,
I do not doubt it is wisest to reap all the advantages of
London life: more especially as every reason will urge us
to pay frequent visits to real country, which the suburbs
never afford. After the two or three years are out, we then
might decide whether to go on living in the same house or
suburbs, supposing I should be tied for a little longer to*

London & ultimately to decide, whether the pleasures of retirement & country (gardens, walks, &c) are preferable to society &c &c. It is no use thinking of this question at present & I repeat, I do not doubt, your first decision was right: let us make the most of London whilst we are compelled to be there: the case would be different, if we were deciding for life, for then we might wish to possess the advantages both of country & town, though both in a lesser degree, in the suburbs. ... Tell me what you think of this reasoning...

After much deliberate talk, (especially with the Lyells) I have no doubt, that our best plan will be to furnish slowly a house for ourselves ... it will be far more economical both in money & time; but not in comfort just at first ... will you rough it a little at first? Again I clearly see we shall be obliged to give at least 120£ for our house; if not a little more...

I do long to be seated beside of you, again, in the Library; one can then almost feel anticipation, the happiness to come... [4]

At the end of November Emma wrote to Charles:

... I really & solemnly think you are quite right about houses & so let us cast off the suburbs & what is more Susan [Charles' sister] *thinks so too & you know what a wise woman she is. I read her what you said on that subject which I did not think was infringing on your wish of keeping your letters to myself. Dear good Susan has undertaken to get all the household linen which will be a great weight off our minds. She came over by coach yesterday & we are enjoying her visit thoroughly. She brings a very good account of Caroline & will stay till Monday.*

The Hensleighs have asked me to go up with them for a week to look at houses with you. I think you thought of this plan yourself once, but I then thought it would be a bustle & not much use. Whether it will be of much use now I don't know, but I am sure I shall like it of all things so

I am a coming. I really think it will help matters if you fix upon 3 or 4 of the most likely houses for me to take a look at with you. ... I want to be strictly incog so don't say that I am coming to those dreadful blabs Erasmus and Robert [Emma's cousin R Mackintosh] for I don't mean to go after any of my friends...

My dear Charley shall I really see you the end of next week. It will be very pleasant I do think. ... I see you want a real good scolding about getting your work done so you must think what a dreadful rage I shall be in if you are not at leisure the week after next to go a-galivanting with me in the flies & omnibusses.

It is very unlucky your having such a quantity of work on your hands...

Caroline says in a note to me that she can wish me no greater happiness than to meet with the same constant sympathy & affection she does & then it will not signify where I live as she finds. That is a wonderful marriage I say for the hundredth time, but I think I kn[ow] one that will turn out quite as happy. ... We are going to walk to Camp Hill this morning with Susan. Goodbye once more write to me soon like a dear old soul. Yours Emma W[5]

In a letter to Emma dated 30th Nov – 1st Dec. Charles had to confess he had yet to find a suitable house, but was still looking in out of the way places.

Emma arrived in London and stayed with her brother Hensleigh and Fanny in Notting Hill. She and Charles looked at various houses without deciding on any particular one, after which she returned to Maer which looked wonderfully fresh and quiet. She wrote to Charles:

... Having now got rid of me I suppose you will give up your intemperate habits & take to your books again. I advise you not to be in a hurry about houses but see what turns up quietly. ... I must go into the school so Goodbye my dear old Charley. Tell me how you are. I do not like your looking so unwell & being overtired when

*I come & look after you I shall scold you into health like
Lady Catherine de Burgh used to do to the poor people.*

Goodbye & write soon. Your affectionately Emma W.[6]

Emma's mention of a school here refers to the Sunday school held
at Maer where she and Elizabeth taught the children of the estate.

In December Joe (Josiah III) and Caroline had a baby daughter,
Sophy Marianne. Sophy was a delicate child.

At the end of December 1838 Charles wrote from Great
Marlborough Street:

My dear Emma,
*I am tired with having been all day at business work.
– but I cannot let a post go by, without writing to tell
you Gower St is ours, yellow curtains & all. – I have
today paid some advance money, signed an agreement &
had the key given over to me & the old woman informed
I was her master henceforth. The minute I put the whole
affair into the Solicitor's hands, he arranged all the
difficulties, ... I am delighted with the house, the more
I see of it; I have just been going over all the furniture
with the inventory. – We shall not have much to buy, –
even the crockery & glasses are very perfect. –*

*I am also delighted to say that the Solicitor, (having
some minutes to spare) looked at the furniture of the
rooms & he said he had just been furnishing his own
house with care & knew the prices of things, & he
maintains the furniture is cheap at 550£ & the rent
extraordinarily low – He examined all the tables
& chairs & said they are made of excellent wood
& must have cost a great deal of money. – In fact
I am convinced we have been most fortunate & I am
in great triumph at having come to so good an end.—
Mr Steward, (my present landlord) says he will let me off
part of the hire of my lodgings, if I choose to move soon,
& as I want a little diversion of body & mind, I think it
very likely I shall begin moving all my sundry rattle-traps
on Monday. –*

I long for the day when we shall enter the house together; how glorious it will be to see you seated by the fire of our own house – Oh that it were the 14th instead of the 24th.

Goodbye, my own dear Emma

Most affectionately yours – Chas. Darwin... [7]

Chapter 18

WEDDING PLANS – NEW HOME

Emma was overjoyed about Charles' news as she also preferred this particular house and wrote and told him so. Life was full of plans and discussions now at the Hall. The marriage date had been set for late in January, not later than the 24th. Knowing that fashion conscious aunt Jessie was anxious to have the details of Emma's trousseau, she found time to write to her on 28th December:

Thank you, my dear aunt Jessie, for your warm congrat-ulations and sympathy with my happiness. I was very glad to return home last Saturday, as I grudge every day away from home now We had a fly every day and used to go into town to look at houses and [buy] *my clothes, and I think I have obeyed your orders, for though I have not bought many things, they are all very dear and the milliner's bill would do your heart good to see. I have bought a sort of greenish-grey rich silk for the wedding, which I expect papa to approve of entirely, and a remarkably lovely white chip bonnet trimmed with blonde and flowers. Harriet* [Jessie's sister] *has given me a very handsome plaid satin, a dark one, which is very gorgeous, handsomely made up with black lace; and that and my blue Paris gown, which I have only worn once, and the other blue and white sort of thing will set me up for the present. Jessie* [Emma's sister-in-law] *and Susan* [Charles' sister] *gave Fanny strict orders not to let me be shabby. (And a grand shawl too.)*

Top Left: *Robert Darwin* by Ellen Sharples

© English Heritage Photo Library
By kind permission of
Darwin Heirlooms Trust

Top Right: *Susannah Darwin
(née Wedgwood)*

Bottom Left: *Emma Darwin (née Wedgwood)*

© English Heritage Photo Library.
By kind permission of Darwin Heirlooms Trust

Bottom Right: *Charles Darwin
(aged 40)*

Reproduced from 'Order of the Proceedings
at the Darwin Celebration held at Cambridge
22-24 June 1909', Cambridge University
Press 1909 CA

... Mama is quite well. I must tell you what sort of a house ours is that you may fancy me. A front drawing-room with three windows, and a back one, rather smaller, with a cheerful look-out on a set of little gardens, which will be of great value to us in summer to take a mouthful of fresh air; and that will be our sitting-room for quietness sake. It is furnished, but rather ugly. Goodbye, my dearest, no more room.[1]

Emma's description of her future home in Gower Street was not very enthusiastic, but her happiness at being with Charles overcame any misgivings she might have had.

Once the house was theirs, Charles couldn't wait to move in. Impulsively, with the help of his manservant, Syms Covington, he packed his belongings and in 24 hours had moved almost everything into No 12 Gower Street. He wrote to Emma about the move and advised her he would be up at Maer for a flying visit early in January:

'I long for the hour of inducting you into the glory, I dare not say comforts, of Gower St. – I wish I could make the drawing room look as comfortable as my own studio; but I dare say a fire & a little disorder will temporarily make things better, but the day of some signal reform must come, otherwise our taste of harmonious colours will assuredly be spoilt for the rest of our lives... '[2]

In her reply Emma sounded piqued that he could have moved without her:

I was surprised indeed to find how soon you had moved into your new house & I don't wonder you feel triumphant. ... You must have found it very interesting putting all your things away & arranging your sanctum to the greatest advantage, & I should have liked very much to have helped you & also to eat your eggs & bacon afterwards. I find it so curiously tiresome teaching the school now – I suppose it is feeling as if it was no use now it is only for a few weeks. Now we are really in January I begin to feel as if something real was going to happen & it makes me dream & ponder a great deal… .

Tell me how your Carlyle dinner went off. We have been living as quiet as mice here since Monday, reading aloud & playing Cassino in the evening, very comfortable I think. Joe came on Saturday & Sunday. We could not fathom what he thought of his daughter or whether he admired her. He says she is still weakly.

Goodbye dearest Charley your affectionate Emma W.

I am reading Mansfield Park which I find very suitable… [3]

In her next letter to Charles Emma had to tell him that the date of the wedding had been changed. She says:

I am very glad you have fixed your day for coming down & I guess we shall see you here on the Monday after. … You will have a few days more time on your hands than you expect my dear Charley as the marriage must be fixed for the 29th instead of the 24th (I always said about the 24th) … I do dislike very much doing what you don't like my dear old Charley & I do hope this is the last time I ever shall, & I wish very much that it could have been arranged otherwise… [4]

Charles visited Maer in January just prior to the wedding and afterwards wrote to Emma on Sunday night 20th January:

… I cannot tell you how much I enjoyed my Maer visit, – I felt in anticipation my future tranquil life: how I do hope you may be as happy as I know I shall be: but it frightens me, as often as I think of what a family you have been one of. – I was thinking this morning how on earth it came, that I, who am fond of talking & am scarcely ever out of spirits, should so entirely rest my notions of happiness on quietness & a good deal of solitude; but I believe the explanation is very simple, & I mention it, because it will give you hopes, that I shall gradually grow less of

*a brute – it is that during the five years of my voyage
(& indeed I may add these two last) which from the active
manner in which they have been passed, may be said to
be the commencement of my real life, the whole of my
pleasure was derived, from what passed in my mind,
whilst admiring views by myself, travelling across the
wild desserts or glorious forests, or pacing the deck of the
poor little Beagle at night. – Excuse this much egotism,
– I give it you, because, I think you will humanise me, &
soon teach me there is greater happiness, than building
theories, & accumulating facts in silence & solitude.
My own dearest Emma, I earnestly pray, you may never
regret the great, & I will add very good, deed, you are to
perform on the Tuesday:*

my own dear future wife, God bless you… [5]

The church where Emma and Charles were to be married was
across the road from Maer Hall, and still stands today, with very little
difference in its appearance. The cemetery around it is fuller, the trees
have grown taller, but the church still stands on the hill overlooking
the Maer estate. A marriage yet again between a Wedgwood and a
Darwin brought the families even closer, and was also a happy, joyful
event.

The service was performed by Emma's first cousin, Allen
Wedgwood, on 29th January 1839. Allen had been given the position
of vicar of Maer by Josiah III in 1825. Later that day, after the
wedding celebrations, Emma and Charles left for their new home in
Gower Street. With Emma leaving Maer, her sister Elizabeth would
have to look after their mother. Bessy was now bedridden and unable
to attend the wedding. Emma worried about going so far away but
was thankful for the railway, which would ease the journey from
London.

Almost immediately Emma wrote from London to her mother. She
sounded homesick:

*It was quite a relief to me to find on coming out of Church
on Tuesday that you were still asleep, which spared you
and me the pain of parting, though it is only for a short*

time. So now we have only the pleasure of looking forward to our next meeting. We ate our sandwiches with grateful hearts for all the care that was taken of us, and the bottle of water was the greatest comfort. The house here was blazing with fires and looked very comfortable and we are getting to think our furniture quite tasteful. Yesterday we went in a fly to buy an armchair but it was so slippery and snowy we did not do much. We picked up some novels at the library. Today I suspect we shall not go out as it is snowing at a great rate. On Monday or Tuesday we are going to give our first dinnerparty to the Hensleighs and Erasmus. I hope the H's will sleep here, we shall see them so much more comfortably.

I came away full of love and gratitude to all the dear affectionate faces I left behind me. They are too many to particularize. Tell my dear Eliz. I long to hear from her. Nothing can be too minute from dear home. I was very sorry to leave Caroline so uneasy and looking so unwell. I am impatient to hear of her and the baby. I don't know how to express affection enough to my dear, kind Papa, but he will take it upon trust.

Good-bye my dearest Mamma

Your affectionate and very happy daughter, E.D.[6]

The happiness of the wedding was followed in February by the sad news that Caroline and Joe had lost their baby. Both parents were distraught. Dr Darwin attended Caroline and tried to comfort her – he had always taken a great interest in the sickly child. After the intense anticipation of the birth of their first child it would take some time to overcome their loss. In her first letter to their aunt Fanny about the death Elizabeth wrote:

I have no heart to write you an account of the wedding, as it has had such a sad sequel. Yesterday Caroline lost her poor baby. ... She is as miserable as anyone can be, but she exerts herself very much, and I think the best thing to counterbalance her own grief will be her anxiety about

Jos. Of course the chief part of his feeling is for her, but he often cannot command himself when he is sitting with her, and is obliged to leave the room. She came into my mother's room to see us two hours after its death, which I took exceedingly kindly of her, and came into the drawing-room this evening to see my mother again and Charles [Langton] *whom she had not seen. She does her utmost not to yield, but she is very unwell and I never felt greater pity for anyone in my life. It is quite affecting to see poor dear Jos's face and hear his depressed voice.*

The Dr [Robert Darwin] *came yesterday at 5, and C. had a good deal of comfort in talking over everything with him, the more so, I have no doubt, from the exceeding interest he has always taken in the poor little thing. The funeral is to be to-morrow – Susan and Charlotte, as well as my father, will attend. They will go to Fenton in the evening and Susan will go there on Monday, which I am as glad of for Jos's sake (who seems to find her the greatest comfort) as for C.'s. It will make him not so unwilling to go as usual to his employment – but what poor Caroline will find to do I cannot think; for the last so many months the thoughts of this precious child and the preparations for it have occupied her in an intense way that I never saw in anyone else. But I will write no more on this sad subject.*

The ceremony was got through very stout-heartedly, and then there was not much more time but for Em. to change her clothes and pack her wedding bonnet and sit a little by the dining-room fire with Charlotte and me before she set off, and I did not much mind anything but just the last. It is no small happiness to have had such a companion of my life for so long; since the time she could speak, I have never had one moment's pain [from] *her, and a share of daily pleasure such as few people have it in their power to shed around them. I am more afraid of my father's missing her more than my mother. They had not to be sure a great deal to talk together, but her sunny face will leave a vacancy...*

Emma's letters to her family at Maer were full of her love for Charles and about how well he was looking after her.

> *there is not so affectionate an individual as the one in question to be found anywhere else...* [7]

A long letter from her mother in February was treasured:

> *A thousand thanks to you dearest Emma for your delightful letter which, from the cheerful, happy tone, of it, drew tears of pleasure from my old eyes. I am truly thankful to find you so happy and still more so that you are sensible of it, and I pray heaven that this may only be the beginning of a life full of peace & tranquility. My affection for Charles is much increased by considering him as the author of all your comfort and I enjoy the thoughts of your tasty curtains and your armchairs hoping your piano is by this time added to them...*
>
> *Caroline has recovered her peace of mind as much as we could have expected. ... She wished to be alone for these two days with Joe whose behaviour to her has been all that is tender and affectionate. The baby was buried yesterday. The coffin was carried by Caroline's two maids in white gowns hoods and gloves and Charlotte and Susan walked after it. Joe intended to go but he was afraid he should not be able to command his feelings and was persuaded to give it up as Caroline did. ... The Doctor's soothing conversation was of great use in calming Caroline's mind. She stayed in the Library the two days he was here and he sat with her all the time, he went away the day of the funeral...* [8]

The piano mentioned in this letter was one chosen by Emma and Charles while venturing out on their first shopping spree. It had been a present from Emma's father. Emma wrote again to her mother on 8th February:

> *I cannot tell you how pleased I was to see your dear handwriting and how much I thank you for writing me*

such a nice long letter. I shall always preserve it with great care. I was very glad to find you have had such comfortable nights.

... Catherine has very considerately sent us a Shrewsbury paper that we may see ourselves in print, and as she drew us up she has all an author's feelings on the subject. Charles is not quite used to my honours yet, as he took up a letter to me the other day and could not conceive who Mrs C Darwin could mean. He has set to his work in good earnest now...

Charles desires his best love to you... [9]

Bessy's loneliness was less acute after a visit from Emma and Charles to Maer when she saw how happy they were together.

Chapter 19

MARRIED LIFE IN LONDON

During the second month of their marriage Emma put some thoughts she had in a letter to Charles, which he treasured. Indeed, after his death, it was found he had added this note: '*When I am dead, know that many times I have kissed and cried over this.*' Emma was preoccupied with thoughts about Charles' beliefs. She knew his scientific mind questioned everything, that 'seeing is believing' and 'not seeing not being able to believe'. She was staunch in her Christian beliefs, while he questioned everything. This aspect of their relationship was the only problem Emma had with Charles. Her letter is unequivocal:

> *The state of mind that I wish to preserve with respect to you, is to feel that while you are acting conscientiously & sincerely wishing, & trying to learn the truth, you cannot be wrong; but there are some reasons that force themselves upon me & prevent my being always able to give myself comfort. I dare say you have often thought of them before, but I will write down what has been in my head, knowing that my own dearest will indulge me. Your mind & time are full of the most interesting subjects & thoughts of the most absorbing kind, viz following up yr own discoveries – but which make it very difficult for you to avoid casting out as interruptions other sorts of thoughts which have no relation to what you are pursuing or to be able to*

give your whole attention to both sides of the question.

There is another reason which would have a great effect on a woman, but I don't know whether it wd so much on a man – I mean E. [Eramus] whose understanding you have such a very high opinion of & whom you have so much affection for, having gone before you – is it not likely to have made it easier to you & to have taken off some of that dread & fear which the feeling of doubting first gives & which I do not think an unreasonable or superstitious feeling. It seems to me also that the line of your pursuits may have led you to view chiefly the difficulties on one side, & that you have not had time to consider & study the chain of difficulties on the other, but I believe you do not consider your opinion as formed.

May not the habit in scientific pursuits of believing nothing till it is proved, influence your mind too much in other things which cannot be proved in the same way, & which if true are likely to be above our comprehension. I should say also that there is a danger in giving up revelation which does not exist on the other side, that is the fear of ingratitude in casting off what has been done for your benefit as well as for that of all the world & which ought to make you still more careful, perhaps even fearful lest you should not have taken all the pains you could to judge truly. I do not know whether this is arguing as if one side were true & the other false, which I meant to avoid, but I think not. I do not quite agree with you in what you once said – that luckily there were no doubts as to how one ought to act. I think prayer is an instance to the contrary, in one case it is a positive duty & perhaps not in the other. But I dare say you meant in actions which concern others & then I agree with you almost if not quite. I do not wish for any answer to all this – it is a satisfaction to me to write it & when I talk to you about it I cannot say exactly what I wish to say, & I know you will have patience, with your own dear wife.

Don't think that it is not my affair & that it does not much signify to me. Every thing that concerns you concerns me & I should be most unhappy if I thought we did not belong to each other forever. I am rather afraid my own dear Nigger will think I have forgotten my promise not to bother him, but I am sure he loves me & I cannot tell him how happy he makes me & how dearly I love him & thank him for all his affection which makes the happiness of my life more & more every day ...[1]

(Emma often used 'Nigger' as a term of endearment because Charles called himself her 'nigger', meaning her slave.)

Emma must have taken quite a while to write this letter. She would have thought through all her doubts and beliefs. The doubts were about Charles, as her beliefs were based on her faith and trust in God. Her diaries often mention going to church on Sunday, whenever possible with some of her children. Religion was part of her everyday life.

Life in London involved dinners and parties but because Charles became exhausted so easily, especially in the evenings, they tried to limit their social engagements. Emma often mentioned Charles' state of health in her letters to her family. To her sister Charlotte Langton on 15th March she wrote:

My Charles has been very unwell since Sunday. We went to church at King's College and found the church not warmed, and not more than half-a-dozen people in it, and he was so very cold that I believe it was that which has made him so unwell.

She then tells her sister her problems with her staff and that she is hoping to part with the cook, and maybe the housemaid too. The letter ends with:

I expect Charles to get quite fond of the theatre, but as to dinners and parties he gets worse I think, and I don't care how few dinners we go to either. Drinking wine disagrees with him, and it is so tiresome not drinking that he can't resist one glass...[2]

Late in May they went back to Maer for two weeks, followed by one week with Charles' family in Shrewsbury. Elizabeth wrote to their aunt Jessie on 5th June:

... I have been enjoying three weeks of Emma's company. She and Charles stayed a fortnight here, and I went on with them to Shrewsbury, Eliza [brother John's daughter] *kindly taking my place here meanwhile; and the feeling that she was procuring me a great pleasure, and the retirement, made her, I think, quite enjoy her week. It was agreed by all the members of the colony that Emma's time was so short she could not be spared to divide any of it amongst them away from Maer, and that they would all come and see her here, so that we had the whole of her visit. It was rather spoilt by Charles being so unwell almost the whole time of his stay in the country, and Emma not very well herself. Charles got some of his father's good doctoring and is much better again, but I suppose he is feeling the effect of too much exertion in every way during his voyage and must be careful not to work his head too hard now. His journal is come out at last along with two other thick volumes of Capt. Fitzroy and Capt. King of the same voyage, but I have not had time to read it yet. It is a great pleasure to see Emma so entirely happy in her lot, with the most affectionate husband possible, upon whom none of her pleasant qualities are thrown away, who delights in her music, and admires her dress. I quite agreed with all your good advice to her on that head, and I even mean to dress well myself, now the credit of the family rests on me.*

... There cannot be a happier or easier task than making the lives comfortable of my father and mother. There never were people who gave so much and required so little. Indeed it often makes me ashamed and touches me very tenderly to see my father get up to pay me some little kind attention that would come so much more appropriately from me to him. We have very seldom been only our own selves since Emma went. Now I have had these three weeks of her company, I feel satisfied and think no more of her loss, and have got rid of the fits of sadness that would

take me sometimes unawares.

The Hensleighs are coming down the end of this month, and Hensleigh will return to town after bringing them down, and I then mean to run up with him and see Emma in her own house for ten days or so. The Hensleighs have just taken a house four doors only from Emma, which Emma very much likes. She will find it a great comfort for they are neither of them idle people to fall into the error of running in and out at all hours. Charles goes to his own room to work after breakfast till two o'clock, so that Emma has a good deal of time to herself in the mornings, which I should think very comfortable... [3]

Chapter 20

FIRST CHILD – FAMILY LETTERS

During the summer of 1830 Emma was pregnant with her first child. Her family at Maer were very happy to hear the news.

Emma usually dealt with all the family correspondence, but when his sister Caroline wrote to them in October Charles replied, albeit reluctantly as he felt there was not much news to relate because of the:

> 'extreme quietness with which we are living':– Camp-hill [Aunt Sarah's home near Maer] is quite gay compared with Gower Street – we see nothing, do nothing & hear nothing, & this to my mind is the perfection of life – I find I cannot stand going out in the Evening – I can just last through the 24 hours if I am quite quiet after dinner. ... I fear poor Emma must find her life rather monotonous. ... The poor thing has been but poorly every other or third day since we came back, which has been a great disappointment to me: But she is, I hope essentially going on well & undeniably growing... [1]

Around that time Charles also wrote to his cousin, William Darwin Fox, again remarking on the quietness of their lifestyle in Gower Street. He added:

> We have given up all parties, for they agree with neither of us; and if one is quiet in London, there is nothing like its

*quietness – there is a grandeur about its smoky fogs, and
the dull distant sounds of cabs and coaches; in fact you
may perceive I am becoming a thorough-paced Cockney,
and I glory in the thought that I shall be here for the next
six months…* [2]

When the baby was due, Elizabeth travelled to London to be with
Emma. The baby arrived on 27th December 1839. Emma and Charles
named him William Erasmus. Immediately after the birth Emma's
mother Bessy wrote what would be her last letter to Elizabeth:

*I received your letter of good news yesterday with great
joy. It cost me a good cry, but such tears are precious and
I was very happy while shedding them. Remember my
love and blessing to both parents of the welcome stranger,
who will, I hope be as great a comfort to them as their
predecessors have been to us. We have been guessing
at his name and have guessed Robert. So no more from
your affectionate mother, as Fanny has been so kind as to
promise a little gossip of her own in addition to this.*

Ever yours, my dearest Elizabeth. E Wedgwood[3]

Charles was not much help to Emma after the birth, as his
inexplicable ill health governed their everyday lives. Any excitement
or stress brought on palpitations and vomiting and then Charles would
always have to withdraw from whatever activity was in progress and
remain in quiet seclusion until he felt better. In February 1840 he
claimed that it was nine weeks since he did a week's work.

As will be seen from Emma's letter to her aunt Jessie on 7th February
1840, she took some time to get over the birth of their first child and
was only now getting back into her usual form. She wrote:

*It seems very odd to me that I should have been all this
time without writing to you, but I have been so helpless
and unable to do anything that I never had the energy to
write, though I was often thinking of it. Now I am quite
well and strong and able to enjoy the use of my legs and
my baby, and a very nice looking one it is, I assure you.*

He has very dark blue eyes and a pretty, small mouth, his nose I will not boast of, but it is very harmless as long as he is a baby. Elizabeth went away a week too soon while he was a poor little wretch before he began to improve. She was very fond of him then, and I expect she will admire him as much as I do in the summer at Maer. He is a sort of grandchild of hers...

Charles and I were both very much pleased at having a visit from Papa, and he looked comfortable in his arm-chair by the fire, and told us that Gower St. was the quietest place he had ever been at in his life; and Elizabeth finds it very quiet after Maer, though she had a little private dissipation of her own, dining and going to parties, but she has a different sort of bustle at Maer.

I was delighted to hear by your letter that your coming to England was positively fixed, and I hope to catch you here and at Maer. Charles and I had been planning to get you to come straight to us when you came to town, and I cannot tell you what a pleasure it would be to receive you both in my own house and show you my own dear husband and child, but I have been telling him this morning that while his health continues in such a very uncomfortable state, it would neither do for him nor you. He has certainly been worse for the last six weeks, and has been pretty constantly in a state of langour that is very distressing, and his being obliged to be idle is very painful to him. He is consulting Dr Holland, but without much good effect.

Feb. 10. Here is a gap in my letter, but I can find time for nothing, as nursing and looking after the baby fills up any number of hours. Charles has been better again these three days, and I hope he has made a turn and will continue mending, and that I shall have the happiness of having you and my dear M. Sismondi with us. I should see so much more of you in the mornings and at odd times, and perhaps he would be going out more than you would like, and then I should catch you. I have not forgotten my happy stay at Paris, and the precious bits of talk I had with you. It was a bright, happy time.

It is a pleasure in writing to you that one's letter is only seen by two, and one may say whatever comes uppermost, and so I will be as egotistical as ever I please. It is a great happiness to me when Charles is most unwell that he continues just as sociable as ever, and is not like the rest of the Darwins, who will not say how they really are but he always tells me how he feels and never wants to be alone, but continues just as warmly affectionate as ever, so that I feel I am a comfort to him. And to you I may say that he is the most affectionate person possible, as much so as your own Sis, and I am sure I could say no more for him. It is a great advantage to have the power of expressing affection, and I am sure he will make his children very fond of him. I have been pretty well coaxed and spoilt all my life but I am more than ever now, so I hope it does one no harm, but I don't think it does.

I have no doubt it will be a painful moment to you when you see Papa and Mamma at first, but I think you will find that Mamma's affections are much more alive than when you saw her last, though I suppose her mind is certainly much weaker. She lights up occasionally very much into her old self. Mr Clifford [old friend] *was very charming and nice to her, and I think his visit at Maer was a satisfaction to him. I was very glad to catch him, as I had been longing to see him again these 20 years, and he was very much his old self, only grown very old. I am glad you like Charles Langton. It is a pretty part of his character his fondness for Mamma. Charlotte told me that he seemed to see through her into what she had been, more than she should have thought possible in a person who had not known her before. I am going this evening to take Fanny* [Hensleigh] *and the children to see the illuminations for the Queen's marriage. I am sorry the rablement have such a rainy day for seeing the fun.*

I have been reading Carlyle, like all the rest of the world. He fascinates one and puts one out of patience. He has been writing a sort of pamphlet on the state of England called 'Chartism'. It is full of compassion and

*good feeling but utterly unreasonable. Charles keeps
on reading and abusing him. He is very pleasant to talk
to anyhow, he is so very natural, and I don't think his
writings at all so.*[4]

During that winter, while Emma nursed her new child, she
complained of frequent headaches. When Charles went to Shrewsbury
to visit his father and sisters in April 1840 he discussed Emma's health
with Dr Darwin and wrote to Emma subsequently:

*You are a good old soul for having written to me so soon.
... My father is appearing very well – I have begun to
extract wisdom from him, which I will now write – He
does not seem able to form any opinion about your case,
– but strongly urges your going on suckling a little for
some time, even at the expense of slight headaches. –
He says you probably will be able to guess with better
chance of truth later about your condition – but that it
will be only a guess. – You will be pleased to hear, that
he objects to the Baby having medicine for every trifle –
He says, as long as the Baby keeps well, & the motions
appear pretty healthy, he thinks it of little consequence
whether it has a dozen or one or even less than one in
24 hours, although he says it is desirable it should be
more than once – He is very strong against gruel but not
against other food – he thinks there is no occasion to go
on with Asses' milk...*[5]

Charles mentioned he was not sleeping very well but believed it
was from Emma's absence. His father could not recommend anything
for Charles' sickness but said he *could* take Calomel.

From June to November that year Charles, with Emma and baby
William, stayed at Maer. Charles was not well for most of that time.
Meanwhile aunt Jessie and her husband stayed at 12 Gower Street
en route to Tenby to visit her sister Harriet Surtees. Jessie wrote to
Emma from Tenby in June:

*... Your roof, my Emma, brought us good luck while there,
everything went to our hearts' content; be it observed that*

Parslow is the most amiable, obliging, active, serviceable servant that ever breathed. I hope you will never part with him…

Give my love to your husband and my grateful thanks for his munificent reception of us, even when not there to do the honours. I hope his silver will not suffer. I found he had left out wine also, in short I never saw such a reception, invisible as it was. It was like having entered an enchanted castle, everything was there before one wanted it, you inspired your servants too I think. When I asked for the washing bills, they said they had orders not to send the linen to the wash till after we were gone. Is not this your very mother? And is it not conspiring against your husband's purse?… [6]

Emma was most hospitable and one of her friends, Maria Edgeworth, later wrote from North Audley Street in December 1840 in praise of her:

Mrs Darwin is the youngest daughter of Jos Wedgwood, and is worthy of both father & mother; affectionate, and unaffected, and – young as she is, full of old times. She has her mother's radiantly cheerful countenance, even now, debarred from all London gaieties and all gaiety but that of her own mind by close attendance on her sick husband … [7]

During their stay in England the previous year aunt Jessie's husband Sismondi had not been very well and in January the following year, from Chene, Jessie wrote to Emma:

… If I had written to you ten days ago I should have told you Sismondi was much better, but within that time his hiccup has returned as violent as ever, and lasts the whole day. He continues to work in spite of it all the morning, and he will walk out, but he will not see anyone if he can help it…

Give our united love to your husband and a kiss to your child… [8]

Emma had become pregnant during the summer of 1840 at Maer and their second child, Anne Elizabeth, was born on 2nd March 1841. Emma wrote again to her aunt in May:

> ... *We are thinking of going to Maer on the 1ˢᵗ June. It will be delightful to find ourselves there but I rather dread the journey for Charles. I wish he would let me and the babbies and nurses go by ourselves and he by himself, but he says it would look so bad he can't consent to that plan.*
>
> *I have taken to playing a little on the piano and enjoy the feeling of health and being able to play with the little boy and walk about and do what I like, without always thinking about oneself which is very tiresome. Before my confinement I could take so little notice of the little boy that he got not to care a pin for me and it used to make me rather dismal sometimes, but he likes nobody so well as Charles and me now, but I think C. is the prime favourite.*
>
> *I must tell you a nice thing of Erasmus as you used not to like him, but it is a profound secret so you must not tell anybody. The other day he wrote to Miss Martineau, thinking that owing to her long illness she might be in want of money, to ask if he could help her. He carried about his letter in his pocket for some days without having courage to send it; but he did at last and poor Miss M. was very gratified by it, though she would not let him help her. She refused very nicely by openly entering on her affairs with him and telling him exactly what she had, to show him that she was not in want. She has nothing but what she has earned. I am afraid she has little chance of recovery, which I am very sorry for. Life was of great value to her, though she seems resigned to quit it. She told him she would let him know if she was in any distress.*[9]

They went to Maer as planned. Charles' sisters took young William – nicknamed 'Doddy' by his father – over to Shrewsbury for a short stay and Charles joined them at the end of June. He missed Emma and wrote to her on 1st July:

I will give you categorical account, and first for my own beggarly self. I was pretty brisk at first, but about four became bad and shivery. I was very desolate and forlorn and missed you cruelly. But to-day I am pretty brisk and enjoy myself. I think my father looking rather altered and aged, though he and the two old chicks [Susan and Catherine] *appear very well and charmingly affectionate to me. Doddy's reception of me was quite affecting. ... When I had had him for about five minutes I asked him where was Mama, and he repeated your name twice in so low and plaintive a tone, I declare it almost made me burst out crying. ... I am grieved to hear my father, who is kindness itself to him, thinks he looks a very delicate child. I felt quite ashamed at finding out, what I presume you did not know any more than I, that he has had half a cup of cream every morning, which my father (who seemed rather annoyed) says he believes is one of the most injurious things we could have given him. When we are at home we shall be able to look more after him. Only conceive, Susan found him when he started in the carriage with his stockings and shoes half wet through; my father says getting his feet wet on the grass, when afterwards changed, is rather a good than a bad thing, but to allow him to start on a journey in that state was risking his health. Last night Susan went into Doddy's room and found no water by his bedside. I tell you all these disagreeablenesses that you may feel the same necessity that I do of our own selves looking and not trusting anything about our children to others...*

Give my kindest love to Elizabeth and to Uncle Jos and Aunt Bessy. Good-bye, my dear. Right glad I shall be to see you on Tuesday.[10]

That year Emma's sister Charlotte and her husband Charles Langton moved to Maer to help Elizabeth in the care of both Josiah II (who had palsy) and Bessy: Charles by now had given up the Church. After ten years of marriage their only son Edmund was born in November 1841. Elizabeth adored him and he restored some vitality to the now quiet life of Maer. In February 1842, Emma went back to Maer to visit her mother and family and on her return wrote to aunt Jessie:

> ... *Mamma very well and cheerful, but decidedly more deaf I think, though I think it is more want of attention than deafness.*

Emma mentions Charles's health:

> ... *every now and then some little bit of overtire and dissipation knocks him up, & shews that he must still be careful...* [11]

Again early in April Emma wrote to her aunt:

> ... *My little Annie has taken to walking and talking for the last fortnight. She is 13 months old and very healthy, fat and round, but no beauty. Willie is very much impressed with his own generosity and goodness to her. ... We don't mean to move this summer, which you will think a good thing – my inclination for the country does not diminish though. Charles is very busy finishing his book on Coral islands, which he says no human being will ever read, but there is such a range for geology that I hope better things...* [12]

Jessie's husband died in June 1842. Jessie decided that as soon as she had settled her affairs abroad she would come back to England and live at Tenby.

Chapter 21

DOWN HOUSE

Originally both Charles and Emma liked being in London but gradually Charles, who had stated back in October that he loved London, now craved peace and quiet and they began to think of moving to the country. By 1842 they were seeking a suitable house not too distant from London. House hunting once more was hard work and they had to cover more ground in the country. To add to their situation Emma was again pregnant with their third child. They eventually found and bought Down House in the village of Downe in Kent for some £2,200.

The house was not their dream home, but they deliberately concentrated on its good features and one attraction was its seclusion and feeling of quietness. Charles wrote to his sister Catherine in July when decisions had been made finally about Down:

> *My dear Catty,*
> *You must have been surprised at not having heard sooner about the House! Emma & I only returned yesterday afternoon from sleeping there. ... Village about 40 houses with old walnut trees in middle where stands an old flint Church & the lanes meet – Inhabitants very respectable – infant school – grown up people great musicians – all touch their hats as in Wales, & sit at their open doors in evening, no high road leads through village – the little pot-house where we slept is a grocers-shop & the landlord is the carpenter – so you may guess style of village – There are butcher & baker &*

post-office. ... House ugly, looks neither old nor new – walls two feet thick – windows rather small – lower storey rather low – capital study 18×18. Dining room, 21×18 – Drawing room can easily be added to is 21×15. Three storeys plenty of bedrooms ... two bathrooms – pretty good office & good stable yard & a cottage...

Emma was at first a good deal disappointed & at the country round the house; the day was gloomy & cold with NE wind. She likes the actual field & house better than I; the house is just situated, as she likes for retirement, not too near or too far from other houses. ... Emma is rapidly coming round – she was dreadfully bad with toothache, headache, in the evening of Friday – but in coming back yesterday she was so delighted with the scenery for the first few miles from Down, that it has worked great change in her – We go there again the first fine day Emma is able & we then finally settle what to do... [1]

But in mid-September, when they took possession of their new home, Emma just wanted to rest; the whole upheaval of moving had tired her. In her diary on 14th September she wrote just one line: '*I and children came to Down.*' Her baby, Mary Eleanor, was born at the end of that month, but there were complications with her birth and she survived only three weeks. Afterwards Emma wrote from Down to her sister-in-law Fanny Wedgwood:

Thank you my dearest Fanny, for your sweet, feeling note. Our sorrow is nothing to what it would have been if she had lived longer and suffered more. Charles is well today & the funeral over, which he dreaded very much. ... I think I regret her more from the likeness to Mamma, which I had often pleased myself with fancying might run through her mind as well as face. I keep very well and strong and am come down-stairs to-day. I have had a good acct from Maer...

with my best love to Hensleigh. E.D [2]

Top: *The Mount*

Left: *Anne Darwin*
© English Heritage Photo Library

Bottom Right: *Down House*
Reproduced from 'Order of the Proceedings at the Darwin Celebration held at Cambridge 22-24 June 1909', Cambridge University Press 1909 CA

Emma's father Josiah II, who had palsy, never recovered his health and to aggravate the situation he fell in the autumn of 1842 and became bedridden. However his mind was clear, unlike Bessy who, by now, was increasingly vague. In July 1843, while Emma was visiting Maer, Jos died peacefully in his sleep.

Two months later Emma and Charles had another daughter. She was christened Henrietta Emma, but she acquired the pet name of Etty, which was used by the family all her life. Etty, when grown up and married to Richard Litchfield, in a book entitled *A Century of Family Letters*, gave a description of Down House when she was young. The house was eventually covered with ivy. About 18 acres of land surrounded the property. Trees and shrubberies sheltered it from the north, with an open field to the south. There were colourful flowerbeds under the drawing room windows. On the lawn were two yew trees where the children had their swings, and there was a sand pit. Behind the house was an orchard and a kitchen garden and beyond that was what was to become the well-known Sand-walk, where Charles had planted trees, such as hazel, alder, lime and hornbeam. It was sheltered and secluded. The children loved to play there, and Charles walked around it almost every day for over 40 years, either deep in thought or enjoying watching his children at play. Emma also loved this wood and in later years cultivated a wild garden there.

Gradually the house was enlarged to accommodate the many members of their families who often came to stay. Emma was always willing to look after more children if there was a need. For instance, in 1844 when Fanny and Hensleigh's youngest child Hope Elizabeth was born, Emma had the couple's five children to stay at Down.

In mid-June 1844, while aunt Jessie Sismondi was visiting Down, she wrote to Elizabeth Wedgwood at Maer:

> *... This place and house I find exceedingly pretty, the drawing room is a charming one and the dining-room is excellent. Emma, always the dearest little hostess in the world, and without any extraordinary out-of-way quality, is the most original little person in her way living...* [3]

Charles, during that year, working at his *The Origin of Species* papers, began to think ahead about the final work. With this in mind, he wrote formally to his wife in July:

... I have just finished my sketch of my species theory. If, as I believe, my theory in time be accepted even by one competent judge, it will be a considerable step in science.

I therefore write this in case of my sudden death, as my most solemn and last request, which I am sure you will consider the same as if legally entered in my will, that you will devote £400 to its publication, and further, will yourself, or through Hensleigh, take trouble in promoting it. I wish that my sketch be given to some competent person, with this sum to induce him to take trouble in its improvement and enlargement. I give to him all my books on Natural History, which are either scored or have references at the end to the pages... [4]

In October that year, Charles went to Shrewsbury to visit his father and sisters. In his letter to Emma, he said that when his sister Susan had voiced her admiration for Emma:

I did not require to be reminded how well, my own dear wife, you have borne your dull life with your poor old sickly complaining husband. Your children will be a greater comfort to you than I ever can be, God bless them and you... [5]

Emma went to Maer as often as possible to see her mother. During one such visit in 1845, Charles wrote to her from Down on Monday 3rd February:

Now for my day's annals. In the morning I was baddish, and did hardly any work. ... But the children have been very good all day, and I have grown a good deal better this afternoon, and had a good romp with Baby – I see, however, very little of the blesseds. The day was so thick and wet with fog that none of them went out, though a thaw and not very cold; I had a long pace in the kitchen garden...

The children are growing so quite out of all rule in the drawing-room, jumping on everything and butting like young bulls at every chair and sofa, that I am going to have the dining-room fire lighted tomorrow and keep them out of the drawing-room. I declare a month's such wear would spoil everything in the whole drawing-room.

Tuesday morning. I am impatient for your letter this morning to hear how you got on. I asked Willy how Baby had slept and he answered 'She did not cry not one mouthful'... [6]

Emma and Charles' second son, George, was born on 9th July 1845. Usually in her diary Emma was brief in her descriptions of everyday happenings but at rare times she revealed how she felt. That month of August was troublesome, as she wrote that during her brother Frank's visit she '*lay in bed 6 days, then got up, had toothache; on 18th drove out – did me harm and on 20th came downstairs second time*'. She wrote to her Aunt Jessie Sismondi on the 27th but made no mention of not having been well:

... My new baby is very comfortable. He is very smiling & fat & big & I think will be rather above an 'average wean'. ... Brodie now looks after the new baby & Etty has her own nurse Bessy.

... Charles had just finished his Journal, which has over-tired him a good deal, and he is but poorly now he has not had the excitement of being forced to go on with his work... [7]

Brodie was the children's Scottish nurse, who stayed with the family until 1851 when she returned to Scotland. However she remained a very good friend and used to visit Down until her death in 1873.

In January 1846, when Emma went again to Maer to be with her mother, she did not realise it would be the last time she would see her alive. While at Maer, in a letter to her aunt Jessie she wrote about her oldest son, Willie:

... He is getting on a little with his reading, and I find it a great pleasure and interest teaching them. But when I am not well I feel it a great anxiety to be looking after

*them all day, or else the small quantity of lessons they
do I think I could always manage. ... My baby [George]
is a real beauty, except for looking red & rough with the
cold. He has fine dark blue eyes, & I can't conceive how
he gets them. He is very placid & sweet but I don't think
he is very robust...*

Emma goes on to say that Susan (Darwin) is worried about
untidiness with the children:

*I might be all day doing that, so I let them accumulate till
the room becomes unbearable, & then call Bessy in to do
it all...* [8]

Aunt Jessie advised Emma to continue educating her children for
now as opposed to having a governess:

*... No governess can do what a mother can for their souls,
therefore if possible, my Emma, keep them in your own
hands...* [9]

Emma replied:

*I certainly shall make a trial of doing without a governess
for another year at least. I am grown so fat & well that
I enjoy every day & feel it quite a novelty to feel well &
strong.* [10]

Shortly after Emma returned to Down, her mother Bessy died,
aged eighty-two. After her death Elizabeth wrote to Emma:

*Oh! How thankful I am that her death was so gentle!
In the evening I heard her saying as I had done before,
'Lord, now lettest thou thy servant depart in peace'. For
her own sake no one could wish her half-extinguished life
to be prolonged. For us it was still a happiness to be able
to look on that sweet countenance, and see a faint gleam
now and then of the purest and most benevolent soul that
ever shone in any face.* [11]

In Emma's private papers found after *her* death, part of a note she wrote, remembering her mother, read:

> *The time I remember my mother with most affection was about the time we came from school, and she and my father came to meet us at Stone and gave us such a reception. I shall never forget her warm glow as she embraced us again and again. Soon after she left us at school again, after the midsummer holiday, she went to Shrewsbury and was ill there for some time. When I think of the grief I felt then at hearing of her illness, I often wonder at my apathy now, but in fact the first fit she had was almost a greater grief than any I have felt since, with respect to her...* [12]

In April Elizabeth wrote again to Emma from Maer:

> *We have been talking a little of our plans. I think we shall come to the conclusion that as we must break up from here, there is little use in lingering, and that we shall probably not stay more than a month. I don't feel that leaving the place (although I shall never see another I shall like anything like it) will be much of a grief. How glad I should have been if Jos or Harry had taken to it; I can't help thinking Jos [Joe] will regret it. It is so unlike any other place, so completely its own self, and with alterations it might be made so very nice a one, and he will find it almost impossible to fix anywhere else...*
>
> *Thank you. my dear Emma, for your invitation, but I think I shall stick by the Langtons at present. Charlotte wishes it, and Charles Langton gives me great confidence he will like it too. It is a great pleasure to see how entirely Charles understood & loved my mother – how he felt the transparent brightness of her character, & how everybody whom we have heard from felt it. There never was anyone comparable to her. Her look & voice are a brightness gone from the world for ever. I feel it a comfort that she continued so unaltered to the last. Till that one day of insensibility she had no look of pain or illness, and I have*

not borne to disturb that image in my memory by any sight since…

Good-bye my dear Emma, you may be sure I shall be very glad to go & see you and dear Charles a little further on. Yours affect. SEW[13]

The whole family, both Darwins and Wedgwoods, felt a great loss at the sale of Maer Hall. It had been both home and a second home to two generations of both families.

In June 1846 Emma and two of their children, William and Anne, were visiting Aunt Jessie Sismondi at Tenby. This was a long journey for Emma, but she had promised her aunt she would go. Charles would have preferred Emma never to be away from him and always seemed to be unwell during her absence.

He wrote:

To-day has been stormy & gloomy, but rather pleasant in the intervals, only I have been sick again but not very uncomfortable. A proof has come from the printers saying the compositor is in want of MS. [manuscripts], which he cannot have and I am tired and overdone.

I am an ungracious old dog to howl, for I have been sitting in the summer-house, whilst watching the thunderstorms, & thinking what a fortunate man I am, so well off in worldly circumstances, with such dear little children … & far more than all with such a wife. Often have I thought over Elizabeths words, when I married you, that she had never heard a word pass your lips which she had rather not have been uttered, & sure I am that I can now say so & shall say so on my death-bed, bless you my dear wife.[14]

In 1847 Emma's aunt Sarah Wedgwood, now seventy-one, left Camp Hill, her Staffordshire home, and came to live near Emma at Down. She bought Petleys from Sir John Lubbock, and lived there until her death in 1856. Etty said of Sarah Wedgwood:

The stated and solemn visits to our old great aunt were rather awful but fortunately rare events. She remains in my memory an old-world figure looking like some old lady in Cranford – tall, very thin and upright, dressed in a scanty lilac muslin gown, several little capes of muslin or silk, & a large Leghorn bonnet with yellow ribbons. She kept several pairs of gloves by her, loose black ones for shaking hands with little boys and girls and putting on coals, and others for reading books & cleaner occupations.[15]

In July 1847 a sixth child, Elizabeth, was born to Emma and Charles. There were now five children in the nursery. Charles went to visit his father in Shrewsbury in October and on the 31st he wrote to Emma:

My very dear Mammy,
I had two wretched days on Friday and Saturday. I lay all day upstairs on the sofa groaning and grumbling & reading 'Last Days of Pompeie'. I have almost made up my mind to stay here until Wednesday, & I shall not go round by Kew, as Hooker will come to us. I have had plenty of time to think of you my own dearest, tenderest of wives. I do love and adore you. I have no doubt I shall be at home on Thursday. Kiss the dear children for me... [16]

Chapter 22

THE POTTERIES – UPPER HOUSE
DARWIN CHILDREN – ANNE'S DEATH

While Hensleigh Wedgwood and his sister Emma Darwin were getting on with their lives in the South, their brother Francis (Frank) and his family lived in Staffordshire where he was the master potter of Etruria. Because of their close relationship, the Wedgwoods and Darwins were united as one family and although not all living in the same area, they always visited or wrote.

By 1847 Frank Wedgwood had decided he could not take on Maer Hall, as it was too expensive to run. He had bought 100 acres of land in the village of Barlaston and built a large, roomy family home, named The Upper House. It was built on a small hill at the edge of the village, with a long drive leading up to it. From the front, looking south and east, green fields met the eye, with mature trees interspersed in the meadows and on the horizon low hills made a gentle background. This new Wedgwood home became the main meeting place for friends and relatives. Frank and his wife Frances' seven children grew up there.

Frank was austere in his lifestyle. Although he was described as 'jolly' within the family, his grandson, Josiah IV, in later years doubted it:

> *He hated Rugby School, and sent none of his sons to public schools ... what we knew was a sober, strong, silent man, who rode into the works every day for 55 years,*

The Upper House

Top: *Upper House*

Left: *Frank Wedgwood*

Bottom Left: *Lucy Wedgwood*

Bottom Right: *Cecil Wedgwood*

*seven miles each way, and so regularly that the cottages
by the wayside set their clocks by his appearance down
the lane.*

*I remember his bedroom of bare boards, with two
dumbells and a tub. He taught me my lessons – French
and arithmetic – but I never knew him either smile or
lose his temper ...[1]*

In 1919 Frank's daughter Mabel (b.1852) gave a talk to young
people in Barlaston. She described the Upper House as a home often
full of relatives and friends; her mother was sociable and loved
entertaining. The house was very comfortable, with roaring fires in
the Staffordshire winter. Remembering how austere Frank was in
those days, her description of a house not too cluttered with ornaments
fits the picture of him. That famous painting by Stubbs of Sarah
and Josiah, with their family – now in the Wedgwood Museum at
Barlaston – had pride of place over the sideboard in the dining room.
Among the few china ornaments was one of the Portland Vases: there
were plenty of books.

Mabel's picture of sitting on the terrace as a popular gathering
place is reminiscent of Charles Darwin's description of evenings at
Maer, where there was always good conversation and music when
desired.

Emma's other siblings were settled in their respective homes:
Harry Wedgwood had gone to live at The Hermitage near Woking;
Josiah III (Joe) at Leith Hill Place, also in Surrey; the Langtons in
Sussex. Elizabeth had a house, The Ridge, built near the Langtons,
along with a small school for children who lived nearby, where she
taught every morning.

The summer of 1848 Charles Darwin's father Robert was seriously
ill and Charles went to Shrewsbury to be with him. On 20th May he
wrote to Emma:

My dear Mammy
*Though this will not go today, I will write a bit of Journal,
which 'in point of fact' is a Journal of all our healths. My
father kept pretty well all yesterday, but was able to talk
for not more than 10 minutes at a time till after dinner*

*when he talked the whole evening most wonderfully well &
cheerfully. It is an inexpressible pleasure, that he has twice
told me that he is very comfortable, & that his want of
breath does not distress him at all like the dyeing sensation,
which he now very seldom has. That he thought with care
he might live a good time longer, & that when he dyed, it
would probably be suddenly which was best. Thrice over
he has said that he was very comfortable, which was so
much more than I expected. Catherine has been having
wretched nights but her spirits appear to me as good as
used formerly to be. Lastly for myself, I was a little sick
yesterday, but upon the whole very comfortable & I had a
splendid good night & am extraordinary well today...* [2]

Again on 27th May he said:

*My dearest old Mammy,
I was so very glad to get your letter this morning with
as good an account of the baby as could be expected.
I am so thankful you had Elizabeth with you; for she of
all human beings would be of the greatest comfort to you.
Her presence is a blessing & joy to everyone.
    I am weak enough to-day, but think I am improving.
My attack was very sudden: Susan was very kind to me
but I did yearn for you. Without you when sick I feel most
desolate. I also doubt whether I shall be able to travel on
Monday; but I can write no more now.
    Oh Mammy, I do long to be with you and under your
protection for then I feel safe. God bless you. C D* [3]

In August 1848, Emma's and Charles' third son Francis was born.
During that autumn of 1848 Charles returned to visit his father as
often as possible, although the long journey tired him. When Robert
did die on 13th November, although Charles set out again to attend
his funeral he arrived too late. However, he and his sister Susan, who
was too distraught to attend the service, stayed at The Mount and
tried to comfort each other.

Robert had been a shrewd and successful businessman and he left
his children comfortably off.

Emma spent most of her time looking after Charles and the children. 1849 was one of the most stressful years for her. She was forty-one, by then had given birth to seven children, the last one, Francis, in August the previous year. By April 1849 she was again pregnant and as usual suffered from morning sickness. In her diary she also made a note most days of how Charles felt – he was often sick, with headaches and flatulence and he was 'languid'.

After his father's death Charles seemed to lose any enthusiasm for work. He was dispirited, his hands trembled and he often felt dizzy. When there was no improvement friends recommended a treatment at Malvern as prescribed in a book by a Dr James Gully, *The Water Cure in Chronic Disease*. Finally, in March 1849 they rented a house, The Lodge, in Malvern for two months, taking their family of six children, a governess and servants with them. The move involved much work and great upheaval for Emma.

Charles continued to suffer from a delicate stomach and extreme tiredness, but Dr Gully's 'hydropathetic' treatment seemed to do him good. On his return to Down he built himself a douche-bath and the butler, Joseph Parslow, learned to be his bathman. During the next couple of years he returned to Malvern for the odd week. On the advice of his doctors, Charles had to give up taking snuff – 'that chief solace of life' – which he found difficult.

In July 1849, the oldest son, Willie, had a fever and had to remain in bed for two weeks. In August, Brodie took Willie and Anne to Brighton, which took some pressure off the nursery. Then in November Anne caught scarlet fever, followed by Ettie and Bessy. Luckily, they all recovered. Christmas came and went but Emma and Charles could not enjoy the festivities as Charles felt unwell and Emma's confinement was near.

A fourth son, Leonard, was born in January 1850. During that year the family visited Emma's brothers, Joe and Harry, in Surrey. During that year, too, the question of a school for Willie arose. They made some enquiries and were slightly inclined towards Rugby.

Up to that summer Anne, in her ninth year, had been a healthy girl with chubby cheeks and happy in her everyday life. Her looks tended towards Wedgwood rather than Darwin. As the first girl in the family, she was a great favourite of Charles and a comfort and companion to Emma. Her younger sister, Etty, followed her everywhere. However, by June of 1850 Anne became ill and never again reached her old buoyancy. By the end of October she seemed worse. She complained of an upset stomach, she cried easily and always wanted to be near her parents. Dr Holland from London attended her, but he was unable to diagnose her illness.

At the beginning of 1851, Anne's health continued to fluctuate. In March they all had influenza and at the end of the month Charles took Anne to Malvern to take the 'water cure'. He had great faith in Dr Gully. Emma was then seven months pregnant and unable to travel. Charles returned home briefly to see her. He went back to Malvern in April and wrote to Emma on 17th:

> ... *Dr Gully is most confident there is strong hope. ... My own dearest, support yourself – on no account, for the sake of our other children, I implore you do not think of coming here. ... Sometimes Dr G exclaims she will get through the struggle, then I see, he doubts. Oh my own, it is very bitter indeed. God preserve & cherish you. We must hope against hope, my own poor dear unhappy wife. C D[4]*

Fanny (Hensleigh's wife) went to Malvern to support Charles and for a while Anne seemed to be getting better. Then she caught a fever from which she did not recover, and died on 23rd April. Immediately Charles wrote to his wife:

> *I pray God Fanny's note may have prepared you. She went to her final sleep most tranquilly, most sweetly at 12 o'clock to-day. Our poor dear child has had a very short life, but I trust happy, and God only knows what miseries might have been in store for her. She expired without a sigh. How desolate it makes one to think of her frank, cordial manners. I am so thankful for the daguerrotype. I cannot remember ever seeing the dear child naughty. God bless her. We must be more & more to each other, my dear wife. Do what you can to bear up, and think how invariably kind & tender you have been to her. I am in bed, not very well. When I shall return I cannot yet say. My own poor dear dear wife.*
>
> *C Darwin[5]*

On Thursday 24th April Emma wrote to her husband:

My dearest,
I knew too well what receiving no message means. Till
4 o'clock I sometimes had a thought of hope, but when
I went to bed I felt as if it had all happened
long ago. Don't think it made any difference
my being so hopeful the last day. When the
blow comes it wipes out all that preceded it, &
I don't think it makes it any worse to bear. I hope you
have not burnt your letter. I shall like to see it sometime.
My feeling of longing after our lost treasure makes
me feel painfully indifferent to the other children, but
I shall get right in my feelings to them before long.
You must remember that you are my prime treasure
(& always have been). My only hope of consolation
is to have you safe home and weep together. I feel
so full of fears about you. They are not reasonable
fears, but my power of hoping seems gone. I hope you
will let dearest Fanny or Catherine, if she comes, stay
with you till the end. I can't bear to think of you by
yourself. No doubt you will have sent Miss Thorley
home to recover her cheerfulness. I will write to her
in a few days to fix her time of returning.
Your letter has just come, and I feel less miserable
a good deal in the hope of seeing you sooner than
I expected, but do not be in a hurry to set off. I am
perfectly well. You do give me the only comfort I can
take, in thinking of her happy, innocent life. She never
concealed a thought, & so affectionate & forgiving.
What a blank it is. Don't think of coming in one day.
We shall be much less miserable together.

Yours, my dearest.[6]

Emma also wrote two letters to Fanny at Malvern on Thursday and
again on Friday. The first letter reads:

Thursday before post time

My dearest Fanny,
The feeling of hope crossed my mind once or twice in the course of yesterday, but as no message arrived I felt as certain as if I had long known it was all over. It is worse to bear than I expected but the hopefulness beforehand made no difference. Now I cannot help all sorts of fears for Charles which I know are not reasonable. Now all cause for exertion is over I know he must be ill & I am sure either you or my dear Cath. If she comes will stay with him to the end & let me have a line every day to Bromley as before. My first feeling of consolation will be to have him safe at home again. I do feel very grateful to God that our darling was apparently spared all suffering & I hope I shall be able to attain some feeling of submission to the will of Heaven. Goodbye my dearest Fanny. ED

What a comfort it is to feel you are there with him. God bless you. I hope Ch will not set off in a hurry I am perfectly well. Tell dear Cath Thorley [governess] with my best love I hope she will go home as soon as she can & I will write to her there. After post your sweet note has given me some comfort dearest F.[7]

The second letter:

Down Friday

25 April 1851

My dearest Fanny,
I cannot tell you the surprise & joy it was to see poor Charles arrive about 6.30 yesterday. I had no hopes that he would be well enough for some days. The journey did not tire him & he had not to wait 5 minutes any where on the road. He is much better bodily than I had any hopes of & not worse in spirits & began to notice the little ones this morning. We have done little else but cry together

*& talk about our darling. He cannot express enough
what a comfort you were & how you mourned for her.
I think every body loved her. Hers was such a transparent
character, so open to kindness & a little thing made her
so happy.*

*Poor darling she went to sleep at last like an infant
without a fear & through her illness I hope she felt
little uneasiness of any sort. From her having filled our
minds so much for the last 9 months it leaves such an
emptiness & from her clinging affectionate nature if she
felt uncomfortable. She was never easy without being
with one of us.*

*Dear kind Eliz is gone to Leith Hill to fetch home Etty
& will be back here in the evening. I suppose this painful
longing will diminish before long. It seems as if nothing
in this life could satisfy it. Goodbye my dearest my best
love to Hensleigh & to Harry if with you. E.D* [8]

In her diary at home in Down, Emma had written down her
progress every day. On 23rd April there was just one poignant entry
on that page, '*Dead*'.

Anne Elizabeth Darwin was buried in the old Abbey churchyard at
Malvern. On her headstone was inscribed 'A dear and good child'.

Emma never really got over the loss of her daughter and could
not bear to talk of her. Her Christian beliefs and her trust in God
and prayer probably gave her some comfort, but for Charles, Anne's
death destroyed any Christianity he might still have had, or any belief
in moral justice. His thoughts were bleak. Shortly after she died,
Charles wrote about his beloved daughter:

*I write these few pages, as I think in after years, if we
live, the impressions now put down will recall more
vividly her chief characteristics. From whatever point
I look back at her, the main feature in her disposition
which at once rises before me is her buoyant joyousness,
tempered by two other characteristics, namely, her
sensitiveness, which might easily have been overlooked
by a stranger, and her strong affection. Her joyousness
& animal spirits radiated from her whole countenance,*

and rendered every movement elastic & full of life & vigour. It was delightful and cheerful to behold her. Her dear face now rises before me, as she used sometimes to come running downstairs with a stolen pinch of snuff for me, her whole form radiant with the pleasure of giving pleasure. Even when playing with her cousins, when her joyousness almost passed into boisterousness, a single glance of my eye, not of displeasure (for I thank God I hardly ever cast one on her), but of want of sympathy, would for some minutes alter her whole countenance.

The other point in her character, which made her joyousness and spirits so delightful, was her strong affection, which was of a most clinging, fondling nature. When quite a baby, this showed itself in never being easy without touching her mother, when in bed with her; and quite lately she would, when poorly, fondle for any length of time one of her mother's arms. When very unwell, her mother lying down beside her, seemed to soothe her in a manner quite different from what it would have done to any of our other children. So, again, she would at almost any time spend half-an-hour in arranging my hair, 'making it', as she called it, 'beautiful' or in smoothing, the poor dear darling, my collar or cuffs – in short, in fondling me.

Besides her joyousness thus tempered, she was in her manners remarkably cordial, frank, open, straightforward, natural, and without any shade of reserve. Her whole mind was pure and transparent. One felt one knew her thoroughly and could trust her. I always thought, that come what might, we should have had, in our old age, at least one loving soul, which nothing could have changed. All her movements were vigorous, active, and usually graceful. When going round the Sand-walk with me, although I walked fast, yet she often used to go before, pirouetting in the most elegant way, her dear face bright all the time with the sweetest smiles. Occasionally she had a pretty coquettish manner towards me, the memory of which is charming. She often used exaggerated language, and when I quizzed her by exaggerating what she had said, how clearly can I now see the little toss of the head, and exclamation of 'Oh, papa, what a shame of you!' In the last short illness, her conduct in simple truth was angelic. She never once complained; never became fretful; was ever considerate of others, and was thankful in the most gentle, pathetic manner for everything done for her. When so exhausted that she could hardly speak, she praised everything that was given her, and said some tea 'was beautifully good.' When I gave her some water, she said, 'I quite thank you'; and these, I believe, were the last precious words ever addressed by her dear lips to me.

We have lost the joy of the household, and the solace of our old age. She must have known how we loved her. Oh, that she could now know how deeply, how tenderly, we do still and shall ever love her dear joyous face! Blessings on her.

April 30, 1851[9]

Also recorded in *Emma Darwin: A Century of Family Letters* (edited by Etty) is a description of a small packet of memorials of Anne, found 45 years later in Emma's papers. The packet contained a half-finished piece of woolwork, a child's writing case, a lock of brown hair, some texts in Anne's handwriting and two ornamental pocket books, a thimble and other small personal mementoes. In the same packet was a copy in Emma's handwriting of a letter sent by Charles to Mrs Thorley, the governess's mother. It was a 'thank you' to her daughter for her support at Malvern.

After Anne's death, Charles and Emma felt vulnerable about their children's health and were wary of any signs of sickness. The health of Etty was a puzzle. She was eight in 1851, and they had always been anxious about her health. Like her father she tired easily, but despite various consultations with the family doctor nothing was ever diagnosed. Emma worried about her and consequently allowed her to lead a very gentle, easy life, with people always looking after her. Perhaps because of this solicitude, Etty lived to be eighty-four. Two months after Anne's death, Horace was born on 13th May and once again Elizabeth went to Down House to be with Emma and her family.

Chapter 23

THE GREAT EXHIBITION
THE ORIGIN OF SPECIES

Later in July 1851, Charles and Emma went to London for the first of many visits to the Great Exhibition in Hyde Park. They stayed with Charles' brother Erasmus in Park Street. Members of the Wedgwood family were there in strength, as their pottery was on show in the famed Crystal Palace. The building, containing nearly a million square feet of glass, with miles and miles of space for exhibitors, rose like something from a fairy tale in the south of Hyde Park. Queen Victoria had formally opened the Great Exhibition on May Day 1851. The Crystal Palace was the brainchild of her consort, Prince Albert, and although he was ridiculed by all and sundry he persisted with his dream and on the great day the Queen was proud of her beloved Albert.

Three years later, when the Crystal Palace was moved to Sydenham from Hyde Park, on the day Queen Victoria officially reopened it, Charles and Emma were present. Their daughter Etty wrote about her mother:

> She was calm over music, deeply as she enjoyed it. But one of the very few times in my life that I saw her lose her self-control was when Clara Novello sang the solo verse of God Save the Queen at the opening of the Crystal Palace. My mother broke down then and sobbed audibly. The scene was extraordinarily impressive – the standing

crowd, the Queen and Prince Albert present, and the
wonderful volume of the rich soprano voice, sustained
and round and full, filling the enormous building ...[1]

Emma and Charles had finally decided in 1881 they would send
William to Rugby. In September, twelve-year-old William left Down
and went away to school. Charles wrote to him in October advising
him on how to behave. He added:

Mamma was to start for Shrewsbury and Barlaston on
Saturday, but the baby is not quite well, so she has put
it off for a week. Georgy is terribly disappointed, for he
now likes as much going from home, as he formerly did
not care about it... [2]

Emma did eventually visit her brother Frank in Barlaston early in
1852 and when she returned in April Frank came with her to visit his
relations in the South.

Aunt Jessie had written to Emma in January. She was getting old
and had become increasingly deaf. Now she used an ear trumpet to
help her to hear. Many Wedgwood women suffered from deafness –
Julia ('Snow'), Hensleigh and Fanny's daughter, was deaf from birth
but it did not hinder her from leading a full life.

Jessie and Emma continued to write frequently to each other, and
Jessie was always keen for Emma to visit her in Tenby. Emma had
hoped to go in 1852, but postponed taking the long journey. Jessie
died early in 1853 and Emma was full of regret for not making
that trip.

Three years later Emma's aunt Sarah Wedgwood died at 'Petleys'.
She was eighty years old.

During all these years at Down, Emma's husband Charles – apart
from writing many other papers – was engrossed in writing *The
Origin of Species*, started in 1831 and published in 1859. In his
autobiography, he wrote of how his mind changed during those
30 odd years.

Up to the age of thirty, or beyond it, poetry of many kinds,
such as the works of Milton, Gray, Byron, Wordsworth,
Coleridge, and Shelley, gave me great pleasure, and even

as a schoolboy I took intense delight in Shakespeare, especially in the historical plays. I have also said that formerly pictures gave me considerable, and music very great delight. But now for many years I cannot endure to read a line of poetry; I have tried lately to read Shakespeare, and found it so intolerably dull that it nauseated me. I have also almost lost my taste for pictures or music. Music generally sets me thinking too energetically on what I have been at work on, instead of giving me pleasure. I retain some taste for fine scenery, but it does not cause me the exquisite delight which it formerly did ... if I had to live my life again I would have made a rule to read some poetry and listen to some music at least once every week; for perhaps the parts of my brain now atrophied would thus have been kept active through use. The loss of these tastes is a loss of happiness, and may possibly be injurious to the intellect, and more probably to the moral character, by enfeebling the emotional part of our nature.[3]

This lack of interest in the arts, especially music, must have saddened Emma. She played the piano daily and used to love to go to the theatre, but this was a rare treat since living at Down. Charles still liked to read popular fiction, or to have it read to him, and this they shared. Emma supported Charles in every aspect of his work but could not agree with his philosophy of life. During lectures at the British Association, he said to her: 'I am afraid this is very wearisome to you.' She replied, 'Not more than all the rest.' This reply amused him.

She looked after Charles with tender loving care and arranged her days so that she could be with him when he needed her. Charles was *never* fit – and Emma's constant support made it possible for him to produce his life's work. With her growing children she was never gushing, but always there for them and treated them all as individuals. She once said, 'I do not feel my sons are my sons, only young men with whom I happen to be intimate.' The children, while growing up, were free to learn many things by themselves: how to get up on a horse, fall off and eventually discover how to ride, and the same with bicycles. They were allowed to roam extensively in the fields and woods around their home, while Etty was known to go walking quite a distance alone. Their education was not a big issue for Emma. She taught them the Bible and when she went to church on Sunday, Etty usually accompanied her. Over the years they had many governesses with whom they had happy relationships. Emma was homely, generous, intelligent – all those things, but all her life she was untidy – and yet got things done with little fuss.

After the birth of Horace in 1851, both Charles and Emma had thought this would be their last child and for four years this seemed to be so. But by April 1856, she became pregnant once more. Always in her diary when she realised she was pregnant she used to write '*I began to be bad*' and on the 17th April she wrote those words again. Another entry on 19th July said '*Bad day for me*'. Usually the diary entries were mostly brief, about Charles' condition or appointments and always what the weather was like. Her sister Elizabeth always came to be with Emma when she was *enceinte* and that November she arrived. On 6th December Emma, now forty-eight, after a difficult confinement, gave birth to her last child, Charles Waring.

A pregnancy practically every year – at least until 1851 – cannot have been easy for Emma, despite the fact that she had nurses and servants at Down. Charles wrote to his cousin, William Darwin Fox, after the birth and said that Emma had produced their sixth boy '*under blessed chloroform*'. However, this new baby was never strong, never learned to walk or talk and at the age of two he died of scarlet fever. Emma and Charles mourned their child, but also felt it was a happy release for him.

Although Emma's everyday life was mostly dedicated to Charles and their large family, she still found time for her charity work. In the lending library for children in the village, she gave out the books every Sunday afternoon. She helped people who were ill, using her simple medicines. She had a red book of prescriptions inherited from her father-in-law, Robert Darwin, and kept a special cupboard for medical supplies.

In 1859, *The Origin of Species* was published. Charles said, 'It is no doubt the chief work of my life.' What a relief that must have been in the Darwin household. Emma had helped Charles with all the proof sheets for the first edition. The full title of the work was *On the Origin of Species by Means of Natural Selection, or The Preservation of Favoured Races in the Struggle for Life*. Very briefly, his theory was that all species, made of variable populations, maintain their existence through sexual reproduction and that the preservation of favourable variations and the rejection of injurious variations was by natural selection, and that such variation was the origin or foundation of different plant and animal species. Having sent the book to the publisher, he also sent a draft to his closest friends. The book, one of the most radical scientific treatises of the 19th century, sent shock waves through society, that continue to this day.

Once the book was finished, Charles collapsed and fell ill. They all went to Ilkley in Yorkshire – he for the water cure. But it was October and the weather was cold and miserable. They were happy to return home to Down after a short stay.

Criticism and praise of Darwin's theories appeared hard and fast both in the press and in correspondence addressed to Charles. His brother Erasmus wrote: '*For myself I really think it is the most interesting book I ever read...* ' Charles Lyall called it '*a splendid case of close reasoning*', Joseph Hooker commented on '*its curious facts and fresh phenomena*' and Thomas Huxley wrote '*I do most heartily thank you for the great store of new views you have given me.*' The fact that these friends supported him and approved his book gave him great satisfaction and happiness.

Some time after the publication of *The Origin of Species* a letter written by Emma to Charles with a note added by Charles – '*God bless you. C.D. June, 1861*' – contained the following:

> *I cannot tell you the compassion I have felt for all your sufferings for these weeks past that you have had so many drawbacks, nor the gratitude I have felt for the cheerful and affectionate looks you have given me when I know you have been miserably uncomfortable.*
>
> *My heart has often been too full to speak or take any notice. I am sure you know I love you well enough to believe that I mind your sufferings, nearly as much as I should my own, and I find the only relief to my own mind is to take it as from God's hand, and to try to believe that all suffering and illness is meant to help us to exalt our minds and to look forward with hope to a future state. When I see your patience, deep compassion for others, self-command, and above all gratitude for the smallest thing done to help you, I cannot help longing that these*

precious feelings should be offered to Heaven for the sake of your daily happiness. But I find it difficult enough in my own case. I often think of the words, 'Thou shalt keep him in perfect peace whose mind is stayed on thee'. It is feeling and not reasoning that drives one to prayer. I feel presumptuous in writing this to you.

I feel in my inmost heart your admirable qualities and feelings, and all I would hope is that you might direct them upwards, as well as to one who values them above everything in the world. I shall keep this by me till I feel cheerful and comfortable again about you, but it has passed through my mind often lately so I thought I would write it, partly to relieve my own mind.[4]

In 1862 Emma's sister, Charlotte Langton, died at the age of sixty-five. This was a great loss, especially to their sister Elizabeth, whose whole life changed. She left Downe and bought a house at 4 Chester Place in London, near Hensleigh's home. Later that year Charlotte's widowed husband Charles proposed to Catherine Darwin (Emma's sister-in-law). Catherine was then aged fifty-three. The speed and choice of Charles was criticised by the families, but the marriage went ahead in June 1863. Sadly, Catherine was to live for only another three years. She died in 1866, the same year as Charles Darwin's unmarried sister, Susan.

For the Darwins, visits to London were rare, but in 1866 Charles felt slightly better and in April they went to stay with Fanny and Hensleigh. Emma wrote to her aunt Fanny Allen on 28th April. She tells of Charles going to a 'soiree' at the Royal Society with all the important scientific men in London, at which he was presented to the Prince of Wales:

My event was nearly as wonderful, going to see 'Hamlet with Fechter. The acting was beautiful, but I prefer anything to Shakespeare, I am ashamed to say... [5]

Emma and Mrs Thomas H Huxley had become friends and in the spring of 1867. Emma offered to look after the Huxleys' seven children while Mrs Huxley accompanied her husband on business. A letter found in Etty's papers, written by Mrs Huxley, said:

Towards your mother I always had a sort of nestling feeling. More than any woman I ever knew, she comforted. Few, if any, would have housed a friend's seven children and two nurses for a fortnight; that the friend, myself, should be able to accompany her husband to Liverpool when he was president of the British Association; & in early days of our acquaintance, just after we had lost our boy, she begged me to come to her & bring the three children & nurse, & I should have the old nurseries at Down. ... What wonder that I had for always the most grateful affection... [6]

In 1867, the Darwin boys, George and Frank, were up at Cambridge. Emma missed them and endeavoured to visit them whenever she could; she enjoyed meeting their friends and being shown around the city.

Emma and Charles sometimes went to visit Emma's sister Elizabeth at her small house at 4 Chester Place, usually when Charles had business in London. This was also convenient for socialising with the Hensleigh Wedgwoods, and Emma went to the theatre a couple of times. Although she really enjoyed being in London, she also loved to return to the quiet of Down House.

During 1868 Elizabeth decided to move for the last time, buying Fromer Lodge, in the village of Downe. She was happy there with her garden, her dog Tony and her faithful servants. The greatest comfort was being near to her dear sister Emma.

That summer Charles, Emma and Erasmus Darwin rented a house in Freshwater, Isle of Wight, as did Hensleigh and Fanny Wedgwood. The house belonged to a Mrs Cameron, sister of Lady Somers. They had a busy social life – among the people who called were Tennyson, Longfellow and the poet's brother-in-law Tom Appleton. When Emma returned to Down in August, she wrote to aunt Fanny:

I must go back to our last day at Freshwater. Mrs Cameron very good-naturedly took me & Lizzy to call on Mrs Tennyson. It was pouring with rain, & the more it rained the slower we walked, so when we got there we left our dripping cloaks in the hall. Mr Tennyson brought in a bottle of light wine & gave us each a glass to correct the wet.

Mrs T. is an invalid, & very pleasing and gracious. After sitting a reasonable time Tennyson came out with us and shewed us all about, and one likes him, and his absurd talk is a sort of flirtation with Mrs Cameron. The only Tennysonian speech was when he was talking of his new house; I asked where it was, & he answered half in joke 'I shan't tell you where', also telling that the Illustrated News wanted to send an artist to take him laying the first stone. Charles spent a very pleasant hour with him the day before. We ended in a transport of affection… [7]

For the past couple of years Charles had been occupied in writing *The Descent of Man*. In 1870, when Emma sent proofs to Etty to read (Etty was on holiday in Cannes with the Langtons) Emma wrote of one chapter: '*I think it will be very interesting, but that I shall dislike it very much as again putting God further off.*' The book was published in 1871 and the reviews, on the whole, were favourable.

Chapter 24

ACHIEVEMENTS – LOSS

The Darwin children were now adults and Emma had more time to think of other things, and of course look after Charles. She had always kept up with both English and foreign news and was an avid reader, always interested in the political climate.

At Down, Emma had made a happy and secure home environment for her own family and any relatives who came to stay. Because there were so many relations there never was a need to look elsewhere for company. Although the Darwins were on good terms with the villagers, they rarely mixed socially with their neighbours, apart from Sir John Lubbock. However in relation to Charles' work many people came to Down, either for a day or a weekend – only relations stayed longer. The most frequent visitors were: the botanist Sir Joseph Hooker, a close friend of Charles; biologist Thomas H Huxley; geologist Charles Lyell and botanist Asa Gray.

In the early 1870s at Down House, a verandah with a glass roof was added. It opened out of the drawing room on to the gardens and became a favourite meeting place for family and friends.

William was in banking in Southampton where he had a 'little villa'. In August 1870 Emma, Charles and family visited William and while there Emma wrote to her aunt Fanny Allen:

> *We are very comfortable here with William in his little villa which is cheerful though Cockneyish. We see plenty of Wm as he leaves for the bank at 9.30 and comes home before 6, & often takes a ride with Henrietta upon*

Tommy, who does double duty here. Charles rides in the morning, and there are a great variety of pretty rides & walks within easy distance.

William is a very pleasant host, always cheerful & agreeable. We talk & read of nothing but the war. I think L Napoleon's fate might make a tragedy if he was not such a prosaic character himself. I can't help hoping that when he is kicked out – which must happen soon – Prussia may be persuaded to make peace. What an enormous collapse it is of a nation, tumbling headlong into such a war without a notion of what the enemy was capable of. Lenny [son Leonard] tells us that almost all the Woolwich young men are "French", tho' he owns it is chiefly because they long for war, & they think that more likely if France wins. Lenny himself is a staunch Prussian.

... I have been reading Lanfrey's memoirs of Napoleon I. It is refreshing to read a Frenchman's book who cares nothing for la gloire, & it makes one ashamed of Louis Philippe for giving in to such baseness as bringing the body from St Helena & making a sort of saint of him. I mean to skip all the Russian retreat, as it is too horrid. I should like to know what impression the book makes in France. Some people (F Galton) are of the opinion that truth or falsehood in a nation is merely a question of geography, & that the nations who have not got the article do pretty well without it. I think France shows the contrary. There is no national value for truth, and Napoleon I employed the most elaborate system of lies by means of Fouche to gain his ends – the letters are now extant... [1]

Emma's aunt Fanny Allen was engrossed in what went on in the world, so Emma knew she had a sympathetic ear when she wrote of how she felt about war, or any other topical subject. Later that year she wrote again from Down to Fanny about the Prussians:

... I get to hate the war & the Prussians more and more, tho' I must say that a General Napier, whom George met

at the Bunburys', said he believed an invading army had never behaved so well. Certainly Lord Wellington thought his own army in Spain capable of any wickedness. Bad is the best... [2]

While reading the '6th number of Middlemarch' Emma described it to Aunt Fanny as '*strong meat for us after some of our weak diet*'.

The following year, while the Darwins were in London in June, Etty, now twenty-eight, met Richard Litchfield. They were instantly attracted to each other and after a short engagement were married in August. They lived afterwards in London. Charles wrote to Etty:

... Well it is an awful & astounding fact that you are married; & I shall miss you sadly. But there is no help for that, & I have had my day & a happy life, notwithstanding my stomach; & this I owe almost entirely to our dear old mother, who, as you know well, is as good as twice refined gold. Keep her as an example before your eyes, & then Litchfield will in future years worship & not only love you, as I worship your dear old mother. Farewell my dear Etty ... [3]

After her marriage Etty and Richard were frequent visitors at Down and Emma and Charles also visited them in Bryanston Street whenever possible. They did not have any children. In a letter to her mother Etty tells of a séance at Erasmus's house when Mrs G H Lewis (George Eliot) was present. Emma was more curious about the novelist than the outcome of the séance.

Whenever Charles felt fit enough to travel he and Emma visited relatives and there were plenty from whom to choose. During the summer of 1873 they spent a week at Abinger Hall, the home of Mr T H Farrer, afterwards Lord Farrer, who had recently married Euphemia (Effie), second daughter of Emma's brother Hensleigh. This relationship was further strengthened when, in January 1880, Horace Darwin married Ida Farrer, only daughter of Lord Farrer – and Effie's step-daughter – despite opposition from Ida's family. Ida and Emma became great friends and Ida was like another daughter to Emma.

Horace, Emma's youngest living son, was not very strong and had always been over-protected by his mother and older brothers. The whole family felt that he would not achieve much in life but they were proved wrong. He became a successful scientific engineer and lived to be seventy-seven years of age.

Many people were curious about Charles' attitude to religion and over the years he had various letters questioning him on this. He had no objection to giving his views so long as they were in a private letter. He wrote to a Dutch student in 1873:

> *It is impossible to answer your question briefly; and I am not sure that I could do so, even if I wrote at some length. But I may say that the impossibility of conceiving that this grand and wondrous universe, with our conscious selves, arose through chance, seems to me the chief argument for the existence of God; but whether this is an argument of real value, I have never been able to decide. I am aware that if we admit a First Cause, the mind still craves to know whence it came, and how it arose. Nor can I overlook the difficulty from the immense amount of suffering through the world. I am, also, induced to defer to a certain extent to the judgment of the many able men who have fully believed in God; but here again I see how poor an argument this is. The safest conclusion seems to me that the whole subject is beyond the scope of man's intellect; but man can do his duty.[4]*

And to a German student in 1879:

> *I am much engaged, an old man, and out of health, and I cannot spare time to answer your questions fully, – nor indeed can they be answered. Science has nothing to do with Christ, except in so far as the habit of scientific research makes a man cautious in admitting evidence. For myself, I do not believe that there ever has been any revelation. As for a future life, every man must judge for himself between conflicting vague probabilities.[5]*

When Francis Darwin was twenty-six, he married Amy Ruck from Wales. They arranged to live near Down, as Francis worked as secretary to Charles – though he had trained to be a doctor but then decided he did not want to practise. Their son Bernard was born in 1876 but Amy died in childbirth.

Francis, bereft without Amy, moved back to Down with his new son. Emma welcomed them back, as having a baby once more in the nursery was wonderful. All her life afterwards she and Bernard had a close and special relationship.

At this time Francis's brother, Leonard, was in the Royal Engineers, while George Darwin was studying law.

Aunt Fanny Allen, with her keen intellect still intact, lived to be ninety-four. As well as being deaf, her sight was also failing, but otherwise she remained a bright old lady. She left this simple note, headed '*Miss Allen's message*':

My love to all who love me, and I beg them not to be sorry for me. There is nothing in my death that ought to grieve them, for death at my great age is rest. I have earnestly prayed for it. I particularly wish that none of my relations should be summoned to my bedside.[6]

Every evening for many years, Emma and Charles played two games of backgammon. They kept a score of wins and losses and whenever Charles was losing, he was heard to say 'Bang your bones!' He wrote in a letter to Professor Asa Gray in January 1876:

> *Please give our very kind remembrances to Mrs Gray. I know that she likes to hear men boasting, it refreshes them so much. Now the tally with my wife in backgammon stands thus: she, poor creature, has won only 2,490 games, whilst I have won, hurrah, hurrah, 2,795 games!*[7]

In 1877, Emma and Charles' eldest son William was engaged to Sara Sidgwick. They were married in November and continued to live at Basset. William had first known Sara in 1868 when she was at Keston with her brother-in-law and sister, Mr and Mrs Charles Norton of Cambridge, Massachusetts.

The historical and political philosopher, Thomas Carlyle, a friend first of all of Erasmus Darwin and a frequent guest at the Hensleigh Wedgwoods, also became a friend of Charles Darwin. Charles thought Carlyle had the best mind of any man he knew. From Southampton, William, who also admired him, wrote to his mother in March 1879:

My dear mother,

... Our drive with Carlyle was interesting but it was difficult to catch all he said. He talked about a number of things especially about his "French Revolution" [1847], which I happened to be reading. His face was quite in a glow with an expression of fury when he talked of it, & he raised his hands & said it was the most wonderful event in the world, 25,000,000 rising up & saying "by the Almight God we will put an end to these shams". He also talked of the frightful difficulty of rewriting the 1st vol. when the manuscript had been burned; he said it was the hardest job he had ever had, that he had not a scrap of note or reference of any kind and it was like trying to float in the air without any wings, or some metaphor to that effect. He also said that he thought at one time that he should have gone mad with all the horror & mystery of the world and his own difficulties if he had not come across Goethe. ... He said that Goethe always carried about with him a feeling of perplexity of things & of the misery of the world ... so I said that Goethe had not felt the French Revolution anything to the extent that he had, then he smiled and said that was true, & afterwrds he said that Goethe had always been prosperous while he had had to struggle with many difficulties. ... He said that G. was far the greatest man living in his times, that he was very kind to him, and that every 3 months or so a box of curiosities, books, etc. used to come to him in Scotland. He spoke with real sorrow in his voice that want of money prevented him ever seeing Goethe

... As we came away he asked after my father, & said with a grin 'but the origin of species is nothing to me... [8]

Emma's oldest brother Josiah III (Joe) died at Leigh Hill Place in 1880, aged eighty-five. Also in November of that year, their sister Elizabeth, now eighty-seven, died at her house in Downe. Since she had come to live nearby, Emma had always watched over her.

After Joe's death, Charles and Emma went to Leith Hill Place to visit Caroline, his widow. She was now eighty and crippled by arthritis.

Caroline's unmarried daughter Sophy cared for her. Her younger daughter Margaret, who had married the Revd Arthur Vaughan Williams, was now a widow and had returned to live at Leith Hill Place with her children, two daughters and a son, Ralph. It would have given Emma, with her love of music, great pleasure if she could have foreseen eight-year-old Ralph's future worldwide fame as a composer.

The Lake District had become a popular place for family holidays – one year when the Darwins went to Coniston for a month they met John Ruskin; Etty and Richard Litchfield went too. Etty wrote about her parents:

> *During this visit they also had the interest and pleasure of making friends with Ruskin. I remember very well his first call on them and his courteous manner; his courtesy even included giving my father the title of 'Sir Charles'. Ruskin spoke of the new and baleful kind of cloud which had appeared in the heavens, and his distressed look showed that his brain was becoming clouded ...*[9]

Erasmus Darwin, aged seventy-seven, died in 1881. He was buried at Downe and was deeply mourned. Ras, who never married, was popular with both his own generation in the family and with his cousins, his nephews and nieces. In his will he left his large fortune to his brother Charles. He had lived a life of leisure with very few, if any, responsibilities. He was a popular figure on the London social scene and had many friends: his best female friend was Hensleigh's wife Fanny, and also he had a strong friendship with the author Harriet Martineau. This latter friendship had been a subject of speculation within the Darwin family – it was hoped that Ras would not marry her – they all knew their father's feelings towards her.

Harriet Martineau, two years older than Erasmus, had died in 1876. A devout Unitarian, during her life she wrote on social reform and was influenced in her thinking by Jeremy Bentham and John Stuart Mill. She lived with her mother in Westminster and was part of the social scene of the mid and later 1880s. She travelled abroad to Europe and the USA, but her health was not great and she felt more comfortable in London among her friends.

In December 1881 Horace and Ida had their first child, a son whom they named Erasmus.

Chapter 25

CHARLES DARWIN'S ILLNESS AND DEATH

The first hint of any trouble with Charles' heart came late in 1881, when Emma mentioned his irregular pulse to their doctor Dr Andrew Clark. He said this showed a derangement of the heart but didn't imply that it was serious. Charles experienced his first 'heart pain' that month and from the beginning of 1882 he did not exert himself or walk any distance in case the pain returned. Instead of going for walks during March, he and Emma sat in the orchard each day and enjoyed the first signs of spring approaching. During those early months both Dr Clark and Dr Norman Moore came to see him. However, by April it was obvious that Charles was seriously ill.

On the 19th April, the family had to accept that the end was near. Etty and Francis sat with Charles while their mother had a brief rest. Charles said: 'You are the best of dear nurses.' Shortly after that Emma and Bessy were called to his bedside. He peacefully passed away at half-past three on that day. He was seventy-three. A week later he was buried in Westminster Abbey – all their sons were present but Emma did not attend. She had said her 'Goodbye'. His friends were his pall-bearers.

Emma was then seventy-four. Looking after Charles during the 43 years of their married life took up most of her time – now he was gone she was lost and heartbroken. After Charles' death she wrote some remembrances of their last few days together: Charles said *'It is almost worth while to be sick to be nursed by you.'* On Tuesday 18th April at midnight he woke her up saying, *'I have got the pain, and I shall feel better, or bear it better if you are awake.'* Later he said, '*I am not the least afraid of death. Remember what a good wife you have been to me.*'[1]

Charles had written in his autobiography when he addressed his children:

> *You all know your mother & what a good mother she has ever been to all of you. She has been my greatest blessing, and I can declare that in my whole life I have never heard her utter one word which I would rather have been unsaid. She has never failed in kindest sympathy towards me, & has borne with the utmost patience my frequent complaints of ill-health & discomfort. I do not believe she has ever missed an opportunity of doing a kind action to anyone near her. I marvel at my good fortune, that she, so infinitely my superior in every single moral quality, consented to be my wife. She has been my wise adviser & cheerful comforter throughout life, which without her would have been during a very long period a miserable one from ill-health. She has earned the love & admiration of every soul near her.*[2]

In his study of his father's life, Francis Darwin said:

> *In his relationship towards my mother, his tender and sympathetic nature was shown in its most beautiful aspect. In her presence he found his happiness, and through her, his life – which might have been overshadowed by gloom – became one of content and quiet gladness.*[3]

Francis wrote of his mother's reaction immediately after Charles died on that April day:

> *She was wonderfully calm from the very first and perfectly natural. She came down to the drawing room to tea, and let herself be amused at some little thing and smiled, almost laughed for a moment, as she would on any other day. To us, who knew how she had lived in his life, how she shared every moment as it passed and sympathised with every feeling, her calmness and self-possession seemed wonderful*

then and are wonderful now to look back upon. She lived through her desolation alone, and she wished not to be thought about or considered, but to be left to rebuild her life as best she could and to think over her precious past. This wish for obscurity and oblivion came out in her eager desire to get the first sight of her neighbours over, and then as she said 'they will not think about me any more'[4]

Among the many letters of condolence received after Charles' death, there was a special one from Emma's niece, Lady Farrer ('Effie'):

Your marriage made the strongest impression on me as a young girl & influenced me deeply in my ideal of married life. I felt from childhood your & Uncle Charles's exceptional happiness together; & now that the tremendous wrench of parting has come, sympathy in your great happiness seems almost the stronger side of my feelings for you, although when I turn my thoughts to your life without him no words will do to say what I know it must be for you ...[5]

Emma slowly came to terms with her husband's death. Her own health also was no longer good and she used a bath-chair around the grounds when much distance had to be covered. Here are some extracts from her letters later that year. To her son Leonard shortly after Charles' death:

It is always easier to write than to speak, and so, although I shall see you soon, I will tell you that the entire love and veneration of all you dear sons for your F. is one of my chief blessings [In their teens the Darwin children told their parents that in future they would not call them Mamma and Pappa but F and M and so it was], *and binds us together more than ever. When you arrived on Thursday in such deep grief, I felt you were doing me good and enabling me to cry, and words were not wanted to tell me how you felt for me... .[6]*

And again later to Leonard:

I have very little to tell you except how beautiful the weather is ... I feel a sort of wonder that I can in a measure enjoy the beauty of spring. I am trying to get some fixed things to do at certain times... [7]

To her son William in May:

Your dear letter was a great happiness to me. I never doubted your affection for an instant, but this has brought such an overflow of it that it makes me feel that you could not spare me, and makes my life valuable to me – and in every word I say to you, I join to my dear Sara.

Two or three evenings ago they all drew me in the bath-chair to the Sand-walk to see the bluebells, and it was all so pretty and bright it gave me the saddest mixture of feelings and I felt a sort of self-reproach that I could in a measure enjoy it. I constantly feel how different he would have been. I have been reading over his old letters. I have not many, we were so seldom apart, and never I think for the last 15 or 20 years, and it is a consolation to me to think that the last 10 or 12 years were the happiest (owing to the former suffering state of his health, which appears in every letter), as I am sure they were the most overflowing in tenderness... [8]

During Charles' last years a typical day would have been an early breakfast, then attending to his post between 9 and 10 am and some reading aloud, followed by work until midday. He would spend a little time in the drawing room before going for his favourite stroll round the 'Sand walk', usually accompanied by Emma. Lunch would be at 1 pm, a look at the newspaper, then letter writing by dictation which Emma usually undertook. Around 3 pm he would go upstairs to rest and have reading aloud, then a further walk with Emma, followed by some more work, then another rest and more reading aloud. Evenings were spent in the drawing room. Emma sometimes played her beloved piano.

In her diaries, Emma kept notes of Charles' condition when unwell – more frequent than not there were many nights when he was too uncomfortable to sleep. In her diary she also recorded his medication. One item that recurred most of their life was referred to only as the 'blue pill', which also features in her diary as something she took quite often too. (A mention of a blue pill, containing Mercury and other ingredients, can be found in pages 215-216 of *A Manual of Materia Medica and Therapeutics* by J Forbes Royle MD FRS and Frederick W Headland MD BA FLS, published by John Churchill & Sons, London in 1865.)

To her daughter Etty in May, Emma said:

> *I am trying to make stages of the day of something special to do. It often comes over me with a wave of desolate feeling that there is nothing I need do, and I think of your true words 'Poor mother, you have time enough now'. The regularity of my life was such an element of happiness, and to be received every time I joined him by some word of welcome, and to feel that he was happier that very minute for my being with him...* [9]

In a later letter to Etty she said:

> *... But life is not flat for me, only all at a lower pitch...*

Down House without Charles was a lonely place. Only Elizabeth (Bessy), Francis and his son Bernard lived there now with Emma. Bessy was very dependent on her mother and very shy. While growing up Etty enjoyed the most attention from everyone, as she was outgoing and bright. She knew how to get other people to do things for her and all her life she had servants to wait on her. After Etty was married and moved to London, Bessy was a willing companion to her parents. Now, with her father's death, it was a comfort for Emma to have her near.

Horace and Ida lived in Cambridge, as did George, still a bachelor. Leonard, now with the Royal Engineers at the Staff College in Camberley, married Elizabeth Fraser, the sister of a brother officer, in July 1882.

Emma took a good look at her life and the prospects for just herself and Bessy at Down, knowing Francis would not be with her forever. Lonely, empty days stretched before her, but Cambridge beckoned and she decided to buy a house there to be near her sons and her grandchildren.

Towards the end of 1882, Francis, who had been his father's secretary and who was *au fait* with all aspects of Charles' life and work, undertook to edit his autobiography and letters. Emma was apprehensive about this daunting work but she was pleasantly surprised when she read the result. She wrote to Etty from Cambridge January 1883:

> *I have been reading Frank's [Francis] notes on F. and I am quite delighted with them. The picture is so minute & exact that it is like a written photograph, & so full of tender observation on Frank's part. The whole picture makes me feel astonished at myself that I can make out a cheerful life after losing him. He filled so much space with his interest, sympathy & graciousness, besides his love underlying & pervading all. I think Frank has done so wisely in writing down everything.[10]*

As recorded in her diaries Emma wrote letters most days. The most frequent recipient was daughter Etty. She wrote from Down on 7th July in 1883:

> *I took a holiday from letters yesterday and loitered about the haystack, etc. Our strawberries are grand, and there are some in the house who certainly enjoy them. I found we were spending 5s. a day on cream and milk, so Mrs B and I were equally shocked and are not going to be so magnificent. To-day I have a nice novel and nice work, and I mean to fill up my time by looking over the wine and doing any other unpleasant thing I can think of ...*

And again on 20th September:

> *... Yesterday such a lovely day, every leaf shining. Bernard spent almost all day on his tricycle, going to the end of the kitchen garden and back whilst Frank timed him with his watch. He is now gone out alone and I am going to time him presently. Old women are turning up, so good-bye my dear.[11]*

Chapter 26

CAMBRIDGE – SECOND HOME FOR EMMA

Having decided she would spend the summers at Down and the winters in Cambridge, Emma spent some time house-hunting during her visits to her sons and finally found The Grove on Huntingdon Road, a mile from the city centre, and there she lived from October 1883. The house was surrounded by gardens with trees and meadows which she loved.

Francis worked at the Botany School in Cambridge and in the summer of 1883 he became engaged to Ellen Wordsworth Crofts, a lecturer at the all-female Newnham College. They were married in the autumn of that year and with Bernard, initially lived at The Grove. Eventually both Francis and Horace built houses on the land surrounding The Grove and called them Wychfield and The Orchard respectively.

Coming to the end of summer at Down, knowing that a certain way of life was ending and that her hours would be filled with very different occupations, Emma felt sad that she would not be at Down to live through the changing seasons, or to visit the dear old Sand-walk whenever she wished. Then she would think ahead to the beauty surrounding her new winter home in Cambridge and, characteristically, she would feel optimistic about the future. Down would still be there next summer.

That summer her diary recorded many visitors, and she herself visited London, Camberley and Cambridge. She was rarely alone. She remained at Down through September until 6th October when, accompanied by Etty and her husband Richard, she went to Cambridge and moved into The Grove on the 11th.

Emma, for the first time in her married life, had time on her hands. She had always been a person who hated to waste time, and was impatient when she had nothing to do. In Cambridge, because she had become familiar with the city and had also met various people during her previous visits to her sons, she very soon found her own social circle with whom she dined or entertained at The Grove. This new awareness of having time to be herself, to relax more easily in company and in conversation, was stimulating and, she had to admit, exhilarating. Now, in her new life, without Charles, she spent some time reading, and she loved cards and played whist. Playing patience also gave her great pleasure and she played it before going to bed at night. She did needlework and, of course, had her *Peggywork*. This comprised long strips of knitting in thick wool, pulled the wool over the pegs of a wooden frame. Afterwards the maids would sew the strips together to make rugs. Most of all she often saw her sons and their families and if Etty did not come to Cambridge, Emma would sometimes go to London to stay with her.

Emma's visitors included Charles' old friends Sir J D Hooker and Lady Hooker. In his own *Life and Letters* (1918), he said that when *A Century of Letters* was printed in 1905 it brought back memories of his very first visit to Down. He wrote to William E Darwin on 19 February 1905:

> *I often recall with deep feeling your Mother's winning reception of me on my first visit to Down in 1843. ... On these visits your Mother did everything to make me feel at home. Often I worked in the dining room, (latterly in the billiard room) through which your Mother often passed on her way to the store closet in the end, when she would take a pear, or some good thing, and lay it by my side with a charming smile as she passed out. Then in the evening she always played to me, and sometimes asked me to whistle to her accompaniment of some simple air! Those were happy days to me.*[1]

Emma got immense pleasure out of books and ordered a dozen at a time from the London Library. Having read Mrs Sandford's book on *Thomas Poole and his Friends* she wasn't impressed, especially with some letters of Coleridge, whom she did not admire – and wondered why her father had liked him. When her niece Snow (the nickname of

Julia Wedgwood, the first-born of Emma's brother Hensleigh and his wife Fanny) wrote *The Moral Ideal* in 1888, she enjoyed reading it and discussing it with the author. From an early age Snow, usually with some of her siblings, spent some time at Down during the summer and as she grew up the friendship between herself and her aunt Emma strengthened. There is an account in *A Century of Family Letters* of an escapade involving the children. Hensleigh was very ill in the autumn of 1842 and for some weeks Emma looked after three of his children, Snow, Bro (James) and Erny (Ernest), aged nine, eight and five. Their nursery maid was Bessy Harding. One day the children and Bessy, got lost in the woods and Snow and Doddy (William Darwin) were separated from the others. She eventually got back to the house from over a mile away, dragging him along, both covered in mud. Emma wrote to Fanny on 6th November:

> *... Snow will tell you of our agitation of the children losing their way. I was afraid of nothing worse but their all sitting down to cry together. They had only Bessy with them, and Snow and Doddy missed the rest somehow and she brought him home from more than a mile off, dragging him along up to their ankles in mud. She kept him from being frightened or crying and from crying herself, and behaved like a little heroine. Charles and Parslow met them a short way from home and learnt as much as Snow could tell them of where the others were. They then found that Bessy and Annie and the 2 boys had been enquiring at a farm-house, and in about half-an-hour Charles found them and took them in to the farm-house for slight refection, and got a man to carry Erny on his back and Annie in his arms and they all came home in very tolerable spirits. Bro kept up his heart very well. It was in our own valley, but I had given them leave to go into Cudham Wood, which was rash of me, and I have forbidden it in the future. I was easy as soon as I saw Snow, as then I was sure Bessy would be hunting after them. Poor Bessie had been carrying Annie for 3 hours...* [2]

Snow grew up with a keen intellect, serious and thoughtful, and had always searched for spiritual understanding of life. Being the daughter of

Hensleigh and Fanny, there were many opportunities to meet interesting people at their frequent social gatherings. She was small in stature, of slight build. Her deafness since childhood, instead of being a hindrance, became a challenge. She had many friends, mostly intellectual, and she was a prolific letter writer. She found it easier to write than to converse. She had a great admiration for Harriet Martineau as they had much in common, including literature, social reform, and moral issues. Harriet too was deaf but they conversed by sitting opposite each other and lip reading. Although Snow was much younger than the pioneering nurse Florence Nightingale, they also became friends. 'Meta' (Margaret Emily) Gaskell, the novelist, Elizabeth Gaskell's daughter, was a good friend too. In 1855, while doing secretarial work for Mrs Gaskell, Snow made a decision to be a writer and was encouraged by her family and others who knew her. She was also a talented artist and many paintings remain as reminders of her frequent travels abroad. At thirty-three she wrote her first essay, 'A Life of Wesley', a study of religious ideas. Her greatest work, completed in 1888, was *The Moral Ideal*, an ethical history of the world's civilisations.

Once in 1864, at her parents' house, she met for the second time Robert Browning, who had been widowed two years previously. Their friendship grew and over the next year they met and corresponded regularly. But because of unkind gossip, Snow decided that to be proper she must end the friendship. She worried in case the poet thought she was chasing him, and she wrote and said she wished the visits and letters to end. That decision caused her unhappiness and regret for the rest of her life. A book entitled *Robert Browning and Julia Wedgwood; a broken friendship as revealed in their letters* was printed in 1937. Snow remained single and died in 1913.

Snow visited Emma in Cambridge and in the summers at Down and they had much to talk about always.

Emma's last unmarried son, George, at the age of thirty-nine met and fell in love with an American, Maud Du Puy of Philadelphia. Maud was a niece of Sir Richard and Lady Jebb, and was staying with them in Cambridge when she met George Darwin. Emma liked Maud on sight and after she visited The Grove in 1884, Emma wrote to her:

My dear Maud,
This is only a line to wish you goodbye. I have been
so vexed at George's attack, which is so ill-timed and

*prevents the enjoyment of your last days together. How
I hope he may be able to accompany you tomorrow to
Liverpool but I am afraid it is very doubtful.*

*Your visit here was a great happiness to me, as
something in you (I don't know what) made me feel sure
you would always be sweet and kind to George when he
is ill and uncomfortable.*

*No doubt you will send a telegram to George on your
safe arrival and he will forward it to me. I hope you will
have a happy meeting with all your dear ones at home.
I am glad to think you are such a good sailor.*[3]

The couple were married in America and on returning to Cambridge,
George and his bride went to stay at The Grove while they looked for
a house. After much renovation, they moved into Newnham Grange at
the end of May 1885. Over the next ten years they had four children
– Gwendolen Mary being the first, born in 1885.

In later years Gwendolen (married to Jacques Raverat) in a
book she wrote about her family called *Period Piece* gave vivid
descriptions of a childhood spent at Down. She remembered Emma
as grandmamma, who was by then a very old lady. But even then her
hair was the colour of tobacco, like Gwen's father, George. Gwen
described grandmamma's elaborate headgear, put on by her Highland
maid, Mathison.

*First there was a black silk lining cap; then a white lawn
cap, with beautiful crimped and frilled edges and long
lawn strings; and then, if she were going out, yet another
black hood over that.*

She remembered picking flowers with her aunt Bessy and
'*arranging them in water on the green iron table in the old study
where The Origin of Species had been written.*'[4]

Gwen Raverat, writing of Bessy in retrospect, remembered her as
being stout, clumsy and unsure of herself, but on the other hand being
wise, though vulnerable. She was kind and in later life, especially
after her mother died, she did charity work in Cambridge.

A memorial statue to Charles Darwin was unveiled at the Natural
History Museum in London in 1885. The ceremony was well attended

by members of the family, but Emma declined to be at such a large gathering. However, on 29th June from Down she wrote to daughter-in-law Sara:

> *I came on Friday. Having spent 2 days at 31 Queen Anne St one of the mornings I went to see the statue. The situation is unique and I liked the attitude, but I do not think it is a strong likeness. ... However I never expected to be satisfied with the likeness, & the general look of dignity & repose is of more consequence. It was a dismal day on my arrival* [at Down] *but I was glad to wander about alone before the others came. ... I loitered about a great deal, & got to the end of the Sand-walk on my own legs, a great improvement in my powers of walking on last year ...[5]*

In 1885, Emma wrote to Frank about a part of Charles' autobiography:

> *There is one sentence in the Autobiography which I very much wish to omit, no doubt partly because your father's opinion that all morality has grown up by evolution is painful to me; but also because where this sentence comes in, it gives one a sort of shock and would give an opening to say, however, unjustly, that he considered all spiritual beliefs no higher than hereditary aversions or likings, such as the fear of monkeys towards snakes.*
>
> *I think the disrespectful aspect would disappear if the first part of the conjecture was left without the illustration of the instance of monkeys and snakes. I don't think you need to consult William about this omission as it would not change the whole gist of the Autobiography. I should wish if possible to avoid the giving pain to your father's religious friends who are deeply attached to him, and I picture to myself the way that sentence would strike them... [6]*

Whilst at Down in the summer of 1886 she wrote to Etty and mentioned baby Gwen:

She is a most remarkable & interesting child, so intent, and watching one's face, not like some busy and animated children who are so intent on their own aims they never look at you – not merry at all.

She enjoyed the company of her grandchildren. Again in a letter to Etty the following summer she said:

Gwen and Nora [Horace's youngest daughter] *tottered about hand in hand, Nora often tumbling over. Gwen was quite tipsy. She came again yesterday, and rushed about with her arms out, laughing whenever she was caught...* [7]

Top: *The Grove, Cambridge*
Messrs. Bidwell & Son, Land Agents and Surveyors, Cambridge

Chapter 27

EMMA'S LAST DAYS –
RELATIVES IN THE NORTH

Life in the Potteries seemed far removed from life in Cambridge, yet Emma's Wedgwood relations in the North were always in touch. After her mother died, Emma did not visit Staffordshire as frequently as before but always kept in touch with her brother Frank, and sometimes went to visit him and other relatives at Barlaston. Frank was a true family man who visited his numerous relatives whenever he could. In 1885 Frank, now eighty-four, and Hensleigh, eighty-two, went to see Emma at Cambridge. Frank and Emma loved a good debate – or argument – about politics. Gladstone was always a favourite topic. Frank, who had championed Gladstone for over 20 years, changed his opinion of him in the early 1870s because he did not now agree with Gladstone's politics. He campaigned for Disraeli and in 1874 Gladstone was out and Disraeli in. Emma enjoyed every minute of their discussions, especially as she was for Gladstone. She remembered meeting him early in 1875 when he went to visit Charles at Down and how much Charles was impressed by him.

Between the years 1885 and 1891 Emma lost her three brothers, Harry, Frank and Hensleigh. Hensleigh's wife Fanny, who lived such an exciting and full life, had died in 1889. Emma was now the last living child of Josiah Wedgwood II.

Frank's sons, Godfrey, Clement and Laurence were all involved in the factory. In 1870 Frank retired as head of the company and allowed his sons to take charge. He and 'Fanny Frank' had had seven children, four daughters and three sons. Frank and Fanny's marriage had not been without its problems. Fanny had always been unsettled in their marriage – at one stage, against his wishes, she went to America for a prolonged visit. She hated staying still and always wanted to go visiting; in their sixties they practically lived separate lives. However, in their seventies, after Frank retired from the company, they did go on holidays together. On one such holiday (in 1874) in Guernsey, Fanny stumbled when carrying a candle to her bedroom and fell, setting her dress on fire. She suffered severe burns and died eight days afterwards. Her sudden death was a great shock to her family.

Clement Wedgwood was most like Frank in temperament. He married Emily Rendel and they had five children. They called their second son Josiah IV after his great-grandfather.

As the years went by Emma continued to find great pleasure in reading – novels were the most relaxing. Jane Austen was top of the list. She went back to her books again and again. She enjoyed Sir Walter Scott; Mrs Gaskell was as popular as Jane Austen; Charles Dickens and W M Thackeray less so. She felt guilty sometimes when she thought of how much time she spent reading, but then she would remind herself that she also read much non-fiction too, of some of which she could be most critical. In her frequent letters to Etty, she discussed whatever she was reading at that time. In the summer of 1886 from Down she wrote:

> *I am very much interested in Morley's Life of Rousseau.*
> *... He ought to consider himself as a sort of sign-post for*
> *the public. Morley's sense of morality and propriety is*
> *very strong, and he glosses over nothing.*

Later when she read H.M. Stanley's *Darkest Africa* she wrote to Etty:

> *I have nearly finished Stanley's Darkest Africa and it must*
> *be the most tiresome book in the world, so confused and*
> *diffuse, with immense long conversations verbatim that*
> *end in nothing. His contempt for Emin's [Pasha] taste for*
> *Natural History is very comical, and certainly he does*
> *not fall into that mistake himself. He observed nothing.*

In 1891 to Etty:

Top: *Sandwalk at Down*

Bottom Left: *Charles Darwin*

Bottom Right: *Emma Darwin*

Reproduced from 'Order of the Proceedings at the Darwin Celebration held at Cambridge 22-24 June 1909', Cambridge University Press 1909 CA

I am much interested in De Quincey's letters, or rather in Dorothy Wordsworth's to him. There must have been something very engaging in him to have received such nice, wholesome letters, full of the children. ... Such a loathsome crawling letter of Coleridge to De Quincey, declining to pay his debt.

In 1891 in her letter she said:

I am reading Lowell's Essay on Wordsworth after Shairp [Sharp] and he suits me much better. He is rather caustic and amusing, and his writing is as neat as if it was French, also he does not soar higher than I can reach.

Gradually as she grew older, Emma found she tired quickly at large gatherings and although she enjoyed being part of groups of interesting people, be they family or friends, she knew when to retire. Her increased deafness also irritated her in crowds – voices sounded like one long cacophony. Each year, as spring lengthened into summer, she began to look ahead to being at Down again. She always went there in June and usually stayed four months.

She used her bathchair to get around the grounds at both The Grove and Down House. At Down House, every summer at the first opportunity she would revisit her favourite places, the Sand-walk and the gardens. At the end of summer these were the last places she went to say *au revoir* until next time.

In the autumn of 1891 Etty became seriously ill after mistakenly taking a dose of poisonous linament instead of medicine. Her arms were paralysed. Emma worried about her and in one letter from The Grove on 25th October she wrote:

I should be much less uneasy while you were at hand and every improvement would be noted and give me constant happiness.

Also when you were able to bear the open air, getting out of doors for five or ten minutes here would be easier and more satisfactory than in your own house. In spite of this my real wish is that you should do what would be really best for you.

Etty did eventually go to The Grove, where her health improved and her mother cared for her as if she were again a child.

In July 1892 there was a General Election and Emma's son Leonard was standing for Lichfield as a Liberal-Unionist. She listed every seat lost and gained. Leonard was elected. Emma was excited, and in July wrote to him:

> *I am quite bursting with things I want to say. I hope we shall see you soon or they will evaporate...*[6]

From Down she wrote to Leonard and his wife Bee on 23rd July:

> *I must tell you how your two delightful letters warmed my heart. We shall have a happy meeting on Friday and I have asked George and Frank to rush over for a day. They will not have a brother elected to Parliament every day in the week. William laments that he cannot come, also Horace. I always feel how your father would have enjoyed it. ... Yours, my two dear ones. E.D.*

In August when writing to Horace's wife Ida she said:

> *... I am so intensely interested in the debates that I must put myself on stoppages or I shall wear out my eyes ...*

Emma began to slow down, at least physically. Letters were not so frequent but she did manage to write every day to either her children, distant relatives or to her friends. She still read as avidly as ever. In December 1893 she wrote to Etty asking for the seventh volume of Walpole and '*A dozen of those pearl or red pins for my peggy.*'

Emma's sons living nearby saw her most days and with their wives and families shared their everyday lives with her. She enjoyed getting to know her grandchildren. Etty was always in touch and went to stay with her mother frequently. At The Grove Bessy was also a good companion.

By 1894, although socially there were always people coming and going, Emma spent more time resting and did her best to avoid catching cold. Her doctor, Dr Allbutt, was a frequent visitor at The Grove and when at Down Dr Moore was in attendance. In her diary on 24th March 1895 she wrote: *'Gt storm at 2 the elm down plus 6 chimneys'* and on the 25th she wrote to Etty:

> *I wonder whether you had our yesterday's storm. It increased in violence all morning and was at its height about two. I looked out to see the trees swaying and remarked on the big wych-elm; I looked away for a minute, and then looked again and saw it was down. Then came a great noise, as if a great weight falling, and we saw part of a chimney down near the north corner. Frank and Bernard soon came in to see if we were frightened. They said some trees were down across the road. Then came another great bang and we settled to go down to the drawing-room. Eventually two stacks of three chimneys each were blown down. We shut the south-west window [shutters] and felt more quiet there, not that I was frightened. It is so bright and calm I hope I shall go out and see the damage, especially the big tree.*

From The Grove in May 1895 she wrote to her daughter-in-law Sara, William's wife:

> *I cannot easily express the happiness your note gives me. To keep such warm affection as yours all these years, and also to know that you feel the same as ever to Ch. fills me with gratitude.*
>
> *I think it is a surprising thing that at 87 I should feel stronger and better in every way than I did at 85.*
>
> *My best love to my dear William who is as steadfast as you.*
>
> *Yours, my dear daughter in heart*
>
> *Emma Darwin*

Returning from Down at the end of that summer she read Balfour's *The Foundations of Belief.* Writing to Etty in October it is still clear that her thinking was as sharp as it was all those years ago when she wrote that letter to Charles about her beliefs and his doubts:

I have finished Balfour. Of course I don't do the book justice, but the last two or three pages seem to me very inconclusive. I can agree with him that the belief in a God who cares is an immense safeguard for morality; but I do not see that the doctrine of the Atonement is any additional safeguard – yes I do see it partly. Also I am surprised at his considering that morality is impossible without some religion, which he gives as an axiom not to be disputed. I quite agree that the remains of Christian feeling make us unable to judge of the present race of agnostics...

One of Emma's many good deeds to the poor was to give out penny bread tickets at the front door of Down House – this she had been doing for the past 50 years. However, in the spring of 1896 she agreed to discontinue this custom. She wrote to tell Etty in April:

I have written to George to ask him to diminish the bread tickets while they are at Down, which will make it easier for Mary Anne. I think there always used to be a great burst of tramps in the spring, and once I found the yard full of hearty Irishmen refusing to go away, till I sent for the policeman. ... I have found Voltaire's Louis XIV very pleasant and short, leaving out the battles. Voltaire seems so impressed with his magnanimity and generosity, as if a despotic King could be generous. V. seems really to forget where the money came from.

The following month in her letter she used the word 'shop' as her name for The Cambridge Scientific Instrument Company where her son Horace was the head:

I liked seeing the Shop on Sunday. It is a perfect situation, surrounded with gardens and so quiet. I did not mount up to the show-room. Horace's room is so nice and airy and quiet It made me think more of him to have such a shop...

As usual Emma went to Down for the summer of 1896. And as usual, the Darwins and Wedgwoods spent some time there. She loved being surrounded by her family and her extended family and still enjoyed playing the piano for the children. Her diary was full of names (usually just initials) of visitors, and every day people came and went – some stayed overnight or for a few days. That year there seemed to be more visitors than ever and Emma also went out and about to old haunts. She wrote to Etty on 29th June:

> On Saturday I took a drive into Holwood. It looked a new place to me from the growth of the trees; especially the band of beeches along the paling, which I used to despise as such poor-looking trees. The mare is perfect on grass and up the hills, not pulling and straining. I went in and out among the green drives, and I shall go again and never drive anywhere else.

On 5th September she wrote:

> On Thursday I made John take me a circuit in the chair by Down Hall and the Cudham Lane. I was glad to see the Cudham Lane once more. It looked ever so much deeper with high hedges and trees grown. I came back over the big field and through the Smith's yard. I felt the sharp wind over the bare field quite like an old friend.

Up to 24th September she completed her diary each day. There were no entries on 25th or 26th. On Sunday 27th she wrote '*bad mg from 3 am. till 6 p.m. ex.night.*' On 28th she seemed to recover and wrote what would be her last letter ever – to Etty, saying she was well. But she was not well and Etty went to Down on Thursday 1st October. On the following evening Emma wound up her watch as usual, then fell back in her bed and never recovered consciousness. She was eighty-eight years old. She was buried in the small cemetery near Maer Hall near her mother and father. Her house in Cambridge was eventually sold and Bessy went to live in a smaller house.

After Emma died Down House was let for a while and eventually went out of the family. In 1996, with the help of The Heritage Lottery Fund and the support of The Wellcome Trust, Down House was purchased by English Heritage. It is now a memorial to Charles Darwin's life, his family and his work.

PART II:

DYNASTY AND DESTINY

Chapter 28

THE POTTERIES

Every ending is a beginning. So it was for Emma Darwin, whose death in 1896 marked the end of one generation and the start of another.

Emma, a scion of the Wedgwood pottery family and the widow of Charles Darwin, world-renowned author of *The Origin of Species*, which expounded his theory of evolution, had seen her sons make successful careers.

William was a banker in Southampton, Leonard was president of the Royal Geographical Society in London, and George, Francis and Horace were all scientists in Cambridge.

Emma's daughter, Henrietta, lived with her husband Richard Litchfield, who worked in London in the legal branch of the Ecclesiastical Commission. Henrietta's sister Elizabeth, who was unmarried, lived in Cambridge.

Unknown to them, the next bearer of the founder's name was to become famous in a very different context, by becoming an MP and falling foul of the Edwardian era's strict divorce laws.

Meanwhile, further north, the sons of Emma's brother, Frank, continued to run the vast Staffordshire pottery empire, begun by Josiah Wedgwood in the mid-18th century.

Frank Wedgwood, master potter succeeded his father, Josiah II, who, after a prolonged illness, died in 1843. Maer Hall, his home, where he grew up, was too expensive to run so Frank bought 100 acres of land in the village of Barlaston where he built a large, family home, and named it The Upper House. He and his wife Frances (known within the family as Fanny Frank) reared their three sons and four daughters at The Upper House.

In 1894 there were cousins from three different branches of the Wedgwood family employed in the pottery business at Etruria, and it was no longer easy for one or two family members to inherit the responsibility of running it. Also, there were more people to share any profits; only the family owned shares.

Godfrey, Frank's oldest son and senior partner, was diligent and gave the business the best of his abilities, but he knew his limitations and would have preferred a life without all his inherited responsibilities. His younger brother Clement was much more enthusiastic about the pottery business: he was an astute businessman, spotted new trends in manufacturing and had the courage of his convictions, knowing exactly when to introduce new methods.

Godfrey's first wife Mary Hawkshaw, bore him a son, Cecil, in 1863, but died shortly afterwards. Godfrey married again in 1876, this time choosing his first cousin, Hope, and they had one daughter, Mary. When Mary was five, the family engaged a governess, an Irish girl called Lucie Gibson. Cecil fell in love with Lucie and they were married in Cork in July 1888 and two daughters were born to them – Phoebe and Audrey. Cecil's sole ambition was to work in the family business and this he did – his father happily retiring.

Clement married Emily Rendel in 1865 and they had four sons and one daughter, Cecily – a fifth son, Harry, died young. Cecily, who grew up a beautiful girl, cherished by her brothers, married Field Marshal Sir Arthur Money with whom she went out to India to live. But she was to die in Poona in 1904 aged only 28. Emily and Clement's second son Josiah IV, born in 1872, was called 'Siah' by the family. Emily's sister, Frances Elizabeth had married Charles Synge Christopher, Lord Justice Bowen. Frances and Charles had one daughter, Ethel. Thus Siah and Ethel were first cousins, and were to go on to cement the family connection further by marrying. Emily was well educated and made sure her children had a classical education. They lived at Barlaston Lea – a property on grandfather Frank's land, adjacent to the Upper House. The boys at thirteen went to Clifton and afterwards to Cambridge, except Siah, who 'finished' in Dresden, where he stayed with an aunt, Rose Franke, and learned German.

Their grandfather Frank died in 1888. Their father, Clement, died the following year.

Top Left: *Josiah Wedgwood IV 1890*

Top Right: *Ethel Bowen 1892*

Left: *Ethel Bowen Wedgwood with her daughter Helen. The mother of the Gracchi 1901*

Above: *Ethel, son Josiah (V), daughter Camilla*

Photographs are courtesy of Sir Andrew Huxley

Josiah IV's family name of Siah was changed to Jos as he grew up. He started work in 1890 at Armstrong's Elswick shipyard in Newcastle upon Tyne. Emily's brother, Hamilton Owen Rendel was a partner in Armstrong's and he was happy to employ his nephew Jos. However, it was then decided that Jos should go to the Royal Naval College at Greenwich and study naval architecture. He moved to London and lived with his uncle, Sir Alex Meadow Rendel, and family at 44 Lancaster Gate, where he met many influential people.

Where the Wedgwoods were clannish and inclined to be aloof, the Rendels were extrovert and loved all the intellectual pursuits London had to offer. They welcomed young Jos with open arms and were only too eager to introduce him to their many friends.

Meanwhile Jos pursued his studies from 1892 for three years. He had hoped to make the Army his career, but failed the medical examination.

One weekend while at home with his parents in Barlaston, his mother asked Jos to meet his cousin Ethel off the train, as she was coming to visit them for the first time. Jos was reluctant as Ethel's reputation had travelled before her – she was a blue stocking, difficult, looked down her nose at her country cousins and was easily bored. But he was not intimidated by her, and they became friends. In London they attended Fabian Society lectures, and took long walks in Richmond Park, wishing they did not always have to have a chaperone. Ethel urged Jos to help her to understand his college studies, so that they could discuss his work. Later in life, Jos wrote in his Memoirs that in Ethel the admixture of Bowen and Rendel had produced a brain beyond compare.

At the beginning of their courtship, early in 1893, many letters passed between Jos and Ethel and it was apparent they were impatient in their separation. On 8th March 1893 from 14 Albert Hall Mansions, Kensington Gore, Ethel wrote to Jos:

Dearest cousin of mine, I do like to get your letters; but <u>please</u> for both our sakes don't let your own imagination run away with you. Remember that I <u>ought</u> to be strong enough for both of us; and that I am <u>not</u>. I haven't strength to stand against you, and I am so lonely that your affection upsets me unreasonably.

Keep a sane head, dear, for both of us ...

Jos replied from the Naval College on 12th March:

> *Dearest Ethel, ... I am always thinking of you, but when with you I have nothing to say to you, or say the wrong thing. Believe me I mean to work hard for you & deserve your love. You have been very kind to me and oh I love you ... I remain yr loving cousin Josiah Wedgwood*

Jos's impetuous courtship of Ethel was causing concern within their families, as it was felt they were not observing the proprieties. Eventually Ethel's father wrote to Jos asking him to behave with decorum when visiting. He stressed that Jos must behave like a gentleman and not see Ethel alone. In May 1883 Ethel's mother, Frances wrote inviting Jos and Ethel to their home in the country in Colwood, Hayward's Heath, Sussex, she added:

> *It is for Ethel's sake the absolute necessity of keeping up proper proprieties.*

Jos behaved and having gained the blessing of their respective parents, the couple became engaged.

At Greenwich Jos had been made assistant constructor in the drawing office at Portsmouth Dockyard. He and Ethel were married in mid-1894. They honeymooned in Europe and on returning to London made their first home in Hyde Vale, Greenwich. In July the following year their daughter, Helen was born. Helen was Emily's first grandchild. Ethel wrote to her mother-in-law to tell her of her pregnancy:

> *My dear Mother,*
> *I want to tell you our wonderful news myself. We are expecting to have a little child, about next July. We are very very happy, & can't quite believe it. I had been having what seemed a bad bilious attack, so Jos took me up yesterday to see R Brinton & get set straight, & that is how we learnt it.*
>
> *We want you not to tell anyone (except Uncle H) yet, while it is still such early days. I shall tell nobody except my mother.*

> *I wish you could see Jos's radiant face. Couldn't you come here next week for a bit? By the beginning of next week, the household will nearly have tided over its upheavals, & we shall be able to make you right welcome. We both much want you to come.*
>
> *I am very strong & well except for bouts of that horrid sickness. RB told me to keep pretty quiet while it lasted, so I am being very prudent.*
>
> *You must <u>guess</u> how happy we are.*

Your very loving daughter

Ethel Wedgwood

In the next three years their daughter Rosamund, first son Charles and then Josiah V were born. But the fledgling family unit soon faced a major upheaval that would affect all their lives.

The South African War began in 1899. Jos joined up immediately. When he embarked for South Africa, Ethel went too, leaving the children with Emily their paternal grandmother. Ethel managed to have some time with Jos in Africa, but had to return home when she found she was again pregnant. Ethel wrote two letters to Jos in March 1901:

> *... I never knew how I loved you, till I found how small the big events of life were beside it ...*

and

> *... My dear you know my faults & you know that I love you faithfully through this world & into the next, & that no human being, nor time, nor distance, nor anything else can come between us. I am your loving wife Ethel Wedgwood.*

Their daughter Camilla was born in March 1901.

The war lasted 18 months and when it was over and the soldiers went home, Jos stayed. He had fallen in love with the country and wanted to make his and his family's future there. He searched for suitable employment but without success and finally had to return home but he did not give up his dream. His persistence paid off and eventually he applied and was successful in getting a position as resident magistrate of the districts of Ermelo and Carolina, Transvaal, in South Africa. He and Ethel emigrated in March 1902 with Helen, Rosamund and Charles, again leaving young Josiah and Camilla with Jos's mother Emily. Helen had her seventh birthday at Wellington.

Ethel initially enjoyed the life in South Africa – so different from London – but after 18 months she began to fret. Their furniture and books, all their household belongings had arrived from England. Seeing them placed in their new home, the Residency, suddenly made it all feel so final and permanent. She was homesick and became unwell. She appeared to have heart trouble but the doctors could not find anything seriously wrong. Jos decided they would go home for a visit, so he took six months' leave and returned to England and Barlaston.

When it was time to return to South Africa, to make the long voyage easier Jos sent the three children ahead with their governess, Morag Hunter. The crossing for Jos and Ethel was rough. Ethel was seasick and at Grand Canary she refused to go any further. Jos, at a serious crossroads in his life, had to decide whether to go on alone to his work in Ermelo, knowing that that would be the end of his marriage, or turn his back on his career and return to England. He chose England and Ethel. Morag and the children were told to return to Barlaston. When they came back to England in 1904 they did not have a home, and Jos had no prospects or plans for the future.

Jos's uncle Hamilton Rendel had died in 1902. He left most of his large fortune to his sister Emily Wedgwood and her children, including Jos. This legacy from his uncle made life easier for Jos at a critical time in his life and gave him some space and choice in what to do in his career.

Eventually, after living briefly in Barlaston at the Old Hall, Jos and Ethel rented a flat in London, and found a house in Weybridge for their children and staff. By now Jos, a staunch Liberal, was active in politics and won Newcastle-under-Lyme from the Conservatives in 1906, a seat he occupied for 35 years. Ironically, at that time Godfrey's son Cecil – Jos's first cousin – was head of the Wedgwood works and a strong supporter of the Conservative party. He and Jos agreed to differ over politics.

Jos's 1940 autobiography *The Memoirs of a Fighting Life* tells the story of his life in politics.

Chapter 29

ETHEL'S DIARIES

From an early age Jos and Ethel's children, when with their parents, had meals with them, except late dinner. Politics were high on the menu and this helped them to understand something of current affairs. Helen always loved politics and hoped to become more involved when she grew up. There were always governesses to supervise both the children's upbringing and their education, although at times Ethel gave them lessons, but she was most impatient. Jos taught them mathematics and history. A favourite governess, Morag Hunter, remained with the family until the end of 1908. After Morag the new governess was Florence Willett who also became a good friend to all the children, and who was later to re-emerge in all their lives in the most surprising way.

Ethel was much involved in Jos's political career and spent much time at the House of Commons. In 1906, Jos's first year in the House, Ethel kept an everyday diary.[1] Whenever her husband was away, at meetings, etc., she wrote to him practically every day. At that time Jos was Private Personal Secretary to Lord Walter Runciman (1st Viscount, Liberal statesman).

Ethel was passionately interested in political debate and was present in the House on many occasions. She advised Jos on many subjects and kept up to date with all the legislation that was current. Her diary is detailed each day about the business in Parliament and – apart from the actual political issues – is colourful and illuminating about the men and women with whom she mixed. Both she and Jos led a very busy social life.

During that year the children and their governess, Morag Hunter, lived in rented accommodation in Weybridge and on most weekends Ethel and Jos would take the train to Surrey to be with them. Ethel was working on the translation of Joinville (Jean Sieur de) *The Memoirs of the Lord of Joinville*, a French historian (1224 – 1317)

On Friday 4th May the diary read: '*Bertha Synge came to tea, also Ella Coltman & old Mr William Darwin ...*' The following day both parents went to Weybridge until Monday afternoon. '*Lucy Martineau came to tea on Sunday & spent two hours playing paper games with the children & us. ... Helen, to her great joy finished her first French book with me, Le Conscrit, and has now got a Jules Verne for private reading as a reward.*' On Wednesday 9th May, Rosamund and Helen went up to town to spend a day with Ethel – '*... who arrived under Emma's escort at Waterloo about half past ten, looking charming in their cool summer hats & coats. They insisted on going to the National Gallery ... at 6 I sent the little girls under maid Emma's care off from the station.*'

Saturday 12th May: '*Lunched on Thursday with Mrs Erskine Childers in their nice little flat in Embankment Gardens. Her husband is hoping to get his vol of The Times Hist of the War out by August or at any rate before the Official Hist ... saw Adeline & Ralph Vaughan-Williams for a few minutes ...*'

Friday 11th May: '*JCW dined with me here, & then came Master Potter Burton on his way to France to talk Workmen's Compensation with JCW. I gave them tea, & then left them & went to bed ...*'

Friday 22nd May: '*... went to Albermarle Club & had a talk with Cousin Effie* [Euphemia] *over the proposed new life of old J.W.* [Josiah I] *which they would have liked Jos & me to undertake – but we have too many irons in the fire already ...*'.

Jos and Ethel visited their friends the Lambs in Liphook, Hampshire at the end of May. They were in the company of Mr & Mrs John Collier. Mrs Collier was the second daughter of Professor Huxley, and John was a painter and brother to Lord Monkswell. Ethel described Borden Wood as a '*lovely place with a marvellous view down a wooded cleft on to distant downs. Mr Lamb loves horses & farming & botany & so forth. The house is big, full of light oak white paint, pretty & warm & bright & they have some lovely things in it ...*'.

Ethel mentions in June that her Joinville translation has come out and is looking extremely nice. '*I can't think why the whole world is not reading him ...*'.

In September of that year Ethel, with Rosamund, Helen, cousin Mary (Wedgwood) and Morag Hunter went to France for a holiday but they returned three weeks earlier than planned as Ethel was 'out of sorts'. She was actually pregnant at that time with their sixth child.

Jos wrote to his mother in the Spring of 1907:

> *The children will be with you soon. Ethel herself is getting on well. Maud Gladstone is up here now & has been very kind having Ethel much down in her flat & to meals.*

Elizabeth Julia, pet name when young 'Betsy', was born in London on 1st May 1907; at that time the family had a flat at Great Smith Street. Helen wrote to her mother in June 1907 giving her all the news from home, home then being a rented house, Taylors, in Ockley, Surrey.

Taylors
Capel
June 19
1907

Dear Mother

It was very wicked of you not to come down to us, we had got everything ready, and had picked ever so many flowers for you and Betsida.

Yesterday we three girls, Morag, and Father went up to see the dentist. Camilla had three teeth out, Rosamund and I only had the shape of our mouths taken, but I have got ever so many to be stopped. He kept my plate, to alter it, so as to make room for my 12 year old molars, which

> are coming through.
> After the dentist two
> went to the Houses of
> Parliament, and were
> introduced to ever so
> many members, and
> Father showed us many
> more; then we saw over
> all both Houses, and
> the cript; we met Mr
> Harold Cox who said he
> was very glad to meet me,
> as he would convert me
> and I would convert
> Father, he also said he was

> sorry that we had all
> fallen into the same
> mistakes,
> Then we had tea on the
> terrace,
> We saw the speaker go
> into the House, he looked
> so ridiculouse in his tight
> stockings and long
> train,
> Your loving daughter
> Helen Bowen Wedgwood

On 23rd October, Ethel wrote in her diary about celebrating Jos's brother Ralph's last bachelor day by all dining at the Metropole Hotel:

> *He & Felix in excellent spirits & very full of fun, Frank*
> *& I got into a S. African mood, & Felix talked Argentine*
> *Spanish, smoked large cigars & drank Crème de Monte.*

The next day, Ralph's wedding day everything went off as usual in St Margaret's:

> *... The bride & bridegroom looked happier than I ever*
> *saw two look before in the same case ...*

Ethel and Jos spent the last six weeks of that year with the children at Taylors. This was a busy year during which Ethel seemed to thrive on all the activities involved with her husband's political career.

Chapter 30

JOSIAH IV AND ETHEL – LIFE'S UNCERTAINTIES

Much of the contents of Ethel's diaries during those years to 1912 are similar – details about political proceedings in the House, references to meetings, social engagements, everyday items about the children. Some notes stand out, for instance in 1908 when Parliament opened on 29th January – Ethel wrote on 7th February:

Jos dined with the League of Y. Liberals, Churchill spoke in the Masterman style, Jos followed and talked Land Values, with great eclan. Helen & Rosamund went to tea with Winifred Lamb ...

Saturday 8th Josiah & I went off early to Victoria & Albert Museum as he is to be on the Committee of re-arrangement, & we wanted to have a look over the place, which is jumbled in the extreme. Then on to Mrs Green's to lunch. Jos was cross because he hates the Irish question & had specially been asked to meet Sir Horace Plunkett. However he was cheered by finding Mr Philip Morrell one of party. Sir Horace prosed hard all luncheon, & nearly made Mrs J.R.G's hair stand on end by declaring he didn't care a bit about Home Rule, and that it has nothing to do with the real question – i.e. the Agrarian trouble. A young Sinn Feinner with long hair & brown eyes, sat next to me ... Sir H.P. gave his version of the quarrel with the Irish parliamentary party, whom he declares are anxious to keep the peasantry ruined in order to make them discontented.

*Mon. Feb. 10ᵗʰ: "In the afternoon I took the 4 children
to Linden gardens by special invitation to tea at the
Coltman & Stevenson gymnasium, left them there & went
on to Eaton Place to Mrs Evelyn Cecil's who had invited
me to meet Miss Gertrude Bell ... sat next to her & told
her how immensely I liked her book, & asked her about
her next enterprise ...*

Jos and Ethel with their family moved to 2 Phillimore Gardens, which remained their London address for the next three years.

Josiah and Ethel's last child, Gloria, was born in 1909.

From an early age Jos discussed politics with Helen and she was interested in everything that went on. She had a vivid memory of, when only fifteen, being in the Ladies' Gallery and hearing part of the 1909 Budget Debate, with Winston Churchill speaking. Her father addressed her as an equal, always loving, but never condescending. The whole family became actively involved in canvassing for the Liberal party whenever the need arose.

In 1908 Jos built a bungalow three miles from Barlaston, in the middle of a wood on a quiet hillside and within easy reach of other relatives. The house was built on part of Josiah's cousin Godfrey's land; Godfrey and Hope lived at their home, Idlerocks, nearby. Still pining for southern skies, Jos built his new home to look like a South African ranch house, with many rooms and a passage right through the middle. It was built of wood and Jos, who had designed it, called it Moddershall Oaks, but it was known by all the family as the Ark. Camilla and young Josiah did not live permanently with their parents until the Ark was completed. They stayed mostly at Barlaston Lea or Halsteads in the Lake District, their grandmother Emily's home before marriage. All the children loved being together at the Ark, their first real home, and although they also lived in London and elsewhere later, it was to prove a haven for many years.

Between 1910 and 1912 Helen went to stay with Mr and Mrs Lamb at Liphook, to study with their daughter Winifred. During that time Helen worked towards the entrance exam to Cambridge; her parents had put her name down for Newnham. Helen shared Winifred's governess, and masters from the nearby school, Bedales, also came over to coach the girls. At that time Helen's brother Charles was at Bedales and later in 1911 their younger brother, Josiah V, joined him.

Top: *Moddershall Oaks (The Ark) 1908*

Above Left: *At the Ark — family portrait 1908*

Above: *Michael Stewart Pease*

Left: *Helen Bowen Wedgwood*

Photographs are courtesy of Sir Andrew Huxley

While at the Lambs there were many letters to and from home. In one letter from the Ark, Jos wrote to Helen on 16th May 1910:

> *... Mind to try to be agreeable, not out of a desire to be popular, but because it is the best training for unselfishness. ... Rosamund & Camilla have been in the woods all day, chiefly gazing in rapt adoration at a square yard of tumbled soil which they call their gardens.*
>
> *Tomorrow we go for an expedition in motor & on foot to Swynnerton Old Park with lunch in our pocket, & we shall bring Betsy back from the Lea ... Leonard & Mildred Darwin are also at Idlerocks, & indeed many others. Goodbye my dear little girl.*

> *Your loving father Josiah C Wedgwood*

Helen wrote to her father in October:

> *I miss bicycling dreadfully, & I hope I shan't be quite out of practice when I come home ... Your v l daughter H B W*

Her mother wrote to her on 2nd June 1911 from Phillimore Gardens, mostly about her father and politics:

> *Tomorrow we are going to the Ark ... I was pleased to hear from someone who was at Mrs Lamb's garden party 'What a nice eldest girl you have got; so you see pretty behaviour is its own reward, and also brings gratification to one's mother. Ever love your affectionate mother Ethel Wedgwood*

A further letter from Ethel later in June talked about the Coronation. They also went to a Buckingham Palace garden party. Ethel wore a hat with white ostrich feathers and a new green gown with Chinese embroideries.

On 18th November, Josiah wrote from the Ark to Helen:

My dearest Helen,

... I am so glad that you are making an outside interest for yourself that I should be the last to talk exams to you. At the same time you will recognise that a Uni education would be invaluable if you are to help the Cause in the best way. Thinking what a chance there is of going for the Cambridge Fabian Society, I suggest that you amuse yourself by seizing on points in the daily papers. Write letters to show them up, & send the letters & points to me. I want to see that your arguments are sound before you go on the stump. You will be able to help me lots, & when next I am in town, I will tell them to send you Land Values every month.

I only went to town for yesterday & have just got back. You are exactly like your mother. Yours JCW

On 28th March 1912, Helen had a letter from her mother. This was the time of the miners' strike and everyone was worried about the outcome:

R [Rosamund] & I are going down tomorrow to see if we can be of any use, & to see exactly how things are. Do write to me at the Ark. We may come back on Monday as I don't like leaving your Father who is over-strained & tired & has the big Free Speech Defence at the Opera House Kingsway on Wed. as well as all the rest.

... I hope you won't think I have done wrong, I have sold some diamonds. I do not see that they would be of any good ever to any of you, but if you or the other girls ever feel that it wasn't fair towards you I shall think it quite reasonable to give any of you their share's worth. They fetched £80. Best love.

Try & not let all this hinder your work. It is a sound & safe thing to go on doing routine work when one feels in a little commotion.

My dear love to you, Yours ever EW

Helen replied to this letter at the end of March from Liphook. It is obvious she cares very much about what is happening in the country and is familiar with the latest news:

Thank you very much for your letter. I am glad you sold the diamonds, I rather hoped you would do something of the sort. I was rather wondering whether anything I have got would be any good for selling, but I do not know whether they would get much, and the best ones were given to me by Grandmother & I think they were given her by Lord Armstrong, so I don't think the money they would get would be worth the sacrifice.

I saw the manifesto of the Free Speech League. Father must be frightfully busy with all this work; but I expect having such a lot to do keeps him from worrying at all.

Do you think the coal strike will come to an end soon? and do you think that the miners have really gained anything by this Bill? Because it doesn't seem to me there is much in it; the real fight will come when the local boards settle what the minimum is to be; and then the trouble will come all over again.

Also I can't quite understand why if the miners' ultimate object is to take over the mines themselves, they didn't buy out the owners, which Mr Lamb says wouldn't have cost more than the strike and would have saved a lot of trouble.

Of course, really just getting rid of the owners wouldn't do much good, because the landlords would still get royalties, & rents would rise, but the miners haven't apparently seen that, & only say they wish to get rid of the owners, so I cannot see why they didn't buy them out. (Mr Lamb <u>says</u> the owners wd be willing to sell, but the miners know coal-mining doesn't pay, at least not regularly!)

Work is going steadily along. I think we are to have a few days' holiday after tomorrow, then the German lady you told Mrs Lamb of is coming.

It is perhaps well I should have this work, but you can't think how difficult it is to set to it, to appear interested in all sorts of things, when one is all the time wondering about the Potteries, & Father and everything else; and what makes it worse there is nobody I can talk to about it; still I have had such a fine number of letters – two or three or four every day – that I know anything that is going on.

Thank you very much for writing, & for enclosing letters; it does make such a difference. Anyway the only thing I can do now is to pass that exam, which is a step towards working.

You will be glad to get to the Ark. It must be looking lovely now I should think. If you plant any flower seeds, cornflowers ought to do there, & they make a fine show, also shirley poppies.

Please kiss the babies for me.

Your loving daughter Helen Bowen Wedgwood

Helen wrote to her father on 1st April 1912:

What a pity it rained in London yesterday, it must have rather spoiled the Trafalgar Square meeting – however you will be having another at the Opera House.

... I wish you could see my garden now. It is a <u>dream</u>. Everybody spontaneously admires it.

... Nothing at all has happened except that I went to see the boys on Sunday, & we had a glorious talk, & made any amount of plans. ... They are also very much looking forward to their holidays.

Winifred's and my holidays end on Wednesday, when a German lady is coming to coach us in German Literature. Also Miss Burne wishes to start me on Hydrostatics. I know my brain will burst long before the exams.

Do you think the strike will really end with this ballot, because it seems to me they will all be out again over the local settlement of the mine? It also seems to me that if the soldiers are going to play football with the miners as they are at Cannock, they won't be able to shoot them afterwards, even if there is a disturbance.

... Goodbye dearest Father

Your loving daughter

Helen Bowen Wedgwood

Helen had taken the Cambridge Intermediate part of the examination for Newnham, after which she attended Bedford College in London. where she studied for the science exams. These she passed that summer. As a day girl, she stayed with her parents in the capital.

Chapter 31

POLITICAL FRIENDSHIPS

Because of what was to happen in 1913 extracts from some of the letters written by Ethel Wedgwood during the following 12 months are quoted here, which make one wonder how someone could change so drastically in just under a year. During that time the name of Harry de Pass occurred in many letters as will be seen in the following correspondence. He would appear to have been the person who went ahead of Jos to set up political meetings, and was an enthusiastic 'Single Taxer'. There is no known evidence of a physical relationship between Ethel and Harry – but suddenly he appeared frequently in her life. From subsequent letters between Helen and Rosamund, it is obvious they resented his growing friendship with their mother, which preceded her dramatic decision to end her marriage to Jos. But in April 1912, Jos, all unknowing, wrote to Helen, amused at Ethel's new ideas about diet:

> ... *Your mother would like to drop all food & is rapidly narrowing the margin of consumption – if I may so put it. The fault lies with the abominably healthy appearance of that good Single Taxer, Mr Harry de Pass, who gave us lunch in St John's Wood last Monday. It* <u>was</u> *a beautiful lunch & looked so nice. ... Tomorrow we three are going to row up the river from Hampton Court, & pretend we are the castaways of civilisation. We shall take books & cigarettes & – of course – lunch ...*

In a note from Rosamund to Helen in July Rosamund mentioned that 'H de P' came to supper at seven o'clock the previous evening, and later that month she told Helen that Harry would be arriving at the Ark to stay a few days.

Ethel wrote from the Ark to Josiah on 21st August 1912:

Dearest Husband,

I gather Mr Kinloch joined you yesterday. You will see from Harry de Pass's letter & the enclosed 'Scotsman' (which someone sent you) that Shaw [George Bernard] *has promised to join the group.*

... I hope you will remember that R & I should be very much disappointed if this Paris visit were given up, & that you will tell these people if they want to have you as Speaker they must arrange a date after Oct. 8.

I think the plans we have for Paris and our introductions there will be of real service to you & instructive to us all just now, or I should not be so keen about it.

The days have been busy since you went, mostly with domesticities, overhauling & ordering all the family clothes for the autumn & winter, etc. etc. & letter writing, reading aloud to the girls & the babies, etc.

This afternoon I hope to get some writing done before old Miss Gaskell & Cousin Euph. come down to tea. ... Goodbye dearest

Your wife doesn't forget you at any rate!

Love to Helen & the boys & greetings to Mr Kinloch ...

Again from the Ark, a letter to her husband two days later:

Dearest,

You will see from Harry de Pass's letter that he is urgent you should join the brotherhood in Edinburgh instead of going to Wales. If Shaw is really fighting straight on T.L.V. [land valuation tax] *it seems to me you cannot be away and that they will want all our men.*

H de P's suggestion that we might make our trip to Edinburgh seems to me a good one.

Wire me on the enclosed form if I shall meet you at Harrogate (or where) with the car on Wednesday or Thursday afternoon, and we will have our honeymoon in Edinburgh a nous deux.

I don't propose to take any of the children with us. The two big girls must be both here to look after things in my absence & Camilla is too young and would be in the way.

Remember that I don't know the address in Harrogate.

... Please write also to H de P on the enclosed form whether to expect you on Thursday/95 Princes' Street, Manchester ...

Your most loving wife   Ethel W

While she was away in Edinburgh, Ethel wrote to Rosamund:

Dearest R,
... Harry de Pass is settled in Dalkeith ... I won't say: are you all good & happy, but if you are not let me know.

Also if Helen & you find the family too much responsibility or are in any way bothered I will come out at once, & you must be sure to tell me.

Give my dearest love to Helen. I hear that she looked after everyone & darned their socks indefatigably & in short was an angel; & that Siah [Josiah V] enlivened all the way with jokes.

Give both boys my love, Betsy & Gloria shall have picture postcards.

Your ever loving mother

Ethel Wedgwood

On 2nd September Ethel wrote again to Rosamund from Edinburgh:

... Father & I are off to join H de P & breakfast in the Edinburgh tea room – ... & then on in a motor to Mid

Calder where H de P is going to quarter himself among the shale workers. ... H de P is most kind to us and looks after us beautifully. We should be quite lonely without him ...

On 23rd September Rosamund wrote to Helen from Paris:

... H de P is coming, I expect, on the 1st. He may come back with us so you will probably see him in London as there is a Single. Tax kind of gathering from 5th–8th ...

Harry de Pass did indeed join them in Paris.

Back in London, on 12th October Ethel wrote to Rosamund who was now at the Ark:

... We shall be down on Saturday, Father, I, H de P about 2 o'clock ... George Lansbury & H de P have made friends & we are all four dining together on Monday at the House of C ...

On 7th November Ethel wrote to Rosamund at the Ark. Helen was staying in London with her mother at that time:

... My darling Rosamund, returning to lunch at 2 to which also Harry de Pass came. Afterwards Father went back to the House, & H de P & I sat talking over the fire for ever so long till we were surprised to find it 'tea-time' ...

In her letter to Rosamund on 11th November Ethel gave a vivid description of a big meeting in Trafalgar Square, the best for 20 years, with an estimated 20,000-30,000 present:

... Father opened the ball, middle plinth, Keir Hardy on East Plinth (facing Strand) ... Both Father & H de P spoke excellently ... Then we came off home to tea with Mr Evans of the "Nation" & H de P and sat & talked and about 7 had a long bus ride to Hackney, where I was speaking to the Anarchist Club. Father & H de P would come too (which made me feel very nervous!) ...

On 12th December Ethel wrote to Rosamund, about a meeting at the Westminster Palace Hotel that afternoon with Josiah, which included the writer Hilaire Belloc. The only women present were Ethel, a Mrs C Sanderson (strong on suffrage) and Mrs Dora Montefiore Taylor (*Daily Herald*), Harry de Pass, Oliver F Lodge, and, Mr Evans, sub-editor of the *Nation*.

> *... We had a nice little lunch party here ... of Mr Oliver Lodge, whom we all like much. He is a communist Anarchist of the Wm Morris school, an artist & writes a little ... H de P joined us for an hour & was – of course – very helpful & kind with all the arrangements and people. I am very glad that he and Mr Lodge seem to have taken to one another, they have so much in common in ideas, & differ so much in education & habits & are both so nice in rather the same way that I hope they will become friends ...*

In May the following year Ethel wrote from Ronda in Spain to Josiah in London. She was at a conference arranged by Joe Fels an American politician. Harry de Pass was also there. Ethel had addressed the conference delegates in Spanish:

> *... As for Harry, they are all at his feet – especially the young men who stand round in a ring ...*

At the same time, she sent a postcard to Rosamund:

> *Dearest Ros,*
> *The Congress, thank goodness, is over; though it was quite good fun, and we had some storms to keep us awake. But it is a real strain following – or trying to follow & watch proceedings in an unfamiliar tongue.*
> *Yesterday H de P & I had a perfectly lovely walk right round along the tops of the near hills & tomorrow we are going further afield, up into the mountains with a mule & a donkey for me.*
> *Sunday to G Algeciras & sail for home on Monday in the "Persia", London on Friday. "Free Speech Defence"*

meeting on Saturday & on Sunday Monday I shall be at the Ark with you all, but meetings on a good many evenings Monday included. H de P has meeting also in the constituency mid week so have a room ready for him. I don't know Father's movements. Dearest love to you all.

After writing to her children so positively, what happened next must have come as a bombshell to them. For between May and July 1913, Ethel Bowen Wedgwood decided her marriage was over and left her husband, taking 'the babies' with her to London.

Chapter 32

JOSIAH'S FAMILY – HELEN WEDGWOOD

The break-up of a family is distressing and sensitive for everyone concerned. Josiah IV loved his wife and continued to do so for some years after she left him. Ethel's thoughts are hidden, and only her actions help to give some idea of how she felt. Certainly she was adamant and determined to have – and go – her own way. Even her oldest daughter described her as brilliant and hard, like a diamond.

It is understandable that the Wedgwood family wish to leave much unsaid about Ethel's change of heart in 1913 and these sentiments must be respected. However, it *would* enhance the story if Ethel's voice could be heard.

Through the many letters which passed between Jos, his daughters, Rosamund and Helen, and his sons Josiah V and Charles, one can see the puzzlement, the heartbreak and the frustration that existed within a family which, up to then, had been strong and united. Until 1913 Jos had a full, eventful life, with a supportive wife and loving children. Suddenly it all changed – his wife left him and the whole framework of their family life was shattered. It changed the lives of their children, but particularly those of his oldest daughter, Helen, and the 'babies' Julia and Gloria, who had been taken by Ethel.

Helen had always had a close relationship with her father. She resented the way her mother hurt him and afterwards found it hard to understand or forgive her.

Jos said that Ethel had a brilliant but restless mind, forever seeking further knowledge. She had begun to read the works of the Austrian philosopher Rudolf Steiner (1861 – 1925) After studying his writings on life – and death – she decided the way she lived was not right for her, and made a decision which caused heartbreak to many people, but most of all to her husband.

Ethel became an anthroposophist. Dr Steiner describes anthroposophy, as a:

> *path of knowledge to lead the spiritual in the human being to the spiritual in the universe. This path does not lead into remote mysticism but directly into the most practical of human endeavours.*
>
> *The philosophical outlook of Steiner embraces such fundamental questions as the being of man, the nature and purpose of freedom, the meaning of evolution, the relation of man to nature, life after death and before birth.*[1]

At the age of twenty-one Steiner had been invited to edit the works on natural science of philosopher/poet Goethe. He was recognised as the leading expert on these writings. His contribution to these studies is still recognised today. The home of the worldwide Anthroposophical Movement in Dornach, Switzerland, is still called the Goetheanum in honour of Goethe.

In 1940, when Jos wrote his Memoirs he said of Ethel:

> *I owe to her seven children and twenty halcyon years. If one could repeat, I would do it again with eyes open, knowing the end; and what is more, I believe she would, too. It was living in a typhoon; but it was living, living breathlessly, dangerously among the gods. She was a really great woman – certain, decisive, enthusiastic, utterly intolerant of stupidity and of the second rate; cruel, when (as too often) she saw cause; logical, and yet stone blind to everything she did not wish to see. People supposed that she dominated my mind, as she did my heart. I do not think so. Decisions were all mine, but she outdistanced me each time racing for the goal.*

Ethel's departure to London with Gloria and Betsy was traumatic for the rest of the family and initially it was thought that this was but a phase in her life. Jos's mother, Emily, did not think it was serious and said she had every confidence that the couple would be reconciled.

Helen and Rosamund, being the oldest, were aware of all that was going on between their parents and about the problem with the 'babies'. They were suddenly catapulted into adult responsibilities and their emotional involvement made attitudes and loyalties hard to define. Rosamund became a kind of go-between as she sometimes had to be with her mother to help with the youngsters. In a letter to Rosamund on 13th July 1913, Jos, now staying with his mother Emily at Barlaston Lea, wrote in a postscript:

> *Could you not make some arrangements for me to see my babies on Tuesday morning? If I could not be allowed in the flat, ... I might come to 34 Bedford Place. I don't want to see your mother, but she has no right to keep my children from me.*

During the latter half of 1913, the family were still optimistic and hoped that Ethel was going through a phase and would again return to them.

In October Helen went up to Newnham College, Cambridge for her first year at university, not knowing what was going to happen to her father, brothers and sisters. She and Rosamund, although not wanting to alienate their mother, also wanted to show their father that they loved and supported him. Gradually, as their letters show, their support for their father strengthened and, like him, their main concern was the fate of Gloria and Betsy. But when lawyers became involved, emotions had to be put on hold and practicalities faced.

In October Helen wrote from Newnham to her father at Barlaston Lea:

> *... I do hope you are not too lonely at the Lea. Come to Cambridge as soon as possible, there are plenty of trains to and from London. Let Mother go her own way as much as possible, she might be working out something which we cannot understand and she so often acts from some deep reason, which is not at all the obvious one ...*

In a later letter during the autumn term, Helen tells her father about her everyday life and lectures, but again there is that anxiety about the family:

> *... Can't you have Ros with you more often? I am afraid you will be knocking yourself up or something ... Lloyd George's speech doesn't seem up to much. I didn't see any definite announcement, did you go and fix your evil eye upon him? He is a slippery fish.*
>
> *... The Fabian Society has collared me, I am afraid. I shall try to get out of it as the sub. is 7s. 6d per annum, but they have good Lecturers down, also the canvasser tactfully remarked that I might do them good, also I wanted to shock you ... On Sunday I went to lunch at the George Darwins', Margaret and Billy were there and also two undergraduates. Margaret is very jolly, she is just back from Oxford ...*

During that time Helen's younger sisters were sometimes at Barlaston Lea with their grandmother Emily and sometimes with Ethel in London.

Helen enjoyed being at Newnham. Apart from being happy in Cambridge she was lucky in that living there were Emma and Charles Darwin's three sons, George, Francis and Horace – Josiah IV's first cousins. By 1913 they had grown-up families with homes of their own. George had two daughters and two sons; Francis a son and a daughter; Horace a son and two daughters. Helen therefore had many relatives nearby and was always welcome at the various Darwin homes, with many invitations to lunch.

Jos knew how unhappy Helen felt about her mother, but he also knew how concerned she was about the babies and he was apprehensive about her ultimate decision about the future, as will be seen in his letter to her at Newnham College, written on 10th November 1913:

> *... But, dear Helen, you might out of common humanity send me on the letters your mother sends you. You will have either to trust me, or her; you cannot do both. Remember it isn't a joke, or a sensation to us, but pretty*

bitter earnest, & the butterfly will get squashed if it tries to flirt with both.

In her reply Helen ignored his remarks about her mother but wrote at length about her everyday life at university. Her casual note about spending some time with Ethel gave the impression that she thought there was still a chance of a reconcilation:

Thank you very much for your letter. I am afraid I have not written for quite a long time; but I have so many engagements & the days go by so fast, that I do not realise how time goes.

On Sunday I went to lunch with Mrs Lucas, wife of a professor of physiology, she has three dear little boys, & we ate off Wedgwood china. (She explained that her husband was friends with all the Darwins, & that they believed in encouraging family trade, so that three sets of Wedgwood were given them at their wedding). She also lent me some books on the land, which are quite interesting; – one called "The Awakening of England" by F E Green, very down on the landlords, & dealing largely with market gardens, at least as far as I have got, the other called "A change in the Village" by G Bourne.

On Monday there will be a land debate, the motion being "that this house approves of L George's speech at Swindon" or words to that effect. I was going to have been a recorder on one side or the other; but I couldn't second the motion, & they already had somebody to second the opposition, so I shall just get up & speak during the debate. (I have 2 mins I believe). Have you any suggestions as to any special points I had better make?

I shall spend a week or 10 days with Mother at the beginning of the holidays, although I am very anxious to come back to the Ark, but I don't want to disappoint her; and anyway much as I loathe London I shall be able to do some Xmas shopping there.

... How is the anti-Lloyd Georgian land campaign going. The papers are confused & skimpy.

... I went to tea last Sunday at the Horace Darwins, where there was a large party of very nice undergraduates & girls, including Kitty & Fanny Farrer. We had family tea ...

Please give my love to Ros, the babies & Grandmother. Your very loving daughter Helen Bowen Wedgwood

PS. The enclosed is a letter from Mother. I also had a letter from Inez Maskelyne about her [Ethel's] stay in Bath, simply saying that she took the chair at a meeting & stayed with the Tollemaches.

There has never been any definite record of Ethel Wedgwood leaving her husband for another man. Her reasons had always been that she had had enough of her life in politics with Jos and that as she had ceased to love him she could not live with him. However, the continuing presence of Harry de Pass in her life seemed to worry both Helen and Rosamund.

With Helen away at University, Rosamund had the responsibility of being with 'the babies' and her mother and also of being there for Jos, when he needed her. When she learned of Helen's planned visit to London before Christmas, she referred to it in her letter to her in November. She calls Julia 'Betsy', her pet name. In this letter the problem of divided loyalties is apparent. Rosamund was practical, and saw where she was needed most, she rarely had a chance to please herself. It is hard to believe that Rosamund was only fifteen. The split within her family caused her to grow up very suddenly and it presented her with problems that only an adult should have had to face:

My dear Helen, Father has gone to Glasgow where he has had a magnificent meeting, but how he is I do not know, as he left last Friday. Uncle Felix has just gone away again. He seemed to me (don't mention this to Grandmother or Father, as I have no grounds for my supposition) to be rather worried or tired. It may only have been that he has had a cold. Betsy is getting on well with her work, tho' of course not very fast. Unfortunately I cannot consider that this is due to my teaching. This branch of work will not make my fortune.

My dear, I am seriously sorry that you are going to London for it looks (now that Father has taken us away) rather as tho' you countenanced Harry's going on seeing Mother. I am not coming up, & I wrote & told Mother why, otherwise I should love to be in London with you and her. Of course she will think that Father has "got round me". This is not so, only it seems to me that I cannot (when Mother & Father are as they are at present) be with both, & that it wouldn't be right to leave Father, as I can do more for him than for Mother. Unless of course Mother should be in trouble. If also she gave up seeing Harry, Father would not mind us and the babies being with her half the year. Of course it may be all different for you, or you may be right & I wrong. What is right for one, may be wrong for another. If you have time, I should rather like to have your ideas on this anyway. I am your loving Rosamund

In November Jos's mother Emily wrote to him – a letter from the heart with feelings recognised by any loving mother in the same circumstances, the contents of Ethel's letter to which she refers are not known.

My darling son,
I am sorely tempted to burn this letter I enclose – for I know it will be horrid – if so, dear 'Siah will you for love of me and because I love you so, burn it and make no answer – I am sure you ought to do that now – for your children's sake and for your own manhood & self-respect you must not lose temper or patience above all, save yourself the misery of regrets in after life – what would I not give to spare you all this pain dear 'Siah, but you know all that. I am most thankful that I can help you in any way ...

Good-bye my dear ...

I hate to enclose Ethel's big letter – burn it unread – there are so many to love and honour you – let us always honour you my son. I am ever Yr very devoted mother ECW

At the beginning of 1914, as war clouds gathered over Europe, Jos took his son Josiah V, now in his fifteenth year, to Switzerland for a short holiday. He took this opportunity to talk to him about the situation with Ethel. Young Joshiah wrote to Rosamund from Switzerland on 5th January:

> *Dear Rosy,*
> *... Do you know I was only told for the first time, a little time ago, about Mother. I was quite surprised, as I did not think Mother was such a fool, and so void of duty to others. The worst of it is, that Father misses her. Do you think there is any chance of her coming back and reconcilement between them? I hope there is and I wish I could do something to stop Mother being such a fool. I don't know the exact facts, or what you think about it ...*

Chapter 33

A QUESTION OF CUSTODY

In the new year, when it became obvious as the months went by that Ethel had no intention of changing her mind, serious discussions were taking place regarding custody of the youngest girls and solicitors were consulted. In a letter to Helen, her father wrote from the House of Commons:

> *... I do not know whether your mother will accept my terms for the children. If she does they will be with us whenever your <u>Cambridge vacations</u> are on, i.e. half the year ...*

Ros wrote to Helen in early March 1914 – their father had gone to America to preach Single Tax as a memorial sermon for Joe Fels, the American politician and Josiah's friend. Ros wrote from Branksome Tower Hotel, Branksome Park, Bournemouth:

> *I will tell you all the events of the last few days, as I don't know what you know, & what you don't. ... On Friday Father got a wire asking him to go to a Fels Memorial in America (only English representative going) Saturday 9.15 train. ... Mother was told of plans. Burgess & I packed up the House, & came down here to Grandmother [Bowen] on Monday. Mother ramped but calmed. The Hyde Park meeting was grand, but Mother's presence & Lansbury's absence were oppressing.*

Top Left: *Josiah Wedgwood IV 1919*

Above: *Josiah IV with second wife Florence Willet*

Left: *Michael and Helen Pease 1922*

Below: *Richenda, Joanna, Sebastian Pease*

Photographs are courtesy of Sir Andrew Huxley

Mother had just received the terms to be signed: she thinks (I think) that I know nothing of them, & I don't know if she has or will sign. She did not mention the babies. The terms are:

1. *Babies to be with her during Cambridge term*
2. *Father to have free access to them*
3. *Father to be told if they get ill*
4. *Father to be told three days before they leave London, where they are going (if they go)*
5. *Father to be able to <u>take them away at will</u> without needing to give any reasons for so doing.*

He intends to keep strict watch, but feels he must do this for fear she goes off her head. Everyone thinks she ought to have the chance of righting herself, unless it should harm the babies. We hope she may not want them. I don't like it, but I know not if she will sign. The babies know nothing of London plans.

I know not if I shall go with them part of the time while you are in London, or if we shall both be in our flat, or with Mrs L. until Father returns. Meantime we are happy here. Much love Rosie

A further letter from Rosamund from the same address in Bournemouth to Helen around 6th March:

Few things give me greater pleasure than to visit with you from the 17th if I am not with Mother. I expect I shall not be, as she has said nought that leads me to suspect that I am worth the trouble of seeing once (or possibly twice) in a day. We know not yet whether she has signed ...

Ethel became ill in early spring and while the children went to Barlaston Lea, Rosamund went to be with her.

Jos wrote to Helen on 25th March:

... & I had a letter from your mother's solicitors telling me that the majesty of the Law is to be invoked. I contemplate with some amusement the prospect of being sent to gaol by an anarchist for contempt of Court! ...

Rosamund, at her mother's, heard from her father on 26th March, when he told her to make the most of life. He talks about her allowance and hopes she eats enough.

> *My little girl, I love you & want you ever so much, but I shall probably see you in a week at the Ark, & directly I see any signs of breakdown I shall exercise my parental control (law-given) & brutally drag you from the arms of your adoring mother.*
>
> *Dear, I can't help thinking that she must be nice to you a bit & a little affectionate to you still. <u>Draw it out as much as you can</u>, for it is her only chance ...*

Again on 28th March, Jos at Barlaston Lea wrote to Rosamund. He mentioned grandmother Emily's illness and continued:

> *I saw Crompton [solicitor] on Friday & he wants me to go back to your mother. He is going to see her & you, & if possible you had better have a quiet talk to him. If anybody is to be sacrificed I am obviously the person, but I am fairly confident she would not tolerate me for a week ... Camilla is very well & pleasant in all ways. Gloria & Betsy are also well & cuddlesome as ever. Gloria talks & dreams about her mother in a rather distressing way. I should rather like to send her up for a visit some time soon without Betsy, but it can wait until I see you.*
>
> *Of course if your mother is still in bed, you had better stay with her a bit longer. The boys do not come back till April 7th nor Camilla till the 8th. I will write tomorrow & tell you how the Ark is. Crompton described your mother, on Mrs Whitehead's report, to be at the end of her tether; so she may be very feeble & had perhaps better be induced to stop in London in bed after the 4th – if you can do anything.*

During this time Jos's mother Emily also became very ill and it was feared she was dying. Josiah's brothers, Ralph and Felix, returned home to be with her. Emily gradually became better and by May she was up and improved, but was now much slower, particularly in her speech.

Ethel instigated a law suit around this time. Yet despite all the bitterness, Jos told her she could visit the Ark any time she wished.

In early May, when Rosamund is back in town with her mother, Jos wrote to her from the Ark:

... & a nasty one from the lawyers proposing a timetable when I may see each child. I wrote back saying I would listen to no more proposals & that my last letter went as far as I was prepared to go. I think now she will surely go to law; indeed I believe she meant to all along & was only playing the agreement card. She wants & intends to get Josiah. I shall not stop the babies going now I have offered them, but I dare say she will refuse to have them save on her own terms ...

Jos decided to allow Ethel to have the babies pending a settlement. Meanwhile, Helen was busy living her life at Newnham. She loved it all – the only cloud was the rift within her family. She was due to give her first speech at the Cambridge University Fabian Society on 16th May 1914. Jos sent her a telegram '*Good luck today, demolish them.*' He wrote to Helen again on 23rd May 1914:

My dear little girl, you have written me a capital long letter, & I wanted it for I am very much down in the dumps without Ros & the babies. I have broken off all negotiations with the lawyers, declining to be bound or to bind any of the children. So that need not worry us any more. Mrs Fels tells me your mother is in the 7th heaven with the babies, & I expect she will lavish on them all the affection that she used to waste elsewhere. You & I, outcasts, will have to make up together as best we can.

I am so glad you did so well in the debate; your speech is excellent, & you are coming on capitally. ... I think this first real speech of yours ought to go into the [Daily] Herald ... It is better than any your mother ever did, & much better than I could have done.

Helen wrote to Rosamund after receiving that letter:

Dear little Rosie, How are you getting on? I hear the babies are with you, & that negotiations are broken off. What does that mean? How on earth do they propose to arrange about the babies' time? I hope it doesn't mean that every time they come to us Father will have to carry them off by force; or does M intend to grab them permanently. However I think we can stop that. But it seems very unsatisfactory. I fear that M is making a tremendous fuss of them. I hope that means they are happy, and well. How long will it last? She used to make a tremendous fuss of me when I came home.

Does she seem happy? I hope you aren't being killed between M, Burgess, & the babies. How does Burgess take it?

Father writes rather dismally. Poor dear, I wish he would not take things so hard, and I wish you or I were there to look after him. However I shall be there after the 17th I expect. Do, do try and come down for a bit in July. If it gets very hot I hope M will take the babies to the country. If you or they get run down, try & suggest it to her. She hasn't answered my two last letters, but perhaps that is accident. It is an awful business writing to her when one hasn't the vaguest idea what mood she's in or what she's doing.

Give my best love to the dear babies.

Father seems very pleased with my speech; – I am afraid he is too partial to be a good critic, so I warn you I shall have to depend largely on you. Don't I see myself asking Mother!

... I enclose a letter from Miss Willett. Alas she will not come back to us ...

Florence Willett had been the children's governess but had gone to Australia. When she visited England in May 1913 Helen spent an afternoon with her. The family all wanted her to return to them but she loved Australia and returned to Queensland after two months in England. But soon she was to return, and under the strangest circumstances.

When Helen was eighteen years of age her father had bestowed on her £3,000 with advice on how to invest it and she would sometimes ask his advice. Helen mentioned finances in her letter to him in June:

Dear Father,
You have been treating me very badly, you haven't written me a proper letter for a fortnight. Thank you very much for the documents, etc., does risk mean merely that my income may vary or that a large part of my capital may be lost altogether? I don't think Consuls appeal to me but there might be something in between.

I wrote to Ros the other day about my staying up for the Long [vacation], i.e. for four weeks from July 10. I shall have to stay up this Long or the next, and on the whole this is the best for me, but please say exactly what you would like, as it doesn't very much matter. ... I hope Ros is staying at the Ark for some time, does she seem well? I hope you are having a good rest and are getting on with that manuscript which I am to save when the house is burned! Did you see GRST's remarks re Land Tax in Thursday's "Herald". Isn't he a perfect idiot? I am so glad Frank Smith is having an argument with him, although he is not exactly sound, but it is a good thing to have it talked about in the Herald ...

I have been gay as usual, it is lovely to have so many friends, alas I had to refuse two delightful picnics on account of Mays. [May balls, confusingly held in June] *On Sunday I am going out again with Margaret to lunch with Gwen and Jakes. Last Sunday I 'teaed' at the Sewards, Botany Prof., which has been my ambition for a long time. They are extremely nice people, particularly the Professor and the eldest daughter, ...*

I have been to two extraordinary lectures, one on plant response and the other on Futurism. The latter was excellent and made one begin to see what they have got at the back of their minds. He gave an extraordinarily vivid description of the taking of a bridge at Adrianople as a specimen of futurist poetry.

I shall be with the Darwins till the 18th or 19th and then I thought of spending a few days with the Lambs in

London, when I make a few calls and see how things are
all going at the flat, but if I am to come up for the Long,
I suppose you would rather I came straight home.

Your loving daughter HBW

At the end of that summer Helen, then in London, wrote to Rosamund:

Dear Rosie,
Have you spoken to Mother yet? If not, be careful how
you put it. Do not be too strong, also say as little as
possible about Father needing you. If you are not quite
sure that you must go to the Ark I wouldn't go because
Father is very anxious that you shouldn't lose advantages
by cooping yourself up in the Ark and he is quite right.
Besides if he found afterwards that he had spoiled your
chances, etc., it would make him very unhappy. So if you
are sure you had best come, put it to M that it is because
you cannot stand fashionable, intellectual London life,
etc. and not that F needs you so much. He can quite well
get on without you I think, just seeing him as he does now.
I wouldn't quite break with M, but just say that you want
a nice long time at the Ark.
   I called on Moira Davis yesterday and saw [solicitors]
Crompton as well. He says we needn't be alarmed about
the document, that they won't try to order Charles, or
you or me about and that in the case of the others they
are very unlikely to attempt any sort of compulsion. They
were rather on M's side about the babies, etc. i.e. they felt
very strongly how awful it is for her to have the children
so against her; but I don't think they know M very well,
or what she is like. They still cherish the hope that M &
F will come together again and they say we should try
to bring it about. I can't see much hope of it, but I think
it is more to be wished for than I did before I saw how
lonesome Father was, so we must try and prevent them
riling each other.
   I wish Harry would clear out, they can't possibly
come together as long as he's around, but I am afraid the

Cromptons don't realise how complete the rift between them is at all points.

I am looking forward to seeing you on Tuesday. Give my love to the babies.

Your loving sister HBW

In her letter to Jos in July 1914, for the first time Helen mentions 'Mr Pease'. This is Michael Pease, whom she eventually married. Michael, himself a member of the Fabian Society, was the son of Edward Pease, co-founder of that society. Helen's daughter Joanna, speaking in the spring of 1994, said: '... so Mum went off to lunch with Mrs Stewart, and they were having these Morris dancers, and she looked across the room and saw my father and said God, that's the man I'm going to marry just like that!'[1]

Dear Father,
I think you are a horrid wretch not to have written to me for so long, especially when I wrote to you a long letter. How is the case going? Ros writes that she may be called ... . I hope you and she are comfortable in that hotel, and not worried about things.

I saw the Land Values article in the D.H. [Daily Herald] *but I didn't think so much of it, not because he didn't take quite our line, but because the article seemed to me muddled in its points and not as straightforward and logical as it might have been. I like your criticisms, I think you think those people better than yourself because you are so used to your own writing, etc. that they bore you. I am looking forward to the N.T. next week and especially to Chiza's remarks.*

I am having a very jolly time and going out a lot. It is rather maddening though because if Mr Pease had been in Cambridge I should have met him several times already, such is life. However, I get on very well with a lot of his friends, so I have hopes for next term. Last Sunday I went to see the Cornfords whom I like extremely, and I feel very bucked because they pressed me to come again this Sunday. As their house is charming it rather reminds me of the Ark and as he often goes there you may guess I am pleased.

Yesterday I helped Margaret Darwin take the little Hartleys and the little Stewarts up the river for a picnic. There were several delightful people besides children and we had a jolly time playing French and English charades, and a whole lot of games. The little Hartleys are charming and cousin Molly is a dear.

On Thursday we had a botany expedition, about 15 men and women to Epping Forest by motor bus. It was very jolly and what is more I really learned a little botany. I regret to say that during the two hours it took to get home we sang continuously at the tops of our voices, anything from "Clementine" or "Dixie" to "John Brown's Body".

Goodbye Your loving daughter

Helen Bowen Wedgwood

Do write and tell me how things are going.

On 25th July Helen at Newnham wrote to Rosamund:

... I expect you saw by my second letter to Father that Mr Pease is not in Cambs. It is a great blow ...

Will our case be finished on Wednesday? it would be rather horrid for you having to be called. Just you hammer in our children's point of view. ... Give my best love to them all ... I am perfectly sick of writing to Mother, as she only sends postcards back, and often not that, but I suppose I must go on ...

Your loving sister HBW

A settlement – never satisfactory for everyone – was reached about the children. Ethel had the two youngest children under conditions similar to those detailed by her husband in March of that year.

In August 1914 everything changed once again – on the 4th of that month war was declared.

Chapter 34

PACIFISM AND WAR

England was at war with Germany. From London Jos wrote to Helen (the babies and the boys were at the Ark):

> ... As soon as you get back to the Ark you must go into the food and fuel quarter & economise. I listened all last night & the night before to vast crowds who sang under my bedroom window all about 'The boys of the bulldog breed' ... I hear Germany is a vast sweeping nation, hating the war, & helpless in the hands of the machine ...

He wrote a further letter to Helen in August – he was then at the Ark. The letter was marked 'Strictly Private' and dealt mostly with the financial arrangements now necessary because of his separation from his wife and how these would affect his family affairs. He goes on to say:

> ... As for Charles, I fear you will be very angry, but I have decided to try to get him a commission in the Territorials. He must not loaf, he might as well earn money or at least keep himself, he will be proud of it ever after, he will probably be as safe as anyone else military or civil, the war may well end by general conscription in which case he would be caught anyway. I hope I shall get him in the same regt as uncle Felix.

Don't imagine this is a sad letter in any sense. Some of us have been longing for the revolution to help us off the people's backs; now that sort of thing has come & there is a certain pleasure in facing up to the new conditions.

Your loving fa'her Josiah C Wedgwood

From the House of Commons Josiah wrote to Helen in September:

My dear little girl, I think you had better come back to the Ark on Saturday after all, for I fancy I am going right to the front early next week, & we have much to talk over – & I must see you before I go.

I am expecting a commission as Lieut. Commander R.N., which the good offices of Churchill has obtained for me. I love you very much and hate leaving you.

Your loving father Josiah C Wedgwood

The news was a further blow to Helen and Rosamund, who were pacifists, and very unhappy that both their father and their brother were going on active service. Throughout 1916 and 1917 they were active in their support of people who felt the same way. Their father, himself now an active participant in the war, did not try to dissuade them, but was proud of their respective strengths of belief. He was a fervent believer in the liberty of choice for everyone. In his *Memoirs*, he said: '*I bled for my country, while my daughters sat in police courts holding the hands of conscientious objectors!*' He was being ironic but also philosophical about their differences.

Charles was only seventeen but was glad to leave Bedales school to join the Army, even as a private. Jos was now aged forty-two and also an MP, so he was not expected to go to war, but he enlisted at once. In September, the *Manchester Guardian* reported:

On the first and critical day, when Sir Edward Grey made his statement, not the least vehement and probably the most effective speech from below the gangway was made by Mr Wedgwood. Members of Parliament who have still ringing in their ears Mr Wedgwood's passionate appeal for the working classes that were going to be damaged by the war, will be interested to learn that the speaker who fearlessly attacked the Government then has applied for and been appointed to a commission in the R.N.V.R. Mr Wedgwood, M.P., who used to wear a moustache, is now clean-shaven Lt.-Commander Wedgwood, R.N. If he is as successful in the field as he is in the House of Commons, he ought to have a fine career on active service.

Before he left he explained in the pages of the *Staffordshire Evening Sentinel* his reasons for joining the Royal Navy:

In a few days, I shall be leaving for active service in France. This is only what many thousands of volunteers from North Staffordshire have done already, or soon will be doing, but, as I have not had an opportunity of speaking here since the war started, I want to use your columns to tell my friends and constituents what it is that compels me to go. Liberals, like myself, love liberty. It is a passion: I cannot explain it. 'You cannot argue with the choice of a soul.' My political work has all been directed to the securing of economic liberty for the worker. I must now leave that struggle to others and to my children. There is other more elementary and more painful work to be done for liberty. It has to be done. All who think like me ought to take part.

As proof of his continuing love for his wife, Jos wrote to her in late September from Sheerness:

My dear one, ... I wish you were here to tell it all to, & to share the fun. The worst of being alone is that everything of this sort is flat when bottled up inside oneself. Do you remember Willie Campbell's stories? and Major Cropper's? I wish I could tell all the similar stories I have heard tonight.

I have to write to you to pretend that you know & are still interested. All they found of this gun's crew of the

"Laertis" was the top half of the Captain's body & a pair of boots, after the shell exploded. That is all that is left of me and you, so far as common interests & experiences go. But I love you, dear, and if I prayed for anybody it would be for you, that you might be contented & happy. ... Goodnight my dear. Kiss the babies for me.

Your loving husband Josiah C Wedgwood

In a letter from Helen in October with news of his family she added:

Grandmother is fairly well & going about a bit more. We read her your letters, & she usually likes us to read her other letters as well ...

I enclose a particularly beautiful cutting concerning you. Please be sure to return it, as I want to put it in the [scrap]book.

... I shall think of you specially hard about 11 every night. Dearest do come back safe.

I am glad you wrote to Mother nicely before going; (even though she did write to me kindly to tell me that you had gone to Dunkirk & sounded very cheerful, & that you wd no doubt gain honour & distinction)

The babies are coming down next Wed. with Miss Goss. She will be very useful, as we shall explain our point of view so that she will fit in with us, whilst Mother will think that she is bossing the show through Miss Goss.

Goodbye darling

Your loving daughter Helen Bowen Wedgwood

It is difficult to discover exactly what Ethel Wedgwood was doing at that time, but she was also a pacifist and would have helped in war work when possible. She was in Ostend in the autumn, as will be seen from her husband's letters.

In October Josiah wrote to Rosamund from the National Liberal Club, Whitehall:

Dearest Ros, Your mother is back, as Ostend is evacuated & the wounded brought to England. But it is possible she may go out again to Dunkirk or Havre.

I saw Siah [Josiah V] off & had a good talk with Runciman with whom I am to stop next week ...

P.S. I shall not let the babies go to her in November for more than a week. She is too busy, & never asked after them, or any of you.

And on the 19th October he wrote to Helen:

... I have seen your mother several times since her return from Ostend; but it is like visiting a grave & leaves me feeling that I am paying a society call on someone I never met before or want to meet again. She has been in bed with a cold, & visibly screws herself up to submitting to a kiss at parting. No good! I am sorry for her, & for you all ...

About this time Josiah brought a family of Belgian refugees to the Ark, while he returned to Belgium, leaving his young family and the two resident maids to look after them. When Helen returned to Cambridge in October, Rosamund was left in charge.

From Newnham in January 1915, Helen wrote to her father and told him how all the blinds were down and everywhere was dark:

... Also we had each been given a candle in case the electric light is turned off, so even if the Zeppelin doesn't get us we shall run a good chance of being burnt down just the same. (Luckily most people have already used their candles to light their fires with).

Some people think Girton is safe as Count Zeppelin's great-niece is there, but they aren't taking any chances & are darker than we.

... Last Sunday I supped at the Grange. [Newnham Grange] Uncle Felix, Capt Longstaff ... were there. I hope Mother hasn't been worrying you again. I wrote to Camilla to tell her not to be terrorised ...

(Camilla would eventually follow her older sister to Newnham in 1920, and later become a noted anthropologist at Sydney University, Australia.)

While Jos was stationed in Holkham, Norfolk, Helen visited him in February. Afterwards he wrote to her:

> *My beloved Helen, ... Then too, I wanted to tell you how exceedingly proud I am of you – your person, your dresses, your brains & even your character. You will spot at once that parents' affection is really pride in what they think they have produced! ... I love you parentally & mentally,*

> *Your father Josiah C Wedgwood*

In March of that year Helen wrote to her father and was clearly worried in case her mother would be their guardian. '*Could you make* [Uncle] *Frank our guardian in case of anything happening to you & Uncle Ralph's being away, because we might need someone,*' she added in a postscript.

Helen wrote again from the Ark later in April:

> *The babies look well. It does not seem likely that M will take Burgess* [nanny] *back (though B wrote & apologised, etc.) but Miss Goss will be sleeping at the flat, & M cannot get rid of her, legally at least (she must have nurse* or *governess) & she will not dare to stir without the lawyers having completely tied herself up. The Whiteheads will also keep an eye on them.*
>
> *The children say they do not mind London for itself, as long as M isn't nasty to Burgess, & they know when they will come down, & seem quite resigned to going up, you need not worry ...*

Meanwhile during April Jos was preparing to go to war. His son Charles now joined him as a sub-lieutenant and they went on the wreck ship *River Clyde*, bound for the Gallipoli peninsular. Before leaving Jos wrote to his mother, Emily:

Top: *Helen and Michael's home in Girton* (courtesy of Mr Stewart Huxley)

Above Left: *Hon. Julia Wedgwood and sister Hon. Gloria in Donarch (1922)* (author's collection)

Above: Hon. Julia Wedgwood (Italy)

Left: *Hon. Helen Bowen Pease, Hon. Julia Wedgwood, Cambridge, 1974* (courtesy of Sir Andrew Huxley)

... Presently we are going to sea preparatory to landing on the end of Gallipoli. The Captain is going to run this ship ashore so that troops can disembark, dry-shod, and our guns, mounted on this ship, will cover the landing. It is just exactly the job I should have liked to get ... the captain calls this ship the Wooden Horse of Troy, for it looks like a collier gone wrong, and from it will spring men in thousands armed to the teeth ...

There is always of course the chance that I may be killed. If I am, I should like you to know that I think you the best mother in the world, and that I am infinitely grateful to you for all the unselfish loving kindness that you have lavished on me and mine. I have had, on the whole, a very happy life, and I owe it all to you. My children will carry on our good name and traditions. You and Frank and others will look after them, and I have no fear of their coming to harm. Josiah, I hope, will go into Parliament, and with all the good friends he will have, he will become Prime Minister.

I am at perfect peace with God and man.

A copy of the graphic account of the ship's landing and ensuing battle which he had sent to Sir Winston Churchill he later included in his memoirs.

In May on the field of battle Jos was shot and wounded high in the left groin and was invalided home. He wrote to his children from the SS *Southlands* on 8th May telling them about his injury and that he would now probably be sent home, and hoped to be at the Ark as soon as possible.

At the end of that summer 1915, after discussion with Helen and Rosamund, Jos agreed that Rosamund should go up to Cambridge to attend Moral Science lectures. She went to Peile Hall in Newnham in October.

... The babies have got slight colds but I think we have done rather well to keep them off colds for so long (nearly 3 months) ... . Burgess is unwilling to go back to Mother, quite naturally, so I hope the lawyers will manage to fix up something satisfactorily ...

Jos received his DSO from the King that year; when Helen wrote to congratulate him in November she addressed him as 'Respected Sir'. Jos worked for a while at the War Office but there was not enough action there for him so he was added to the staff of Sir H L Smith-Dorrien, going out to fight the Germans in East Africa. They left England in December 1915.

Meanwhile in November of that year the babies Julia and Gloria went to stay with their relatives the Darwins (George Darwin's widow Maud) at Newnham Grange in Cambridge, together with their nurse. Julia was eight and Gloria six. While in Cambridge they attended school. They stayed with the Darwins until the following summer, going back to the Ark for the holidays. Helen and Rosamund were very near them at Newnham and could see them whenever they liked. Helen wrote to her father on her return to Newnham after the Christmas holidays in 1916:

> *Here we are at Newnham again; the babies arrive tomorrow – no sign from Mother but she does not know they are coming. We had a very jolly Xmas holidays ... The babies are very well & looking forward to Cambridge.*
>
> *I have seen a lot of governesses but did not like any well enough; and as Cousin Maud did not want to have one about while the children were at the Grange, we are not bothering much. I can't find out from Mr Withers whether M will take them with a governess, but am writing to Mr Redford about it, as she will be less riled if it is done through the lawyers than if R & I wrote. She had arranged for Siah to be with her for a week but wrote finally to say she was too busy!! So I do believe she will leave us in peace ...*
>
> *You will be rejoicing over the conscription bill. R & I are preparing to pass buns through the bars to the 'objectors'. The Trade unions are making a fuss, but it is probably all gas & they will never do anything. They never do. You exploiters & "junkers" can usually count on a walkover ...*

Easter 1916 was spent at the Ark. Jos wrote to Helen in April and advised her to get a job when she finished her exams. In May he wrote that he was coming home and would go straight to the Ark.

On 29th May from Newnham Helen wrote a long letter to her father. It is evident that she felt deeply about what was happening during this war and felt helpless and in sympathy with all those men who suddenly had no choice about their future and she was strongly opposed to conscription. At college she had finished her tripos and hoped to get a 'second'.

Dear Daddy,

I have no intention of remaining idle after I go down. On the contrary I shall get something to do immediately – Women's Trade Unions or Agriculture, or possibly peace work which you won't like so well, will you. Well it is pretty certain it will be Trade Unions.

It is all very well for you to be cheerful about getting rid of tyranny afterwards, but I assure you they are rivetting the chains pretty hard. All the best people are getting killed (or shot, e.g. Conelly, Damn them). The new act gives the Tribunals power to exempt a <u>man if he will work under a specified employer</u>. It is illegal to <u>have in your possession</u> any thing which is illegal to publish – oh there's no end to it. And no-one except the pacifists will lift a finger to prevent any injustice however flagrant. We're much worse off than Germany before the war. Conscription is simply leading to a system of barefaced slavery – gangs of men to work & the rest forced to fight.

We always said you could only conquer militarism by worse militarism.

And now that unfortunate Ireland with Lloyd George! as peace maker!!

God's curse on our ancestors who have driven half our generation to hell & death & the other half to slavery & despair. And three times cursed be the <u>old</u> who sit here telling us young ones 'our duty' & occasionally deigning to praise the nobleness of those who are defending their precious skins & property.

It would have made you sick to see the tribunals – seven aged fat old men explaining to nervous young ones the sacred duty of defending them.

The conscientious objectors & the Irish are the only people with a spark of spirit left & by Heaven, they are holding out splendidly! One thing is that people say, now we are so completely enslaved the principal reasons for the prolongation of the war will be at an end, & Northcliffe will stop it!

Don't think it's only pacifists who talk like this – you should hear the remarks of the soldiers in hospital & elsewhere – but they are all perfect sheep.

Our friends, as I say are in process of being arrested – well it is the fortune of war – it is a relief however to us outside that those from here are not likely to be treated as badly as they have been in some barracks – kicked & beaten half to death. Seventeen are in France. They think they will be shot. We hope not but fear. Dear Tennant, when questioned, 'bears things in mind', & 'I will make enquiries', & it is almost impossible to get at the truth.

You see we are bitter. Well, so would you be if you were here. It is hard to see the best people of both sides (pacifists & soldiers) being slaughtered off, & no good coming, but things only getting worse ...

The babies are flourishing as usual. Charles is still waiting for his commission ... & enjoying himself I think, though I have had precious little time to see him, on account of cramming for exams. Ros is very well, though anxious about our friends. She goes swimming in the Cam every morning before breakfast, & frequently on the river in the afternoons. She is more worried about the Tripos people than they are themselves, and a pained expression comes into her eyes whenever she catches sight of one.

We are getting some Newnhamites for the summer holidays; but I shall start work at the end or middle of July I expect, unless you are at the Ark.

No, I won't get into trouble while you are away, but it's not so jolly easy to keep out of it. What a scandal – 'Noted M.P.'s daughter arrested. D.S.O. Veteran's pro-German daughter' etc.

Goodnight dear, I really am not as harum scarum as I sound, in fact I am cultivating a highly respectable demeanour.

By the way it is not true to say I haven't written for six weeks. I write at least once a fortnight. Ros writes nearly every other day, so of course you get more. Yours come most erratically 'the last first' and so on. Much love. Your loving daughter Helen Bowen Wedgwood P.S. Will the censor let this through?

In July 1916 Josiah's first cousin Cecil Wedgwood, head of the family, head of the firm and first Mayor of Stoke-on-Trent was killed at the Battle of the Somme. He was a brave soldier, had been awarded the DSO and showed great courage in battle. Jos's brother Frank succeeded him as chairman of the firm.

In January 1916 the Conscription Bill was passed and the No Conscription Fellowship (NCF) was founded. During that spring term Helen became involved with the NCF. She was still secretary of the Fabian Society, where the majority of members were pacifists. Although passionately involved in the NCF cause, she was determined not to neglect her studies at this stage, after all the work she had already put into her education, and with her exams looming. On 16th June she wrote to her father. Her letters have taken on a more serious tone now and she is preoccupied with the war situation:

Hurrah! I have a second, just what I intended to get when I went up to Newnham. A first would have meant too hard work, & neglecting more important forms of education, and a third is for "the common herd" so I am very well satisfied.

So ends the most marvellous three years of my life, and the really marvellous part has been the last six months. It is wonderful the friends these strenuous times have made. Our Cambridge friends are mostly not in prison yet, but many others we know are. Some of the accounts from the military prisons are terrible. It is simply torture they use to force them into the army. If chaining you to walls with your arms above your head & your toes just touching the ground, or hitting you with sticks for ever so long

& you in your shirt can't be torture, I don't know what is. It is ghastly. A Quaker visited about 26 in solitary confinement in Chelmsford, & they said it would have been much kinder to shoot them at once. It's like Russia. And to crown it all it is illegal to collect information much less publish anything about the working of the Act!

Of course it isn't so bad everywhere, but we know for certain of four places where such things are done, & heaven knows what it is like in places from which we can hear nothing. I tell you though, it is demoralising the army all right. We get a lot of information via the soldiers. Only here & there has anyone given in. Our boys at Cambridge face it calm & smiling. If only to stand beside such men I'm glad I'm a 'pacifist'. Come home soon & try & save us from this hell. The ordinary person simply won't believe us, though we have overwhelming proof; & our people are not ones to whine about nothing.

And what is worse very few people will take up the most flagrant case of injustice (even if nothing to do with a C.O.) They only say "We must win the War", & pass by on the other side. Damn the silly fools. They do nothing for the war except talk about it, & they won't work for liberty or justice at home.

Charles & I are just on our way to London (that is why my writing is so bad), he to Ralph's, I to the Lambs. He is getting into a cadet corps tomorrow or the next day, as he is so bored waiting for the O.T.C. [Officer Training Corps] *It is too stupid to keep him hanging about like this, & very bad for him. Uncle R has done his best.*

Rosie & the babies went to Mother yesterday, quite cheerfully, though sorry to leave Cambridge. We shall all be at the Ark by July 1st.

It is sad to be leaving Cambridge, and sadder still when one doesn't know when, if ever, we will see our friends again, or what they may have to go through.

Still the prospect of work is cheering. I am learning typing & shorthand hard. I am told that my touch is very good & I shall soon be quite professional at the former. Shorthand I fear will take some time.

I am feeling less tired than I did, & a fortnight at the Ark will set me up completely. Then you may look out for trouble, but I won't do anything definite till you come home.

Dear, dear Daddy, I do love you so and you make the most perfect father. If you hadn't been what you are we should have had 'a row in the Ark' long ago, like so many other silly families just now. Luckily we shall always more or less agree in being "agin the Government" which is a very sound basis for mutual esteem.

When R & I are feeling rather tired of things in general we go for a walk & contemplate your virtues & how much we love you, with excellent results.

Sam Walker writes to me fairly often. He also expresses a most flattering belief in my future as a rebel!

I wonder if these letters will reach you. We also wonder why you are coming back from E. Africa.

Goodbye dearest, Your loving daughter Helen Bowen Wedgwood

Chapter 35

THE FIGHT GOES ON …

With the exams now out of the way, Helen remained a while in Cambridge to help in the NCF movement. For two weeks in June 1916 she did some NCF work with Catherine Marshall in London. Catherine's parents had a house near Helen's grandmother in the Lake district and they were all friends. Helen had great admiration for Catherine. Helen and Rosamund attended tribunals dealing with conscientious objectors in Cambridge also, but only as spectators. Later in her life, when the Imperial War Museum interviewed her in 1976 about those days, when asked about these tribunals Helen said:

> *Well, the atmosphere in the court in which I ultimately was a magistrate,* [Cambridge] *the old Shire Hall in Cambridge which is now abolished, I don't remember much. There was a good crowd of us there. We always went to support them. And I feel now rather sorry for the tribunals because it was an impossible position, the chairman of the bench was a very worthy market gardener here* [Cambridge], *for instance. And to have a long argument between the officer of the Crown and a very vocal CO on what was the proper interpretation of the New Testament —- I didn't feel sorry for them then. I thought "Oh, stupid old men"[1], and wrote to father about it and said they were stupid old men. And they were, they were quite illogical you see. ——— And*

whereas they would give exemption or non-combatant service, we never could discover on what principle they gave complete exemption to some and non-combatant service to others.

Helen returned home to the Ark in July and she and Rosamund immediately got in touch with the NCF in Stoke, where members were very different to those at Cambridge – working class as opposed to academics. As far as Helen's immediate fellow-sympathisers were concerned most contacts with the NCF were done on a one-to-one basis – word of mouth. At Stoke Helen was made shadow secretary of the Branch. The month was spent mostly in visiting barracks where COs were held and keeping records of relevant names and happenings. Where necessary members of the NCF would endeavour to help the objectors in prison and support their families either with funds or visits to the imprisoned. At no time would Helen act against the law – if there was a law she thought unfair she would argue against it, but not break it.

After the summer holidays were over at the Ark in September 1916, Jos took a flat in Beaufort Street, London and went back to work in Parliament and at the War Office. In December of that year he went to Washington on military business, returning after a month. The children, big and small, were sometimes in London with him; the babies were sometimes with the Darwins, sometimes with their mother and sometimes at the flat in Beaufort Street.

Josiah V left Bedales in 1916 and became an Officer Cadet in the Royal Field Artillery.

Helen went to work at the Women's Trade Union. She would soon have to decide about her future – a politician or a market gardener? She worked for Mary Macarthur and Margaret Bondfield, members of the National Federation of Women Workers, and helped in the East End to get better conditions for women in factories and shorter working hours, plus more hygienic canteen facilities, protective clothing, and similar benefits. She did this work for three months and learned much about factory politics and the attitude of factory-working women. Helen was also active in the NCF anti-war movement and still visited imprisoned conscientious objectors and wrote reports.

After Christmas 1916 at the Ark, Helen decided she wanted to change what she was doing – not that she disagreed with any part of it, but there were lots of other people equally qualified and it had always been her desire to do science or something 'on the land'; after all, she had gained a second in Natural Science at Cambridge! In January 1917 she went to work for a geneticist Mr Bateson at Merton. She worked for him for three months, meanwhile continuing to go up to London, either for family reasons or to attend meetings.

On 14th March of that year Helen's uncle Felix was killed in action. He was buried in the British cemetery of Rossignol Wood, not far from the field of action. Felix was born in 1877, the youngest son of Emily and Clement Wedgwood, and Josiah IV's brother. Felix became a civil engineer, but as a young man he loved to write poetry and had literary aspirations. In 1910 he published a novel *The Shadow of a Titan* (mainly about South America) and his family was proud of this achievement. However, his greatest love was mountain climbing; he climbed in the Alps and also in Canada. In Canada he met his future wife, Miss Katherine Longstaff, sister of the well known Himalayan explorer Dr T G Longstaff.

In the spring of 1917 'The 1917 Club' (or 'The Soviet Club'), was founded. This was a group of free-thinking idealistic people who had much to say about the present state of the world. They met in a building in Gerrard Street, London, and included pacifists, revolutionaries, conscientious objectors, etc. Some members wore a Russian cross to signify their beliefs.

The Russian Revolution had begun. Helen, Rosamund and their father attended the Russian meeting in the Albert Hall on 31st March. Everyone was exhilarated at this new happening, the beginning of a new Russia and the end of despotism. The conscientious objectors were delighted, too, because it meant the beginning of the end of the war. But this was not to be. Since the Tsar's abdication eight months earlier, the Provisional Government had ruled Russia. In 1917 the communists, led by Vladimir Ilich Lenin, seized power, and promised freedom and equality for the people. The civilian population were still suffering from the aftermath of Russia's involvement in the First World War, when they had fought with the French against Germany.

The ideals of the revolution inspired the people but there was not much fight left in them. The Russian economy was at rock bottom. There followed three more years of civil war – the Bolsheviks (the Reds) and the anti-revolutionaries (the Whites). The Whites wanted to restore the monarchy. At the end of the civil war, in 1921, the victorious Lenin introduced the New Economic Policy.

While Lenin was busy seizing power, Helen made a less revolutionary decision – to work on the land. She had by now decided she could never be a scientist as she didn't have the mind for research, and she saw an advertisement in a Cambridge paper for 'potato pickers'. Helen went to see her Uncle Felix's widow, Kate, in Birmingham and dug potatoes in her garden. While there she wrote to her father on 17th June, mostly about her pacifist work and that she would be finishing this particular job on 28th June and would look for something else, but she was going off market gardening as being too strenuous. She continued:

> *I know I want to stick to the land, & also to get used to being with working people – so I shall rather seek my fortune & go anywhere fate directs, & see what happens. It will be quite amusing as well as instructive.*
>
> *On the 28th I go for the weekend to Nancy Barlow before her marriage & I* think *on the 2nd I will come to the Ark for three days for my birthday, as it is on the way back to Birmingham.*
>
> *... I get on as well as I can with Aunt Kate, but I don't think she really likes me – we just haven't much in common. I don't argue with her, & I do my best ...*

Later on 12th July when writing to her father she mentioned 'Mike Pease'. Michael Pease, born in 1890 at Aberfeldy in Scotland, was up at Cambridge while Helen was studying there. He studied genetics. He was secretary of the Cambridge University Fabian Society, as was his father, Edward Pease, before him.

During July Helen worked in market gardening at Evesham and spent August at the Ark. For her birthday her father gave her a 'lovely watch'. The following month she went to Wales and did forestry work for the remainder of the year in different parts of the principality. She enjoyed the work, which involved assessing the growth of trees in different locations. The work was hard and the living accommodation very basic but despite that Helen enjoyed her time in the forests.

Although the work was rough and often very uncomfortable, Helen was happy with herself. A letter to her father on 3rd December 1917 showed a certain contentment with her lot and an appreciation of her surroundings. Helen could express herself very well and her letters demonstrate her personality. Despite her serious outlook on life she also had a great sense of humour. In this letter from the middle of a forest, close to nature and far from the reality of war, she found time to see and appreciate the beauty surrounding her. She finished by letting her father know she was not missing out on what was happening in his world and ended with a joke.

She wrote from the Miner's Arms, Pont-rhyd-y-Groes, Ystrad Meurig, Cardiganshire:

Dear Father,
You can see by my address in what outlandish parts we find ourselves. This morning we left Aberystwyth at 7 a.m., by moonlight, – train to Strata Florida as it gradually grew light in company with two timber men from Lincolnshire who had a verg poor opinion of Welsh characters & arrived at the little station just as a wonderful green & gold dawn came up. The hills were barely covered with snow & the air like wine. Then five miles across a high plateau with little rushing streams, the sun rose just as we reached the top. It was just like what one imagines the Tyrol; hills covered with larch or spruce, & deep valleys below one with little stone houses, & every now & then little crags of bare rock. The illusion was completed by the men by the roadside who shouted 'Borodachi' (Welsh for "good Morning"). Then a long run down through Yspathy Ystwyth, the road running along the edge of the hill with the Ystwyth below. Yspathy consists principally of a post office, a church & two enormous & very ugly chapels. Now we are settled in very comfortable quarters at the Miner's Arms, quite a big inn & with nice rooms & cooking, thanks to the fact that this is a tourist place in the summer.

The old Welsh women follow us to our plots to pick up firewood & you meet them in the evening coming home with huge bundles of branches on their backs. That & the larch woods in the snow today made one feel as if one came out of a picture in Grimm's Fairy stories.

What a splendid speech Lord Hugh Cecil made on the COs' disenfranchisement. I can't understand, though why they rejected it before, & pass it now so soon afterwards. Oh yes, & I see Punch implies that you must have written your preface to Young India without having properly read it!!!

How is your new job? I hope you are making someone uncomfortable for the good of your country. Our latest landlady thinks our parents must be very much worried about us in this weather, – so I hope whenever you perceive the rain or snow, you think of your poor little daughter lying on the wet ground trying to count rings on larch butts – an awful job & are properly alarmed lest my delicate health should be undermined.

Much love & goodnight. Helen

During that year, whenever possible she attended Quaker meetings as it helped to ease her loneliness. She also corresponded with Michael Pease, who was then a civilian prisoner in Germany. Helen remained with the forestry work until April 1918, when she returned to the Potteries. She wanted to be near the Ark in case she was needed. Also she had been in touch with her cousin Phoebe, the oldest daughter of Lucie and Cecil Wedgwood. Phoebe was described as a genuine socialist – she lived as frugally as possible and gave what she could to the poor. Her donations did not include any capital, because she reckoned that was family trust to be passed on. She never married, although it was thought she had loved someone who had been killed in the war.

Phoebe had been close friends with Jos's children and adopted all their socialist ideas. Cecil, of course, was not a socialist and he and Jos never saw eye to eye. Cecil and Lucie lived at the Woodhouse near Cheadle. There was a political divide between the two families. Cecil resented the free-thinking influence of Jos's family on Phoebe – he even sent her off to boarding school to get her away from the situation. It didn't work.

Cecil did not have long to worry about Jos's family's influence on Phoebe, however. For on that never to be forgotten day, 1st July 1916 in the battle of the Somme, 58,000 British soldiers became casualties: of these, one third were killed, among them Cecil. Head of the family firm in the Potteries, Cecil had been awarded the DSO during the Southern African war. Although given the choice of a staff appointment, he remained with the regiment he had raised, the 8th North Stafford Regiment – known as 'The Potters'.

After Cecil's death, Jos's brother Frank became chairman of the firm. Although Frank was in charge, he also worked for the War Office. Cecil's wife, Lucie, was invited to join the Wedgwood board. Her daughter Audrey asked the general manager if she could help in the factory, which she did, and eventually she was made company secretary. In discussion with Audrey's daughter Ann Makeig-Jones in 1999, she said that the Wedgwood factory had the first canteen in the Potteries before it became a legal requirement.

In 1917 Phoebe was in Hanley, where she planned to do her Women's Trade Union work. She suggested that she and Helen set up house together and this they did at 16 Wood Terrace, Hanley. They were determined to live on very little money (although both were independent financially) and live as much as possible like their working-class neighbours. Helen was still officially Liberal, Phoebe was Labour – ironic given that Cecil had been chairman of the local Conservative Party.

In an interview in later years, Helen reckoned she and Phoebe must have looked an odd pair. '[Phoebe] was very beautiful, tall, big and hair that you wouldn't believe wasn't dyed. It was bright gold, crinkly like Greek goddesses ... one of those rose leaf complexions you only get in Ireland. And I was very dark and sallow and not nearly so good-looking ... her father looked like a Viking ...'.[2]

Helen felt her work in Hanley was worthwhile, as she was doing the kind of work she loved, and could keep her eye on her father's nearby constituency. She happily went to visit his Liberal supporters and she was closer to her beloved Ark. She was busy with the Women's Co-Op Guild in Hanley, the NCF – of which she was local secretary after the secretary George Horwill was arrested – and the Hanley Independent Labour Party. It was during this period of her life she made her first attempt at public speaking, mainly to attract a crowd to listen to the main speaker. The subject then was the Russian situation.

Meanwhile Phoebe carried on with her Union work. Her mother Lucie strongly disapproved of her activities and she was also worried that perhaps Phoebe wasn't looking after herself properly. The girls knew that Lucie could be difficult if she thought her daughter was not eating properly. Doing the 'domestics' was Helen's responsibility. Helen thought this funny because she wasn't much good at cooking and had to really concentrate in order to dish up suitable food – they were both vegetarians. They did go home some weekends to stock up on some decent food and also to save on their housekeeping.

In November 1917, the governess, Florence Ethel Willett was mentioned in Jos's letters to Helen. Florence had tutored Helen and Rosamund in the early 1900s. Julia, then a baby, could not pronounce 'Florence' and called her 'Fingwan' a pet name which the family used for the rest of her life. Florence, when she left the family, went to Australia where she lectured and taught. In May 1913 she came back to England for two months. Helen met her for an afternoon as she disembarked and tried to get her to stay and come back to them. Helen wrote to Rosamund about their meeting:

> *She was completely in love with Queensland and has been trying to persuade everyone, me included, to go out there. I firmly declined, I intend to see England through the Revolution. She is nearly the same as ever, but has had a very sad episode in Australia, which has made her older and also has absorbed her attentions so that she is no longer aware of external events as she used to be. She says she hasn't been really living for some time. I don't know when I shall get a chance of seeing her again. She is looking very well and brown, though thin ...*

Florence had a lot in common with both Jos and the two oldest girls – she was a pacifist and during her years abroad they all corresponded with her. Jos found in her a kindred spirit, and they were true friends. Towards the end of the war, Jos invited Florence to return to England from Australia and letters passed between them. Her replies were favourable. Jos told Helen that he had had 'gorgeous letters' from Florence. He wrote:

> *... I am nervous about F.E.W. [Florence] too, ... but we are both 'on appro' & shall not live together. Really I am rather fed up by 'emotions', & want quiet & peace, glad*

she is deaf. Of course I am like Lloyd George ...

In January 1918 Jos went to Russia via the United States and en route in Washington he was reunited briefly with Florence Willett after a separation of seven years. He took her to see his old friend Mrs Fels while he went on his way. His reunion with Florence was approved by his family.

In November 1918 the war was over and the following month there was a General Election. Josiah Wedgwood parted company with the Liberals and stood for re-election for the seat of Newcastle-under-Lyme as an Independent Radical. He was returned unopposed.

Chapter 36

THE END OF A MARRIAGE

At the beginning of 1919, Ethel Bowen Wedgwood was granted her decree nisi on grounds of desertion and adultery, both entirely fictitious. By the middle of 1918, with no possibility of a reconciliation, and custody of the children officially settled, Jos, on his return from Russia decided to let Ethel divorce him. Legal proceedings went ahead and the news released in the papers was that Josiah had deserted his wife and children, which was, of course, untrue. Many people wrote to or about Jos, criticising his alleged behaviour.

At the beginning of the 20th century, divorce was still not wholly accepted. Although jurisdiction had moved from the Church to the courts, the Church still had the power to show – and voice – its displeasure, which it did with Ethel and Josiah Wedgwood. They were prominent in society, both politically and socially, and the breakdown of their marriage was front-page news. Josiah remained silent until the decree was absolute in June 1919 and only then did he speak out in his own defence. He wrote an open letter to the editor of the local paper, the *Staffordshire Evening Sentinel*:

> *Sir,*
> *When I was divorced, the Rector of Newcastle, with great charity, declined to join in the clerical outcry against me. I made up my mind then, that, in justice to him and to those like him, I must, when the time came, write this letter, however unpleasant it is to publish my private affairs for the whole of North Staffordshire.*

My married life was a very happy one, until in 1913 my wife ceased to love me. She is one of those who believe that to live with a man you do not love is prostitution, and we separated. For many years I kept hoping that she would change, for after 20 years the break always seems inconceivable. I offered to start again in a new country, where no one would know us. It was all useless, and when I came back from Africa in 1916, and failed again, I at last realised that plans had to be made to reconstruct my life and home.

I consulted a colleague, a leading K.C. in the House. He told me that there were only two ways for me to get free and re-establish a home. I could acquire a Scottish domicile, and then divorce my wife for desertion, or I could let myself be divorced by her under English law. It takes (I think) three years to acquire the rights and privileges of a Scotsman, and it would have meant uprooting myself from Staffordshire, so I finally chose the second alternative.

The Law, which the Church will not allow us politicians to change, insists that a wife shall only be able to divorce her husband if he has been found guilty of desertion and adultery. More merciful than the Church, the Law allows "desertion" to be assumed if a Writ for the Restitution of Conjugal Rights is obtained and not complied with. So "letters" were exchanged, and I was duly found guilty of desertion. All the world read in the papers that I had "deserted" a wife and seven children after 20 years of married life.

Such a thing, if true, strikes me as being more blackguardly than adultery. There was no protest from Mr Sinker [vicar of St. George's, Newcastle]; *but I am not likely to forget that day in the House of Commons. I spoke six times that day – on the Education Bill – to a perfectly silent House, feeling that every man was saying: "That is the man who has deserted his wife and seven children."*

The next stage was to get myself proved guilty of adultery. I chose the simplest way – took a suite of rooms at the Charing Cross Hotel, and took a lady there who was not my wife. As a matter of fact, there was no adultery there. It is not exactly a festive occasion when you are carefully providing evidence to end a happy married life. I cannot imagine what sensible people should expect me to be doing with a sitting-room at a London hotel, except to sleep in, or why anyone who has a comfortable flat in London should go to the Charing Cross Hotel at all. But people who knew my children were at Moddershall with me, and saw that the "desertion" conviction must be formal, immediately jumped to the conclusion that the Member for Newcastle was a thorough bad lot, and smacked their lips over "guilty of adultery."

I think Mr Sinker might have been more reticent in the matter, as, had I committed this frightful sin, it would only have been to satisfy the insistence of his Church. And even this avenue to freedom is barred to all but the rich; it has cost me several hundred pounds. Our divorce laws constitute the grossest case of "one law for the rich and another for the poor"; for which again Mr Sinker and his kind are responsible.

Throughout, I have done what I conceived to be the most honourable thing in the most honourable way, and I have had good friends to back me up. But I ask you to observe what happens to a public man who tries to act honourably. Out of 900 similar cases last year, mine was the only one reported. Three times my portrait was in the picture papers; three times I was deluged in anonymous abuse; three times an honourable name was dragged in the mud, and foremost in the hunt is a minister of the Church of England. I thank the Sentinel for taking another line, and for trying to find explanations for what seemed inexplicable.

Whatever my associations may be in the future with those who have honoured me with their confidence for 14 years, I know that at least they regard me as a man of courage. Under the circumstances, they would not have expected me to do other than I have done. And I have my reward, for before these lines are read, I shall have exercised my right to remarriage, and in that I believe that I shall have the good wishes of all that is best in the county of my birth.

Josiah C. Wedgwood

House of Commons

June 24th, 1919[1]

All the leading newspapers of that time reported the divorce, together with Josiah's letter. *The Daily News* on Tuesday 1st July 1919 wrote in more depth about the question of the legality of 'arranged' misconduct in a divorce case:

Apparently Colonel Wedgwood's plan was legal, in the strict sense of the word, and no action can therefore be taken against him in the courts by the Public Prosecution or King's Proctor. Such was the view taken by an eminent authority consulted by "The Daily News" yesterday. ... his present statement is not a sworn statement and does not appear to affect the legal position in any way.

At the offices of the Divorce Law Reform Union, Colonel Wedgwood's action is accepted as a commonplace of the Divorce Court.

"Pretended misconduct on the part of the husband," said Ms Seaton-Tiedeman, honorary secretary of the union, "is part of the regular unofficially recognised machinery of the law. There are solicitors who make a business of arranging evidence on these lines, and high-minded men have again and again found it necessary to accept their services in order to escape from intolerable bondage".

She continued: "A common plan is for a man to arrange to take a lady out to dine with him in a private room, and to have the fact that he locks the door sworn to by a witness. In one case the lady was, to my own knowledge, the man's own sister, but of course the witness was not aware of that. The whole thing proves the criminal absurdity of the law as it stands, and Colonel Wedgwood's courageous act in publishing the facts of his own case is a public service."[2]

The amount of publicity aroused by such a prominent couple's divorce highlighted the absurdity of the legal situation and prompted calls for reform of the divorce laws.

Jos was now free and he immediately married his daughters' former governess, Florence Willett, at Chelsea Register Office on 25th June, two days after the decree of divorce was made absolute. They spent their honeymoon abroad.

Meanwhile Ethel, also free, was still passionately interested in the writings and lectures of Rudolf Steiner. One of her friends at that time – whom she and Jos had met previously – Gerald Kaufman (who later changed his name to George Adams) was also an anthroposophist. In the spring of 1919 Steiner's new book, *The Threefold Social Order*, was published. Ethel and Gerald offered to translate it into English and they were invited to the Goetheanum in Dornach to undertake this work.

Ethel left England for Switzerland, taking her youngest children, Julia and Gloria.

Chapter 37

CAMBRIDGE – HELEN MARRIES

Between March and August 1919 Helen's everyday life was taken up with her political activities in Hanley. She kept a diary and listed the many people with whom she was involved in the Hanley Women's Co-op Guild, the Women's Labour Party and the Independent Labour Party. In April she was elected to the executive of the Central Labour Party. Her enthusiasm and strong belief in what she was doing comes over strongly in her diary entries.

She wrote in her diary in May, whilst thinking of how impulsive her father was in the way he chose to join the ILP:

> *Oh these impulsive men! I shall marry Michael if I get the chance simply to have someone <u>dependable</u> – think of the relief of having a man who wasn't always doing startling things at unexpected moments!*

It was during the middle of 1919 that her parents were in the news because of their divorce. The older children had come to terms with the permanent separation of their parents, but when Ethel took their two youngest sisters abroad, this was a heartbreaking extra blow.

Rosamund – who had done so much to keep the children and the home together – had fallen in love with a Hungarian, Janos Bekassy from Vas. Janos (pet name Doge) had been at Bedales with the girls' brothers and at the outbreak of war he had been interned. Jos arranged his release and gave him work at the Ark; on the Armistice Janos returned to Hungary. In June when Jos took his new bride, Florence, on honeymoon to Paris he left her briefly while he accompanied Rosamund to Hungary to join her fiancé.

Suddenly Jos's family had shrunk from seven to four. Helen went to Cambridge that August and she and Michael Pease had an opportunity to spend some time together. In later years Michael told their daughter Richenda that one day he and Helen went for a bicycle ride around Cambridge and they came to a gate where they sat and talked. It was then he decided she was the one he wanted to marry. Helen had always been in love with him. Jos wrote to Michael before the marriage:

> *My dear Michael,*
> *I am so glad that you and Helen want to get married. She seems very happy, & if a good daughter makes a good wife you should have no reason to regret the bargain. I hope you realise that you are marrying a family not a unit; but anyway they are not very terrible & they know their place! Helen herself will often lose her temper but she is in reality the most affectionate & dependent of females, & with that sort tempers don't matter ...*
>
> *Yours very sincerely Josiah C Wedgwood*

Helen married Michael Pease in February 1920. After their honeymoon they made their home in Cambridge. Michael had been at Trinity in 1909, where he obtained a first-class degree in the Natural Science Tripos and a Diploma of Agriculture. He was a lecturer in animal breeding and later director of the poultry research unit at Cambridge University School of Agriculture.

Life as a married woman, away from all that activity in Hanley, was very different for Helen. Cambridge was familiar territory and she was happy in her new role as Michael's wife. To their delight Helen soon became pregnant and now morning sickness meant that politics – for a change – were not top of her list of priorities. A letter from her grandmother Emily sympathised with her on her nausea and her aunt Lucie (Cecil Wedgwood's widow) wrote in July about knitting patterns and baby clothes. That summer Phoebe went to stay with Helen and Michael at their home in Girton. These two cousins and friends never lost touch and Phoebe always enjoyed seeing Helen and catching up with all the news.

Joanna was born to Helen and Michael at Christmas in 1920.

The following year Helen's grandmother, Emily Wedgwood, died aged eighty-one. She had been a staunch supporter of all her family and was always interested in their activities. When Josiah's children were young they had spent many holidays with her; she introduced the boys to climbing in the Lake District. Jos wrote many, many letters to her right up to the year she died, and she was always keenly interested in everything he did.

Emily would have been proud if she could have lived to see her son Ralph become Chief General Manager of the London and North Eastern Railway in 1922. Also that year, Helen and Michael's first son, Sebastian, was born.

Helen, although now a wife and mother, was still the same politically motivated person she had always been and became part of the political scene in Cambridge. She had joined the Cambridgeshire Labour Party in 1921. In 1923 she was on the Executive Committee, Cambridge Trades Council and Divisional Labour Party – she became president in 1930. She was also a Cambridgeshire County Councillor for Girton division from 1937 and again in 1940.

In London in 1922, the Conservatives and Liberals in a coalition government under Lloyd George agreed to disagree, and as a result Bonar Law formed a new Conservative government, but it did not last long as Mr Law died in 1923. Then Stanley Baldwin was chosen by King George V to form a new Conservative government. Baldwin was Prime Minister for a short time only and on his resignation in 1924 Ramsay MacDonald became the new Labour Prime Minister.

Ramsay MacDonald and Josiah Wedgwood did not always see eye to eye and when Ramsay came into power and formed his new Cabinet, one of the changes he made was to Josiah's role as vice chairman of the Party (which he had been since 1921). Josiah was ousted and given the Chancellorship of the Duchy of Lancaster, with a seat in the Cabinet and complete silence in the House. This was a blow to Josiah. In his book, *Memoirs of a Fighting Life* he referred to this appointment thus:

I took this ridiculous office much in the spirit in which Bismarck recommended Alexander of Battenberg to accept the throne of Bulgaria – "It will always be an amusing episode to remember".

Jos wrote from the House of Commons to Helen on 16th April 1924:

Many thanks for your letter. I am very glad that you have fixed up the candidate for the County and got a good man, but how do you expect me to support a Fabian Socialist? Of course I will do my best to imitate your oratory.

I am going to see Lord Haldane's secretary about the J.P. ship in Cambridgeshire, but I think myself that you are a little too young. I am very glad however that you were recommended by the Labour Party. ... At present things are going quite nicely but nothing will compensate me for being cleared out of the House of Commons.

Later he was elected to the executive of the Party, both in the House and in the country, but again MacDonald neatly removed him from the Party Executive in the House.

In January 1925, when the birth of Helen's third child was imminent and Helen had become a magistrate, she wrote to her father, overjoyed about her new position. At the end of her letter, she said:

... Well goodnight, & mind your licence is in order when next you come down here. I intend to suspend licences on the smallest provocation.

Very much love

Yours Helen Bowen Pease J.P.

She added a postscript that she had acquired a picture of Grandfather Bowen in full regalia: '*the only one I have. I am framing it to celebrate the occasion.*'

Jocelyn Richenda, Helen's second daughter, was born on 25th October 1925. That year was the first break in the silence between Josiah IV and his 'babies' Julia and Gloria, who were now eighteen and sixteen respectively. While in Germany on Government business in 1925, Jos wrote to Michael Pease:

> *... I did spend most of last week at Stuttgart seeing Julia, & quite fell in love with her & her German accent. She did not quite thaw however, & to everything said "Mother would not like it". She is very bescheiden [modest] ... She mealed with me, & has many young friends with whom I ingratiated myself as best I could.*

At the same time he wrote to another of his daughters about the same matter:

> *Magnificent auburn hair brushed straight back a la mamman combined with black eyebrows and eyes the size of saucers ... straight nose, good chin, but the lower lip firm and tight ... So far as I can see, none of these young people laughs. Earnestness is the keynote, chiefly about educating themselves or somebody else. When she opened the door to me she gave me the most perfect automatic curtsey that ever Charlotte did to Werther (if she did); bescheiden is the word. She is surrounded with a court of young friends (both sexes thanks be), who gaze upwards from a kneeling circle. ... Of course like you she is frantically keen on something. In her case it is eurhythmics and the dramatic art. Her whole face lighted up as she talked, beautifully ...*

In 1925 Helen served on the committee of the Cambridge Birth Control Clinic. Helen was the first Wedgwood to be involved in birth control clinics, but not the last. Her sister-in-law Dorothy Winser, married to Helen's brother Josiah V, in the 1930s pioneered the opening of the North Staffordshire branch of the Birth Control Association and despite fierce opposition its clinic was opened in 1936. Cecil Wedgwood's widow, Lucie, was also a great support in this fight. Lucie, way back in 1911, had researched the situation of women who died in childbirth and the number of children who died before the age of five. When, in 1911 the Stoke-on-Trent Infant Health Visitors' Association was founded, Lucie was its secretary and her husband

Cecil was president. Lucie was dedicated to her work for the welfare of mothers and children in the Potteries. She continued to support the work of such welfare clinics for the rest of her life.

In 1999 a letter came to light which is relevant to the way of life in 1910 in the Potteries. The notes written by Dr Dorothy Stevenson, shortly before her death aged eighty-eight, were forwarded to the Wedgwood Museum in Barlaston by her daughter:

The post of assistant school medical officer in Edinburgh was advertised in 'The Scotsman', salary for men £350, for women £300. One could not in honour apply under such conditions. For very many now the salary & status of any medical post are the same for women as for men. I should have applied demanding the same salary.

I applied for the post of school medical officer at Hanley, one of Arnold Bennett's "Five Towns" – there were & are really six, federated in that year, 1910. I was amazed when I arrived at the station for the interview with the committee, & horrified too, for every pottery chimney was belching great columns of smoke from "the pot banks" & of course from the works of all the six towns. The Shelton works lit up the sky at night from their great fires. A good many years later the firing of the china was done by electricity.

Mr Cecil Wedgwood head of the firm, was chairman of the Education Committee. He & Mrs Wedgwood were very kind to me, inviting me to their house in the country, 10 miles off from where Mr Wedgwood rode on horseback to the works every morning. They took me over the works and showed me all the different processes, & to their museum with all the original Josiah's researches and experiments, real scientific work.

Mrs Wedgwood started an unofficial Infant Clinic with two works nurses & me to help her. Infant mortality was very high, especially in the very hot summer of 1911, for these were the days of long-tube feeding bottles, not properly washed & never really sterilised, & baby after baby died of gastro-eniteritis ...

Now in 1925 Helen was involved publicly in child welfare and was aware and proud of the work her aunt Lucie and many others in the Potteries had pioneered.

Helen and Michael Pease worked in harmony together as both had long family traditions in politics and local government administration. At their house in Girton, Michael required a study for his many papers. He bought from the Army a surplus medical hut, which was erected in the garden at Reynolds Close. Within this was his study, and a spare bedroom. Their daughter Richenda (Lady Huxley) in 1999 remembered the other most important garden building – this was the playroom, the children had such happy times. There was – and it is still there – a most effective stove with a picture of a tortoise on the lid. In the winter it was cosy and warm.

Helen's sister Camilla had gone to Australia in September 1927 to work as an anthropologist. Helen wrote to her as often as she could with all the news from Cambridge. In February 1928 she wrote:

> *Ros & Doge* [who now had a farm at Thurston in Norfolk] *came over after the snows had cleared.*
>
> *The children have spent the morning with Michael putting drainpipes into our field across the road. We are planting some of it as orchard ...*

She asked Camilla for a photograph as the only one she could find was taken when she was fourteen.

In March Helen wrote to wish her father a happy birthday and added:

> *... we're just back from the Parish meeting, where our chaps turned up magnificently – about 60 strong, & we licked the other side into a cocked hat; & then they demanded a poll!*

She goes on about the local elections until:

> *Well, it is 10 o'clock & time to milk the goats ...*

Helen's next letter to Camilla, in April 1928, said:

... Michael is standing for the District council, against Mrs Stewart (did you know her? rather nice, old friend of mother's, liberal, very feminist) ...

Michael won the election and was the first Labour man to get on the RDC on a fight (others had got on unopposed). Helen *had* to tell her father:

... There is now hardly an anti-feminist in the place who has not been forced within two months to vote for a woman as the lesser of two evils – not to mention some Tories who have had to vote socialist rather than vote for a woman!

Jos went again to Europe in 1928 and on his return he wrote to Helen on 12th May:

... I have just had the time of my life in Vienna, making love with all the old fervour & increased experience to my secret daughter Gloria. I found her thro' the Zionists there, took Ros out on spec & very nervous, & it went well.

She is a pretty dear of 18, as poor as a Church mouse but not one of the Guild of Poor Brave Things. Such fun I had, especially the last day after Ros had left. Her mother is going to have some job to re-establish the status quo. I know she liked having us, & as they all three live in separate houses, if not places, progress is possible. She is a 'cellist of great promise, also alas an anthroposophist & like all of them unable to explain it. But I adore her & shall certainly see her again.

She does not powder. Her mother has produced something which is quite good, quite happy, & quite useless (for her education stopped at 16). But she has plenty of character, all in the Camilla style, without Cam's nerves and prettily dependent ...

While on holiday at the Ark in July that year, Helen wrote to Camilla to tell her that Gloria their sister was in London with a Miss Pethich, visiting Jos. Helen thought Gloria was a mixture of

Camilla and Charles:

> *... but, as Father complains, quite uneducated as we regard education. However Father has been drumming into her that she must read – & I found Miss Pethich entirely of the same opinion & deploring the way in which mother cuts them off from the interesting circle to which they should belong ... I had to promise to read some of Steiner's works on education (in German too!) in the hope that she will read some standard English works in exchange! ... What I can't understand is that even when she is in Stuttgart (N. B. imagine M letting any of us loose in Vienna at the age of 16!) she lives in separate lodgings from [mother] yet is so much under mother's thumb that she will give up knowing us – though she says she wants to & was obviously pleased to see me – rather than annoy her. Miss Pethich (who appears to be one of mother's ex-slaves) complains that M has a habit of threatening to commit suicide if her articles are not accepted for the anthroposophical magazine, & she wd probably use the same tactics on Gloria, so one doesn't want to force a breach. But I think the month in England has widened her horizon & she will perhaps read a bit more. But really, 18 & 21 is a bit old to forbid people knowing their own brothers & sisters, not to mention Father.*
>
> *I found it very exciting & romantic picking up a sister again after 12 yrs (& was horribly nervous beforehand) ...*

Rachel was born to Helen and Michael in 1928. At this time the two older children, Joanna and Sebastian, were eight and six and Helen, continuing the family tradition, gave them lessons – two hours each morning.

When Joanna was asked in later years about those early days she said:

> *We had the odd maid. We never had a nanny if you know what I mean, which was nice for us, and Mother also educated me and my brother until I was nine. I couldn't*

*cope with my mother's education. It didn't suit me at all,
and when I first went to school when I was nine years old
I then began to learn, which was very late on. My brother
did very well and actually with my mother's help got a
scholarship to Bedales when he was 11.[1]*

In 1930 Jos had some heart trouble and had to rest for six months. During that year his brother, Frank, aged sixty-three, died suddenly and Jos's son, Josiah V, succeeded Frank as managing director of the Wedgwood pottery empire. Josiah V had married Dorothy Winser in 1919. They had been old friends; she had been head girl at Bedales, where they had met.

At the time of their marriage Josiah V was interested in politics and worked for his father as his private secretary. In 1920 Dorothy contracted poliomyelitis and, although she recovered over time, she had difficulty walking. During the years she lived in Staffordshire she worked tirelessly both in health welfare and education. She served as the Manchester University representative on the city of Stoke-on-Trent Higher Education committee and was one of the first members of the Women's Royal Voluntary Service.

Josiah V had studied for a BSc in economics and had joined the family firm in 1927 as secretary. By this time he and Dorothy had had three children, John (1919), Ralph Josiah (1924), and Jenny (1927).

The Wedgwood firm in the late 1920s, had Josiah's uncle Frank as chairman and managing director, Cecil's widow, Lucie, was on the board and daughter Audrey was company secretary, but Audrey was about to leave to get married.

In 1930, when Josiah V took over the reins at the Staffordshire works, he had faith both in his family and in the products the firm sold and this gave him the confidence and strength to move from Burslem and build a new factory. They chose a site in the village of Barlaston, some five miles from the Etruria Works. This was a brave move considering England was still at war. The new factory was officially opened in 1940.

Chapter 38

CHILDREN EVACUATED – LETTERS

Between 1929 and 1939, while the First World War haunted people of all nations, hardship was still being experienced. The great Depression in the United States affected other countries including England, there was a civil war in Spain, and suddenly in 1938 world peace was in jeopardy when Hitler threatened to invade Czechoslovakia. Neville Chamberlain's attempts at keeping the peace failed and by the end of the following year England was at war with Germany. Helen, no longer a pacifist, wrote an impassioned letter to her father in 1939 after the Munich crisis:

> *Dearest Father,*
> *For goodness sake don't let the Labour Party let Chamberlain get away with it! Did you ever see such stupid gush. The worst of it is our own <u>female</u> rank & file are the ones to gush over him. They've had the fright of their lives & seem to think dear C has saved them. God knows why or what he is supposed to have done! <u>The educated Tory convert on the other hand is waiting & hoping to see the Labour Party go for him</u>.*
> *Seriously, do you think a lot of it was stage-managed! The communists of course say so. But that message from Hitler coming so pat, just after he had made his statement & <u>just before</u> any one could get up & criticise, & the working up of war scare to the last point, so that people wouldn't be critical of any means used to get them out of*

it? Anyway of course it is put about now that the wicked Labour Party wanted to go to war.

If you speak you might suggest that out of gratitude to Roosevelt we might pay a bit of our war debt!!

Our D.L. Party sent a message to the Czech legation (drafted by Mike of course), but otherwise they wouldn't make any public pronouncement for fear of being called warmongers. I think we shall emigrate! The spectacle of one's countrymen cheering wildly at having crawled out of a war by chucking their friends overboard is too nauseating & if we are singly going on to lick Hit & Muss's [Hitler & Mussolini] boots & sacrifice Spain, I'd sooner be elsewhere.

And not one word from Chamberlain to show he thinks anybody else except himself & der Hitler "saved Europe".

Damn & blast the folly of the human race.

Very much love Yours affec. Helen Bowen Pease

During all the other tragedies happening abroad, Helen and Michael experienced great personal unhappiness in 1934 when their six year old daughter Rachel, died. There had been a very bad streptoccal virus outbreak and many children in Cambridge died, Rachel among them.

In the following year Dorothy (Dora) was born and in 1936 Helen gave birth to their last child, a boy, Fabian.

By March 1940, when Helen wrote the following letter, she and Michael had decided to evacuate their three youngest children to Canada, where it was hoped they would be safe. This impending separation hung like a cloud over the Pease household.

Helen wrote to her father:

I forgot to write for your birthday; but then you haven't remembered mine for some years nor answered my last letter. However, this failing must be hereditary as I never remember to write my weekly letters to the children unless reminded by Michael, & even then they are usually late.

Well, well, Sebastian writes that he is very shocked by your remarks about leaving German airmen to drown & that he fears you are becoming an old Tory. I have endeavoured to put your point of view, which I largely share, but not quite. I'm bound to say that it is bad enough that Seb. should have to become a soldier & do the sort of things soldiers have to do, but personally, as his mother, I'd prefer him not to be more of a beast than is absolutely essential to winning the war.

I've been reading an entertaining & instructive book "The History of the Englishmen's Food". Did you know that the real reason the Italians ran away at Caperetto was that for six months they had been fed on inadequate rations, deplorably deficient in vitamin B? Now will you offer yourself for a scientific experiment? We will feed you on the same ration for six months & see if you turn into a pacifist! Cobbett, by the way, remarks that the reason the Catholic Church encourages fasting is because it produces docility & slavishness. So tuck into your rations with a clear conscience. (Sugar by the way is not an essential for the red-blooded he-man or she-woman).

We are all well, though I have had Dora down w. a temperature on & off for some weeks. However, she is better now. Joanna has been trying for her Newnham entrance & has successfully got through the written tests. She has just come home for the practical, & the interviews. So we feel a bit hopeful. It will be awfully nice if she gets in.

... Do come down & see us sometime. Why not put in a weekend at the Garden House Hotel? You might just as well come there as go to a seaside hotel & we could all have the pleasure of seeing you.

Do come, if not now, what about Whitsun, only the children won't be here then ...

We are busy with garden & livestock. One of Mike's experiments now is the collection of refuse from 12 houses (separately) sorting it over & weighing etc to see how far the collection of suburban refuse is worthwhile for the poultry keeper. Very interesting from the sociological as well as the hens' point of view. So far it appears you could keep a hen or two on it, but hardly get many eggs.

Very much love. Yours affect. Helen Bowen Pease

In July, after Richenda (Chenda), Dora and Fabian had sailed to Canada from Liverpool, Helen wrote to her father:

... I feel bad enough at our nice happy little family being broken up like this, but poor old Mike is so cut up especially at losing Chenda of whom he is very fond, that he looks really ill. I wish things didn't weigh on him so continuously. I may feel like suicide at times of depression, but I can't be really unhappy for long ...

Initially the three children went to stay with a Dr and Mrs Bell at Chester in Nova Scotia, but eventually Richenda went to the United States to stay with family friends, Mr and Mrs Charles Dunbar in Boston. During the three years while Helen and Michael were separated from these children, many letters passed between them. Richenda kept most of the letters her mother sent to her. Permission has been granted for them to be included in this book. It is interesting to note that the tone of some of Helen's letters to her daughter bears a great resemblance to the type of political information Josiah IV wrote in his letters to her. Again, the two youngest children are referred to as 'the babies'. These letters give a great insight into Helen's life at that time. They are seriously concerned about the war situation and when she and Michael will have their family safe and united again, but also she does her best to 'gossip' about family, friends, chores, etc. For instance, in between writing about refugees and bombing over the Channel she will suddenly revert to home and give details of crops and everyday things, to reassure Chenda that some things remain the same. But always there is optimism and quite often humour in her writings to her daughter. In Helen's letters 'Mama and Grandpa' refer to Michael's parents, and Limpsfield is where they lived.

Helen's very first letter, written on 24th July 1940 said:

My dearest big Chenda

*As I write this I am hoping you are not being seasick &
that you & the babies enjoyed the voyage. We all miss
you <u>terribly</u>, especially Daddy. ... I do hope you are not
weighed down by all your responsibilities & that Dora &
Fabian are good & happy. ... Before you left a postcard
came from Mama, to say Martin & Veronica will be going
to the Dunbars in Boston, & the Dunbars have asked you
too to go to school there with Lockie. We are not quite
sure yet that the Toronto guarantee might not be better,
as you wd be with other Cambridge children there, &
wd be with university people like us, & "in the Empire".
It is awfully kind of the Dunbars. Personally, if you are
not with the Bells, we would rather like you to be with
Quakers. Have you any views?*

*Look after my darling babies. Especially Dora. Fabian
will make friends everywhere, but Dora is more sensitive
than I used to give her credit for, & rather reserved as
well, & she is devoted to you ...*

*I expect you will have a lovely time in Canada, & it
is a great thing to see the World before you have to settle
down. Being in S.Africa even when I was really too young
to appreciate it, was a tremendous education to me, &
you are old enough to get much more out of it then Ros &
I could ...*

*Dear Chenda, we are so proud of you being such a
capable, responsible young lady & to feel we can trust
you with Dora & Fabian, – & that we can trust you to
grow up the right sort of person even without us to jump
on you!!*

On 1st August 1940 Helen wrote:

*... We had <u>such</u> a nice letter from the Dunbars about
the arrangements they were making for you & Lockie,
– you will I gather be at <u>Cambridge</u>, not Boston itself!
Rather funny. So that really seems the best plan. There
will be other English children there besides Lockie &
Martin, & Grandfather has friends there – two of them*

*are schoolteachers, Harriet Wedgwood & her sister!
I will send you a chart to show what sort of cousins
they are.*

*We haven't had any excitements since you left, – not
even any yellow warnings when Daddy was on duty. We
are very busy with the fruit & the honey – a nasty sticky
job that I much prefer to shove off onto you! On Saturday
we are going to Bedales & then to Limpsfield & I shall see
Grandfather in London, – unless of course Hitler decides
to try invading before then, but it doesn't look very likely
just now, though of course you never can tell.*

On the 9th August she followed that letter with the following:

*We've just got back after a very nice weekend at Bedales &
Limpsfield. It was the old Bedalian meeting. Your Matron
(was it?) from the Mount was there and sent you her best
wishes ... Daddy & Joanna (each on their own) created a
sensation by declining to go to the A.R.P. trenches when
there were two warnings that night ... How they expect
the children to work properly or to keep well if they go on
getting them up to go to trenches ten minutes away I don't
know. They have had 37 warnings this term!*

*... On Monday we biked across to Limpsfield, a lovely
day with the west wind behind us. We could hear the guns
going, otherwise it was complete peace. We found Mama
& Granpa well, & Gunter with them, – a triumph for
Mama, as so many of these unfortunate refugees have
been interned <u>and</u> shipped off to Canada & Australia
without even their clothes. It is perfectly disgraceful.
Thank goodness there has been such a row about it things
should be better in future, but that won't undo the wrong
that has been done.*

*We are selling about half a ton of greengages, but
plums are a glut. I am trying to dry some, but it is slow
work as the weather is cool now ...*

*There seems to have been a great battle over the
Channel yesterday. Miss Senser* [a Jewish refugee who
stayed about ten years with the family and was a great

support] *is shocked at me for wanting to see it, – & saying we should run excursion trains & charge for seating on the cliffs. She says it is nearly as bad as wanting to watch the Gladiators in the arena, but I don't think it is the same thing at all. How annoying if one goes through the whole war without seeing one air-fight! ...*

You might find out if it would cost too much in Customs in Canada to send you a rabbit fur coat. If Mrs Bell thinks it would be worth it I will get it made as soon as maybe, so that you can wear it when you go to Boston.

Write & tell us all you are doing & how my darling babies are ...

On 17th August Helen wrote:

... You will have seen we have been having quite an exciting week! However we didn't see any of it here – only one red warning (in the afternoon) and then nothing happened. But we do wish the BBC & press & a lot of people wouldn't be so pleased with things! You'd think to hear them, that just because we've shot down 400 Nazi planes that we had nothing much to bother about, silly idiots.

We have picked & sold half a ton of greengages & I'm now bottling & jamming apricots – a huge crop, and such lovely colours. Joanna has got through a small exam last week, so she is not working so hard & we have a continuous stream of her & Seb's friends in and out all day, – very jolly ...

Then a refugee Czech lady turned up yesterday, very lively & even cheerful in spite of having fled from Czecho to Belgium, been bombed out of Mons with streams of refugees, – <u>met her son</u> in the Czech army <u>by accident</u> in a town in France, & finally got away from S. France with the Czech soldiers on a collier boat & arrived in England!! She is a cousin of Dr Iltis, & had a china factory near Brunn ...

Later in August Helen wrote:

... Things here are much as normal, we pick plums (we've sold about a ton) & extract honey & listen in to what Priestly in a broadcast called the "Merserchmidt – Spitfire serial" & last night Daddy was called up four times by the yellow warning, (but last time he was on duty we weren't called up at all). And of course when there were some incendiary bombs actually dropped near here in a ploughed field he wasn't on duty & we missed all the fun.

However I had a busy day today clearing the loft of inflammable stuff. One would feel rather a fool if an incendiary did drop on the roof & one couldn't get at it. It made me think of the way we used to burn great belts of grass round the house in South Africa in order to keep off veldt fires – a much more exciting job than clearing the loft! as we used to turn out a score or so of people in a line to keep the fire within bounds by beating it with sacks of earth.

... Cousin Maud [Darwin] came to tea & brought a man & wife who are now at Grange Farm. The man is English but brought up in France & they had a big farm near Dieppe. They got away with their two children half an hour before the Germans came, got across France somehow to Bordeaux & so to England. They were very bitter about the rottiness of the French high command, which worked right down so that the officers went off to look after their families leaving the men with no orders, so everything was left undefended & food & ammunition fell unhurt into the German hands.

... Half past ten, & Daddy is out on a yellow warning again. I must go & make some tea & tell Joanna to stop working!

Helen sent off a brief note to Richenda on 29th August as a result of an airmail from Dorothy Wedgwood.

Just got from Aunt Dorothy the entertaining photo & interview of you in the Boston Herald!! But who was the damn fool who told you to say you were not to talk *about affairs in England? That is just the way to make the Yanks think we are beaten, that we are afraid to say the truth. You say next time what we told you, that you are sent to America because you can't fight – yet – & your relations in England can fight better if you are out of the way. Don't you let them come the "poor-little-refugee-rescued-from-bombs" stunt over **you**. We are grateful to U.S.A. for taking our children, not just to save their lives but because it will help <u>US TO WIN THE WAR</u>. I just wish I could have seen you being interviewed, it must have been priceless ...*

After this episode Helen wrote to Harold Nicolson, at the Ministry of Information. He must have replied favourably because in her letter to Richenda on 8th September she said:

... His reply which I enclose will amuse you! Anyway you now have official permission to talk – only it will be a bit out of date by now!!

We are a bit disturbed today over the bad raid on the London docks last night & wondering if more will happen tonight. Of course it is not as bad as we all <u>expected</u> a year ago, & as the Germans lost 1 in five of their raiders it is not exactly a cheap game for them. Anyway if anyone talks to you about the "terrible loss of life in air raids", remember that in the last war we lost <u>an</u> <u>average</u> of 700 of the flower of our young men <u>every day</u> for <u>four</u> years, not counting wounded, and that is far far worse than anything the air raids have done, or I think could do ...

Dear child, we are glad you are having such a good time & are happy. We are all well & fit here, though we miss you all very much. There is nothing you can do to help your country now except grow up to be a good citizen. For the matter of that all most of us here can do is to carry on as usual.

On 23rd September Helen wrote:

... Until yesterday we have had few air alarms here, owing to their being too busy with London. The village is filling up a bit with London families of soldiers & workers stationed here, & I expect & hope we shall have more. Grandmama had an incendiary bomb at the bottom of the garden! She says they hardly know or bother there whether there is a warning on or not now.

Bassy is now "a Trinity Man". They muffed his scholarship syllabus at Bedales, so the best thing seemed to be to start him at college this October, then he will get 2 years before he is 20 &, if he is any good at his subjects, an interesting job in the army. So he swanks round with his hands in his trouser pockets & looks the complete undergraduate. We have chosen his rooms & now I must look up china & tablecloths & spoons etc. Joanna will sleep at home & go in to Newnham in the day time.

Last week we went to Sophy Raverat's [Charles and Maud Darwin's granddaughter] *wedding to a Cambridge Don, he is a zoologist & is now on war work research into glue for aeroplanes! The wedding was in Trinity College Chapel & afterwards in the Common room. The entire Darwin Keynes & Barlow tribe were there, & of course a number of 'well known Cambridge figures'.*

On Saturday we had a whist drive & dance at the Women's Institute, – a joint cttee of village & soldiers is running something of the sort every week. It was a great success – & very hot & crowded! Seb came too & danced. So did I! with three officers & 4 privates, so now! It really is hard on the army that they have to wear such a dingy uniform. The R.A.F. are thus not only the heroes of the country, but turn up in such lovely blue uniforms that the soldiers are simply nowhere ...

Helen wrote on 8th October:

... We've been dreadfully busy this week getting mothers & children from London billetted in the village. There are not yet nearly as many come down as there might to be. I expect by the winter we shall be quite full up what with

evacuees & soldiers. The children yesterday came down with their pockets full of bits of shrapnel as souvenirs. One boy gave me a bit. ... The sirens do go most nights, we suppose when "Jerries" go over. So far we've had scattered bombs, mostly unexpected, & no damage round here. One never realised before what a lot of England is just fields!! I expect the others told you Grannie [Pease] had two near shaves in the same week, with the workshop demolished by one, & a time bomb in the Keen's house & an oil bomb just outside the cottage, so that all their windows are broken & a lot of tiles off. Lucky it wasn't worse, though in another way it was bad luck, as Uncle Nickie says 30% of the bombs dropped in that town & district fell in their road. Anyway they are glad Lockie & Martin are out of it. I think Grannie rather enjoyed the excitement!

Grandfather (Wedgwood) & Fingwan came down here for a week after a bomb fell next to their flat & put the electricity & gas out of order, but they have gone back now.

Grandfather gave a most amusing account of doing Home Guard duty in the cellars of the House of Commons which he says he now knows better than Guy Fawkes. Going to the telephone one night he switched on the fire alarm by mistake in the dark – and he didn't know how to stop it, and it made an awful row & he expected hundreds of police & guards to come rushing – and <u>nobody</u> came!! So there was <u>another sort</u> of row! and now if the House of Commons is burnt out we hope at least it will not be because nobody answers the fire alarm!

Your letter of Sept 8 was very cheering about the babies. Yes, I think we are very lucky to have such good friends, and we are so thankful you are settling down so happily.

... Bassy went into his rooms in Cambridge yesterday. I wish I could have seen him going in to Hall in his cap & gown. He & Joanna have plenty of friends up & will, I think, enjoy themselves in spite of the war ...

In October Josiah IV wrote a general letter to three of his children and Helen copied it and sent it on to Mrs Bell in Nova Scotia and asked her to send it to Richenda.

Dear Children – this is for Helen, Rosamund & Charles, a story of adventure. I write from Ethel Snowden's flat in Dolphin Square, whither we go to shelter & sleep in her absence. It's on the second floor, facing inwards.

So far tonight they have not hit us; but we have had nine bombs in six weeks & are getting perfectly callous. Three on the roof burst on that superb piece of concrete and only wrecked the rooms just underneath; one got the shelter by accident & killed six. Otherwise only an ambulance driver has been killed. On Friday 13th a second bomb dropped on the soap factory 100 yds away & like a volcano all the stone & stuff flew into the air over Dolphin Square. It was at 8 p.m. & we had only just gone down. An iron pipe entered No 903 & smashed the back of my armchair and hurled it about the room. So that balcony window is boarded up. A 2 ton iron girder wandered over the roof & sat up in the middle of the garden.

But last Tuesday was our gala night. One came down within 6 yards of our window & flung F. [Fingwan] into my arms & went through into the garage & destroyed 100 cars. Only three of the Snowdens windows went – but elsewhere desolation & destruction of doors and windows. Another took an adjoining house in St George's Square & covered us with rubble, another missed the front of the Square by a yard & blew in a few more windows, another just across the road in front wiped out all the remaining windows in front; another landed in the west door of the garage & smashed the windows in the west, but not as high as 903, & killed an ambulance driver; a last pitched on to "Granville" & burst harmlessly.

The [Battersea] Power Station & our fortress still stand amid surrounding ruins, but with windows hanging anyhow.

All services still work, & "nothing could stop that

astonishing infantry"!

Jos [Josiah V] spent one night on the floor here – a fairly quiet night, but tonight is as bad as Monday & Tuesday – incessant pounding and I can't hear a single gun. Anyhow I've written 10 letters out of some 50 that await answers.

Florence has two flats to clean now besides cooking all my meals but has got a charing woman to come in & help – one of the few left in the neighborhood.

All I want is to get back at them with interest. They kill about 200 a night only, but the destruction is offensive. All round Coeur de Lion is smashed up & Westminster Hall looks like Fountains Abbey – worth preserving in that condition as a splendid memento. The roof is all right.

The stations are all right too – but woe to anyone who arrives or tries to move after dark. The day raids are of no importance. One never knows whether they are on or off.

Your loving father

J.C.W.

Helen added a note about Dolphin Square for further information:

Dolphin Square is a huge block of modern flats 9 stories high consisting of 10 "houses" (named after admirals) and containing 1000 flats. It stands on the Thames opposite the Battersea Power Station.

Helen and her sister Camilla in Australia always kept in touch. On 23rd October 1940 Helen wrote:

Dear Camilla,
Your letter of Aug 2 came some weeks ago. Events move so fast that ones letters are hopelessly out of date by the time they reach one. I wonder if you are back in Sydney yet? Your description of people regarding Pacifism as a

weakness like secret drinking just hits it off. Personally I think it does them credit on the whole that they are not much more intolerant. I certainly expected that Cos [conscientious objectors] wd. get lynched when the bombing started, but actually people are quite decent. We have a non-combatant corps stationed in the village now – probably for the rest of the winter. The village is a bit 'sniffy' but not unkind, & their officers – regular army men – stick up for them well. Personally I haven't much use for men who are prepared to do almost anything except actually handling the rifle – but there it is; in spite of London in ruins we live & let live. It is extraordinary how one settles down to the fantastic nightmare in wh. we live – not that we here have suffered damage – yet. We only get 'peppered' occasionally in Cambridge; – four bangs went off just now & the house rattled, though no warning was on. Two houses were smashed & a man killed in Cambridge the other day, but it is surprising what a lot of England is fields! But everyone one knows in London has been bombed, though we do not yet know anyone personally who has been injured!! I expect Father has written you a description of the wreckage in & round Dolphin Square. He & Fingwan, [Florence] like thousands of others just go on living among the wreckage. London must be an inferno at night. We can see the horrid red glow from our bedroom & hear the mutter of the barrage – and still our newspapers & letters arrive at a reasonable hour in the morning! In fact the trouble is though we are only 60 miles away the people here are still not properly aware of what is happening in London & refuse to realise that however unpleasant it may be they must fill their houses with women & children from London, – the alternative being surrender & a German army of occupation living on them instead!

Mike is billeting officer for Girton, & as chairman of the public health committee is also responsible for the district, so it is a fairly tough job. The astonishing thing is that though the Londoners arrive tired & dirty they are by no means nerve shattered. I suppose you have to be pretty tough to survive life in the East End even in normal times! And we are all feeling much less depressed than in June & July! Mama & Papa at Limpsfield have had eight bombs just round the house, which broke all windows & fetched some tiles off, but they went on living there though for some days there was a timebomb next door!

Joanna was admitted to Newnham after all, she sleeps here & goes in every day – not a bad arrangement as she would otherwise take no exercise! She is thoroughly enjoying the work. Seb is also up at Trinity. Bedales muffed his scholarship syllabus so it was no use his waiting to take the exam in December, & we got him in at once so that he will have two years before he is 20. He is taking physics, chemistry & mineralogy, so if the war is still on he should get a good job in the Royal Engineers, & in any case will get a good training. He thinks of going in for metallurgy. He is a fine big specimen & looks the typical undergraduate. Eric Whitehead (North's son) is up too, taking more or less the same subjects, so they go round together & seem to be thoroughly enjoying life. That is one thing that makes this war (so far!) much less depressing than the last. One may or may not be bombed, but there is not the awful steady daily slaughter of young life. Jo's and Seb's friends are constantly in & out of this house, which keeps us lively & prevents us missing the babies so badly. We get very good reports of them from Canada, – though at very irregular intervals. Chenda has moved on to Cambridge, Mass. where Nicholas' two children are also, & seems to be having a very good time. Needless to say she had not been 48 hours in the States before she had an interview & photo in three papers: "A lot of reporters came, but the Dunbars only let in three"! Michael misses them badly, especially Chenda & worries a bit. If we had <u>known</u> this country would not be invaded (or defeated!) we would not have sent them, as neither bombs nor food are likely to be bad in Girton. Myself I find it a relief to know they are out of it all, even though my darling Fabian & Dora will be grown out of *all knowledge before I see them again. Tomorrow is his fourth birthday. We've just sent a cable greeting, and Chenda was 15 yesterday.*

<u>Oct 25</u> Today we got a reply cable – very sweet of the Woodroofes. What a weird world it is that in the middle of a ferocious war, with our cities bombarded every night one can get birthday messagess & replies across 2000 miles in 48 hours! A sister of one of Gloria's Czech friends & her little boy have just turned up here from London – very nice. For the present they will stop with us. So I have a large household to cook for! She has been sleeping in shelters in London, – one night in the tube. She has been laying it on to me what a wonderful people the English are ('I never imagined anyone like them – they just say 'we are bombed out of our house, very well we will go somewhere else, or go underground!') A workman in the Tube with his wife & six children said to her 'You are a refugee? Don't worry, we will stand out against them all right'.

I hope you are feeling really fit now. I went to the B.F.V.W. At Home at Mrs Benian's last week & saw a lot of people who asked after you.

With very much love

Yours affect^{ly}

Helen Bowen Pease

Richenda's fifteenth birthday was on 25th October 1940. Helen wrote to her on that day saying she hoped Richenda had received her presents and letters. She continued:

We are all well here & not too much bombed – just a few bangs to rattle the house now & then. Fingwan's letter will have given you some idea what it is like in London, & I sent a copy of one of Father's to Mrs Bell & asked her to pass it on to read to your schoolmates & others. Daddy has been up to the eyes billeting people in Girton

& elsewhere. The astonishing thing is a) that so few leave London, & 2) that though they arrive tired & dirty after <u>6 weeks</u> of sleeping every night in Tube & other shelters, they are by no means nerve-shattered. Of course we lap up the nice things the Americans say about our toughness & I must say it has been a revelation to <u>me</u>. ... Daddy went up to London last week & was appalled at the wreckage. He wasn't in the East End but round Oxford St & Baker St way. Even down here people don't realise what it is like, because the papers don't say much, which is a great pity as it would make the billeting officer's task much easier if people realised. I think I told you we had 22 little Irish Catholics arrived here ...

Being Irish and East End they were quite unmanageable, the trouble started by an angelic looking kid with brown curls, about 6 years old who used the most awful language. They all called Daddy every bad name they could think of. Finally Daddy picked up the said kid & carried her off – she squealing & scratching his face. Her brother rushed to the rescue & thumped Daddy (I must say I admired their family loyalty) so I had to collar him & he kicked hard. We got them parked at last – & 2 hours later they turned up all smiles to ask for apples! The whole gang roam the village & our garden cheerfully & noisily & greet us at the tops of their voices whenever they see us. Dr Hertz who was trying to look them over that morning said to me with a smile "If that is the East End you need not worry, Hitler will never be able to control them!" .... What struck me was that though they were all born in London, they were exactly like the West of Ireland Irish – very talkative & intelligent, quite fearless, ready to knife you one minute & all smiles the next ...

In Helen's Christmas letter of 9th December 1940 she wrote:

My darling Chenda,
Daddy seems to have done most of the letter writing to you lately. We do so enjoy your letters & you are a good girl

to write so regularly. They do arrive in the oddest way, the letters of the 1st half of October arrived after those you wrote in November, although as far as we could see none of them had been censored! But it is so nice to get them all, & we read them again in the right order. The one of Nov 16 came in just a fortnight! I am afraid the ones you wrote between Oct 22 & Nov 5 are sunk. However you seem to have got all the things we sent except Fowles What a shame you had to pay so much for the coat & skirt, we hoped as Joanna had worn it that you would be let off. The book by Ogden Nash hasn't come yet, but I daresay it will ...

I am sending you a pair of gloves (not home made I am sorry to say) & two diaries. I thought you might like to give one to Aunt Anna [Anna lived at Dunbars] as she admires the Labour Party. I expect you rejoiced over Rooseveldt. We all said Chenda will be cocky at her school. All the same do remember you are in someone else's country & it is rather cheek for "foreigners" to be bumptious about their politics ...

If you meet any American film makers you must tell them they must now make different sorts of spectacular films if they wish to impress us here! Most people have seen enough fires & explosions and air battles to make Clark Gable & film earthquakes & fires seem poor & tame. Jane [Joanna] went to see "Grapes of Wrath" but as she said what are the few hundred "refugees" tramping for work there, compared to the millions in Europe, or even our own villages packed with people who have lost everything but their lives. What a world! Well this is not a suitable subject for a Christmas letter.

Joanna & Seb are back from College now, but a lot of their friends are still here so we look like keeping up on huge Sunday lunch parties ...

I hope to be able to send Mr & Mrs Dunbar also the Bells some Wedgwood, but it may not be allowed, as rules about sending things as presents are very strict.

We are all well but miss you & the babies more & more. I do sympathise with the London mothers who came down here & fetch their children back whenever the raids stop for a bit! People say how selfish of them, but I am sure if you were not all too far away I should do the same! Even though I know you are happy & better off where you are, & that it is a fine thing for you to see the world & especially America ...

During the whole of 1940 Helen and Michael Pease wrote often to their children abroad. They sent many books and clothes whenever possible. Although they wished to send presents, particularly Wedgwood, to their good friends in the States, this was not allowed. They were indebted to the Dunbars for having Chenda but were not allowed to send any money. They would repay them when the war was over.

Chapter 39

THE WAR – LIFE IN CAMBRIDGE

Helen, Michael, Sebastian and Joanna were never happy while the young children were so far away. Some things – the garden full of flowers, fruit trees in blossom, a day on the river – made their loneliness more poignant.

Helen and Michael were always pleased when Joanna and Sebastian brought friends home. They had livestock and poultry, plus fruit and vegetables which all helped to put food in the larder. Sunday lunch started in a casual way but gradually it became an institution and Helen did not always know how many people would be sitting around the dining table – all were welcome. Eventually the lunch party became huge. The main course was almost always rabbit pie.

In later years, when Helen was remembered by her nephews and nieces, they all said how hospitable she was and how there was always a warm welcome for visitors. The custom begun in 1940 of a luncheon party on Sunday for friends and family continued for many years.

On 20th January 1941 Helen wrote to Richenda:

> *... Well I'm glad I once went to the Lord Mayor's reception at the Guildhall before those blighters burnt it. It was at the International Poultry Congress in 1930. Aunt Muriel's father was permanent secretary to the Lord Mayor & he showed us round – & we enjoyed seeing the power & pride of London displayed to all those foreigners. Well they are showing its power & pride in another way now,*

& we'll build it up again _still_ unconquered since it was first founded. (Even Wm the Conqueror didn't conquer London you know. He made terms)

This week 'a well-known public school in an East Anglian Town', to quote the weekly paper was burnt out by fire bombs, & the incident was not even mentioned on the BBC! We are told that after the shower of bombs fell everyone was so occupied in watching a big taxi garage blazing merrily that they never noticed the P ... e [Perse] until it was well alight. Anyway our education cttee had been discussing fire watching that very afternoon so it came very apropos, & they are so cock-a-hoop it wasn't one of _their_ schools. And I expect Mr Garner will be ordered to sleep at least two nights in the school here & won't he be cross! I wish to goodness they _would_ burn out three quarters of our village schools, then we might get decent buildings.

Daddy gave me The Drainage of the Fenlands for Xmas – much more entertaining than it sounds, e.g. The Bishop of Ely at one time allowed the bridge & causeway between Ely & Stuntney (the way we go to Ely fr. Cottenham) for which he was responsible, to become useless. He then established a ferry, for which _he_ charged, thus netting a nice little sum for his own use!

On 2nd February Helen wrote:

Mrs Matthews [the family's "prop and stay" who worked for them for many years] *gave me a shock one morning "I see we've sent a telegram to Mussolini" (Good God I thought more appeasement!) to ask him to send the Italian prisoners' ration books because there's too many to feed without'.* [J.B.] *Priestley is giving the Sunday night postscripts again. He is good, & we just wonder who put their foot down & made the BBC invite him back! Do you hear him at all in America?*

You seem to have had a lovely time at Christmas. How frightfully nice of Aunt Camilla! Thanks so much for sending on her letter. Do save & spend the money carefully, because you must remember we aren't allowed to send you anything, & the Dunbars are keeping you entirely. We hope to repay them after the war, but we don't know if we will be able to. So in either case you must be careful. The clothes we sent ought to last you two or three years. If you feel poor beside the American children you must just think & say, that your country is at war & we English must be poor at present. Sorry, this is a motherly jaw that you must expect now & then if you have a mother!

Grandfather Wedgwood & Uncle Jos are planning to come to U.S.A. in April, & he means to come & see you & wants to meet Mr & Mrs Dunbar. I think he is going to write to Mr Dunbar about the possibility of giving a lecture in Harvard. He is not, I hope & believe, giving a real 'lecture tour' in the States; he really is not strong enough; but he wants to speak in one or two places. I gather he will stop part of the time with Lord Halifax.

We are all well & busy. A bomb in "an East Anglian Town" killed 2 people last week, in broad daylight too, damn their impudence! But it is funny to see the difference now from three months ago. Then every one scurried about & went into shelters & wardens rushed round blowing whistles, – & nothing happened! – Now nobody pays any attention except that a few shops put shutters up when the roof spotter signals. I suppose if they machine gun the streets one dodges into the nearest doorway, but so far I am glad to say I have no experience.

I have been reading a history of the Crimean War (incidentally we lost 84,000 from sickness against 4000 killed, so we have improved in some respects!) & it was amusing to read the war correspondents' account of 'what to do when you hear a shell coming,' when now there is hardly a man woman or child who doesn't know that you must throw yourself on your face etc!.

... It has been snowing, thawing & sleeting here, – most disagreeable. However it has kept the raiders off except odd ones in the day time. Daddy & I walked over to Impington Village College today, because it was too bad to bicycle. It really was lovely with the pale sky & the

snow melting so that the dykes were full of water rushing under little snow cliffs.

Feb. 7 I have just heard from Mrs Bell that Grandfather Wedgwood wrote to you (in the early days) telling you not to be afraid of spending as 'Wedgwoods' would pay!! He is the limit! Wedgwoods neither will nor can pay, though I expect Cousin Kennard wd keep you out of the workhouse if absolutely necessary. At present <u>no</u> money can be got across at all; one cannot even send Wedgwood ware to the U.S.A. without proving to the Bank of England that we get dollars back (wh must be handed over to the Govt) So don't listen to your absurd Grandfather. He no doubt wanted to make you feel safe & comforted by saying "the Tribe" would stick by you etc. So they will. But you aren't a Wedgwood in name, and there are an enormous number who are. In any case, financially, you are a Pease, & must beware of Grandfather's airy irresponsibility!

On 10th February Helen wrote:

... We are all well & very pleased over the Libyan victories. Thank goodness we have some generals who evidently know their job! Because even though the Italians are rabbits the sort of fool general from which we have often suffered might have got our men badly lost in the desert. Nothing much has happened here & we are all sort of waiting as we did in August wondering what Hitler will do next, – & hoping that Churchill too may have some surprises for us.

Yesterday we had quite a fine show in the air over the garden, – three of the vast new bombers (we think they are the American ones) sailing through the sky like ships rolling from side to side & round & above them groups of fighters dancing about like gnats. It still passes my comprehension how one can keep anything weighing as much as those bombers (30 to 50 tons I believe) in the air at all, & they didn't look as if they were going so very fast either, but they must do, to keep up. Anyway it was an impressive & cheering sight, – pleasantly contrasting with an awful Sunday in June when we could see & hear no planes round here, & we wondered if our last fighters & even trainers had been thrown into the battle in France!

Last Sunday an unfortunate bomber (not one of those giants) went sailing round & round above the village for six hours. The landing wheel was jammed & they kept up as long as their petrol lasted, trying to get it down. Finally they had to make a "pancake" landing which the pilot managed with extraordinary skill, to the admiring applause of 3 villages. We did not applaud when a damaged bomber returning from Germany crashed into houses in Histon Rd, the pilot & crew having baled out 10 miles away. It is true only 3 old women were killed, but what w. the road deaths, many of wh. are said to be due to furious driving by the army & now the R.A.F. chucking aeroplanes about like this it is a hard world for civilians!! (N.B. This crash, with details of place & time was given out on the wireless so I hope the censor will not say I am giving away information to the enemy).

... We continue to have our usual large parties on Sundays (w. rabbit pie as the invariable first course) ...

On 11th March 1941 Helen wrote to her father:

... Yesterday I was saying to Lady Astor that "Men are a positive menace to any county" – or at least boys are! The entire boy population of our village seems to have been involved in carrying off our precious watering trough for the cows, & launching it on the stream, where it finally sank! After much "it wasn't me it was the other fellow" we finally tracked down the four principally responsible & they retrieved it.

If they had owned up straight away my sympathies would have been very much w. the culprits, because sailing a bath down the stream when it is in flood is a feat that any right minded boy <u>ought</u> to have attempted long ago, – (only not in my cow trough)!!

Yours affct Helen Bowen Pease

In her letter to Chenda dated March 13th to 19th she wrote:

... Last night I bicycled over to Impington College. It was a brilliant moon and an 'alert' on & really felt most romantic what with the lovely night & the feeling of unseen men on the watch all round. At Histon crossing a train came up with lovely puffs of white smoke & went by, an immense long snake of dark trucks.

... Well, thank goodness the winter is over now, & it has not been bad at all. We thought it would very likely be awful with epidemics following the bombing raids. Now we are ready to meet the next blow. I am glad the U.S.A. is to send food, & I hope they get it over here! We have been well fed so far, and it is no good blinking the fact that well fed people can stand up to things much more bravely than underfed ones! So tell them to supply us well against next winter.

Did you know that Geo Rendel, our Minister in Sofia, whom they nearly blew up is your cousin? i.e. he is first cousin to both my father & mother. ... He is a bit like my Father to look at, having the long Rendel head & big jaw.

Here is part of the Wedgwood – Rendel pedigree, to stick in your copy of Father's book. I can't get in nearly all of them! You may remember we met a Jim Rendel in Edinburgh. Do not 'wave' your pedigree about. Ones ancestors though often comforting & strengthening to oneself are not interesting to other people! (unless they are somebody very special!).

Did you hear Grandfather's broadcast to the U.S.A on March 17? ... Good old Rooseveldt. He made a great speech which cheered us up a lot. Not that we are gloomy now by any means, but it is great to feel we & the U.S.A. are really now at one ...

Again on 1st April Helen sounded cheerful:

... Well this has been a cheerful week. Last Monday when the Jugoslavs seemed to have surrendered we all

said *"There, whenever we have a day of National Prayer somebody <u>always</u> surrenders the very next day! The Archbishop should be sent to the Tower!!! However we can't say that now! Uncle Nickie says gloomily that he is afraid the events of this week will give a deplorable 'boost' to state religion! Anyway whether it was the Archbp. or Mr Amery's broadcast (<u>in Serbian</u>!) we have won our first diplomatic victory. May things still be going well by the time you get this. It is a satisfaction to have finally wiped the floor with Mussolini, Garibaldi said "Woe to the Italian who shall not help England in her hour of need", what he would have said about an attempted stab in the back I don't know!*

... It is still disgustingly cold & wet, (wh. may be the reason we have had no air raids to speak of) & of course both cows must choose two successive wet days to calve, & you know our shed won't hold more than one. However all was well, & until I can sell one cow & calf next week we are <u>flooded</u> with milk.

We have started school meals for our own & evacuated school children (over 100 'vacs' now) The numbers swell daily. I go to take a table twice a week. It is really very nice. We manage a good meal for 4d, & now have over 60 children & they seem to enjoy themselves. It takes place in the Village Institute which we have got back from the soldiers. We have a good number of such school feeding centres now, and if Cambridge is 'blitzed', they will come in useful for the population.

... Grandfather doesn't yet know when he will be able to get to U.S.A. It is extremely difficult to get a passage except on <u>vital</u> Govt. work, – & after the things Father has said about him we doubt if Lord Halifax would declare Father to be indispensable in America!!

... I have sold the cow & calf today but I don't know yet what I got. Not much I shd think because she is small. The 3 of them have 'poached' the top of the field badly in all this wet, so, as the pasture is destroyed there we shall probably use it for the extra potatoes we have been ordered to plant.

We are praying those poor devils of Greeks & Jugoslavs are managing to hold out, and that we've managed to send effective help. There is no news to speak of tonight. It is extraordinarily plucky of the Jugs to resist considering how they are placed. And what a difference it may make to shortening the war if only they can! ...

On 25th April Helen wrote:

... We are all well though unhappy about Greece & Libya. Of course, as I said in my last, we knew fighting the Germans in Greece wd be a very different business from licking the Italians, still one did hope for better things even though Churchill always said we should have to be on the defensive all this year. Oh well, one doesn't feel as bad as in last June & July before we knew the strength of the R.A.F. & of our own people at home.

... Congrats on your good results in your French exam. I can't quite get the name of the book you were reading? You say 'Lord Cecil Robert Russell' by his wife, which sounds queer to me. There is Lord Robert Cecil (now Viscount Cecil), great League of Nations man etc. (& the most distinguished of Grandfather's 2nd cousins) & there are several Russells. Cecil Hanbury who owned La Mortala where we had our honeymoon is someone quite different.!

... I am starting to make cheese, – not just the cream cheese, but the real kind that can be kept for the winter.

... We haven't had a bomb in Girton yet, we feel rather neglected as practically everywhere round here has at least one hole to show. The factory got one the other day – in broad daylight too, just like 'their' cheek, but no harm was done.

Our precious village colleges are all untouched (& being what Daddy calls in the 'starfish style' & only one storey it is extremely unlikely that they would be much damaged even if hit) ...

On 29th May Helen wrote:

... I hope by the time you get this that Grandfather will have arrived ... The flat had another near hit just after he left, in the last bad blitz. I am glad I took a good look at the House of Commons & Westminster Hall when I went up to see him off. Blast those Germans. I don't suppose we shall have any historical buildings left by the time the war is over.

I expect you listened in to Rooseveldt's speech yesterday? I listened to a recording of it. It was splendid. One can imagine what might have happened to the <u>world</u> by now if a different sort of man had been President & America had been afflicted with the sort of Govt we had until a year ago.

We have been very busy – this 'double summer time' which means it isn't dark now till after 11, gives one no free time in the evening, – one seems to be doing the cows & ducks etc. until bedtime & as it has been very cold we haven't had the advantage of being able to sit in the garden. I am just getting over a nasty cold, but as it is only my second in a whole year I suppose I can't complain.

... The garden is looking lovely with hyacinths & the fruit blossom, – only it makes us miss you all worse than ever. It is true the 150 evacuee children in the village give us a family to attend to, but it is not quite the same thing!!!

By the way we wanted to send you a bit of jewelry by Grandfather but he had to swear he was taking <u>no</u> jewelry but his tie pin! So don't think it was because we forgot you! And he has got to keep himself in the States by lectures & writing. They are (quite rightly) very particular about everybody in the matter of taking money or valuables abroad. I only hope he won't overwork himself. He was looking forward to the visit like a child going to the seaside! He loves (& idealises!) America. I wish he had got across in time to hear Rooseveldt's speech.

... With very very much love from us all & thank you so much for your nice long letters. We do so love getting them & they cheer us up (in a <u>not</u> very cheerful world!)

In June that year Helen and Michael went to Barlaston to stay with Helen's first cousin Tom Wedgwood. Helen's brother Jos V was Managing Director and proudly gave them a tour round the new Works. The estate was landscaped with an ornamental lake and bridge. At that time in June there were lots of bluebells with other flowers and shrubs.

Michael had to return to Cambridge before Helen and she stayed with her Aunt Kate (Uncle Felix's widow) until the end of the week. She enjoyed a complete rest. On the Friday she went to the Ark to sort out some of Camilla's things in the loft. She ended up at the Lea where her father had been born. It was comforting to be surrounded by so many cousin and other family members.

The following letter on 15th June 1941 is written from 'c/o Mrs Wedgwood, Barlaston, Stoke on Trent, Staffs' where Helen was visiting, this was the home of Helen's first cousin Tom Wedgwood, son of Uncle Frank:

Here I am just finishing a very nice holiday in Staffordshire. Daddy & I came up 10 days ago to Crewe to see his various poultry experiments, & I spent a happy morning watching cheese-making at the Cheshire Agricultural station. It is a bit hard that the girls who make it are only allowed their ration of 1oz a week – with rows of great cheeses ripening in the store!

We stopped with Aunt Kate [Uncle Felix's widow] *(who lives near Crewe) ... Daddy & I lunched at the new Works with Jos* [V] *& Tom & Joy* [Jos's first cousins] *& went all over them afterwards. It happened to be a lovely day & the woods & coppices round, right up to the Works door were full of bluebells. By means of tactful notices Tom has managed to persuade the work people not to pick them. It was so nice to see the crowds of people coming out in to the lovely avenue instead of in to that awful old grimy Etruria street. If only we could have got the garden village built before the war! There have been a few bombs dropped in the Potteries but you couldn't notice it, the place is such a mess at the best of times, it looks normally rather like London after a "blitz"!*

Daddy went home on Monday, where Joanna is keeping house for me, & I stopped till Friday with Aunt Kate, having a complete rest, except for one excursion to the old Works to buy "seconds". Dunlop's tyre people have taken over part of it & they showed me round.

Friday I went to the Ark & tried to sort out Aunt Camilla's [Helen's sister] *things out of the awful mess in the loft. I posted you & Dora some of her books. Aunt Rosie* [Rosamund] *& I lunched in the wood. Doge has gone to his job at Farnborough & Aunt Rosie will go too as soon as they can get rooms or a house there. The Azaleas & Rhodendrons are all out at the Ark & looking perfectly lovely. Then we walked over to the Lea for supper, & I am stopping there. The Lea is full of paying guests – technicians at some of the big works round here. Cousin Tom is not really well yet, but is back at the Works. Susan & Allan his two children (you saw them at the foundation stone laying 3 yrs ago) are each 6 months older than Dora & Fabian, & seeing them makes me miss my dear babies more than ever.*

We all went up to the Works pools & sailed Tom's rubber canoe & had great fun. ... Yesterday I lunched & tea'd with Jos & Ros & went to supper with Jos, to Aunt Iris [Helen's Uncle Ralph's wife] *– who is living in Cousin John's* [Iris's son] *house near Stone. Uncle Ralph was there too, so we had a semi-political evening ...*

Now I am sitting on a bench in the Lea garden as, for once, it is a lovely day & the place looking almost as it did when I played in it forty years ago.

Joanna passed her exam 2nd class!! ...

Back home in Girton on 22nd June, under her address Helen has put 'Invasion of Russia'. She wrote to Chenda:

Just been listening to Churchill's speech. Well, well, poor Uncle Joe. But I'm afraid it means Hitler is pretty sure he can get to Moscow in a month, & its a poor look out for us if he gets the corn & oil & makes himself safe on his eastern front. No one can say this is a dull war!!

289

One of Seb's young communist friends came to lunch, so we all fell upon him for his 'views'. He wouldn't give any – we said because he hadn't had time to get any orders from Moscow. But perhaps he was merely overwhelmed by the Pease voices. Bassy, by the way, has a fine catholic taste in friends, they range from the highly religious to ardent communists. Both he says attempt to convert him without making any impression.

Mike is reading Veronica's [Ralph and Iris's daughter] book on the 'Thirty Years War' which he says is extremely good reading.

I got back from Staffs last Monday after a very pleasant & restful 12 days. I feel ever so much better for the holiday, & very much enjoyed meeting & hearing of the Tribe. ... Idlerocks reminds one of the houses of decaying aristocrats in Russian novels – everyone, including the exiguous staff, a bit cracked. Only instead of discussing their souls they play bridge, while the cobwebs & dilapidations grow & the cows & chickens die ...

In the expressive words of P.G.W. my cows are what-the-helling so I had better go & milk them. It has been blazing hot today & I've put it off till 10.30 p.m ...

In her letter of 30th June Helen mentioned that while at the Lea she had asked Joy to find some family photographs for her as she wished to collate an album for her children so that they would recognise their many relatives. That album now exists and is a wonderful memorial to many relatives. In that letter she continued:

Needless to say it was Mrs Matthews who first brought me a paper with the news of Father's illness – a whole column in the Evening News. But I judge it was just one of his usual attacks. He will get them if he rushes about – the last one he had was in the middle of the blitz with the electric light cut off! So he is safer in New Jersey!

... On Thursday Daddy & Seb & Joanna & I went on the river & we did miss you so much. We took two canoes & got up as far as the chestnut avenue at Harston & had a lovely lazy day – at least I did because I had

strained my arm & couldn't paddle so the others had all the work! The wild roses & the elderflower were out in all the hedges, & many of the pollarded willows have wild rose trees growing in them, so that trails of roses were tangled among the willow leaves and there were numbers of dragonflies, dark blue-&-black ones. Overhead the giant bombers roared – a comforting sound, though you might not think it. They go over us every night to raid Germany & come back in the early morning & we are thankful to hear them when we remember this time last year when the sky was clear & we wondered where our air force was & if it still existed.

... However, thank goodness the Russians haven't crumpled yet. It is a poor look out for us if Hitler gets to Moscow, & if they only can hold him up the war may be over much sooner than we dared to hope ...

On 8th July Helen wrote:

... It has been blazing hot this last fortnight & we have just got the hay in today before a thunderstorm broke; quite a good storm but only a sprinkling of rain here, dash it all. The round bed on the lawn is filled with potatoes – a sample plot to make us look patriotic – really of course Daddy put them there to kill the celandine ...

In her letter of 27th July Helen said:

... It was very sweet of you to send the tea, & it is very good, one little packet makes four cups! A large parcel also arrived from the Dunbars which looks so beautiful in its cases we have stuck them on the dining room bureau as an ornament! It is most awfully kind of them to have taken so much trouble, and it is very nice to get extra luxuries like that, especially as we can then use our ordinary ration for some of the multitudes of visitors & evacuees who are glad of "a cup of tea". Only I feel rather bad about it, because we ourselves, living in the country, are not <u>really</u> short of anything & it is perhaps

taking precious shipping space, however small, for our private luxuries.

... You have got Aunt Kate mixed up with Cousin Lucie, who was Phoebe's mother & died just before the war. Aunt Kate is Uncle Felix's widow (He wrote books & was killed in the last war) & Felicity, Frances & Cecil, whose clothes & toys you all had, are her children. Frances's husband was a clergyman but threw it up to join the air force & is now a rear-gunner & has been to Berlin several times ...

I don't expect you saw much of Grandfather who seems to have been dashing about a lot, – besides getting in to a row by saying rude things about Senator Wheeler! I couldn't get hold of a newspaper which told about it so I don't know the details! He is a terribly impetuous man! Anyway please take note that when you are in somebody else's country you must be careful what you say. It wouldn't matter if he had told the Archbishop of Canterbury to "go & soak his head", but people won't take from a foreigner what they will from a fellow countryman.

I have just shocked Dr Walton, who was urging me to join the 'Soc for Cultural Relations with Russia' by saying that I am bored stiff with Russia! & that they ought to be (& are from Stalin's remarks) jolly grateful to us for not surrendering last year! They would *have been in the soup.*

Thank goodness they are putting up a grand fight. And one can admire people for resisting invasion bravely without liking them in other ways! And hope & pray they may succeed too. What a difference it will make if they do! But it was we English *who saved ourselves & the world last year, & I'm not going to let my communist friends forget it either! ...* [1]

Chapter 40

LETTERS – BARONETCY FOR JOSIAH IV

On 3rd August 1941 Helen wrote from Bedales, Petersfield:

... Daddy & I are down at the O.B. weekend. I am stopping with Cousins Gilbert & Dorothy. Yesterday we lunched with Father at Dolphin Square. He seems to have enjoyed seeing you very much, & also meeting Mr Dunbar. I wish he had seen the babies too but he was offered this place on the clipper & took it while it was open. We didn't realise the Senator Wheeler episode took place at Cambridge with Mr Dunbar! In fact I have not yet seen an account of it, having missed the newspapers here in which it is reported, & Father is a bit sore about it, so I didn't ask him. I hope Mr Dunbar wasn't upset. However somebody in the House of Commons asked Dorothy Thompson whether Father had done harm in America & she said "not at all, a lot of good".

However, as I told Father, it has now passed in to history as a charade episode, along w Alfred & the cakes. When Cousin Maud had her 80th birthday party we acted a Nebuchadnezr & took Darwin (consonants only) – & for 'W' we did Wedgwood (or Wheeler!) Daddy was Mr Dunbar & Hugh Cornford was Father & the rest were reporters, with soft hats on one side of their heads & large notebooks! For the whole word we made Horace Barlow act Darwin – in, I should think, the original black cloak –

293

& a beard. Daddy put bowls of flowers all over the carpet & the rest of us were worms & wriggled about while Horace examined us. Quentin Keynes' brothers Milo & Stephen were there & Bill's & Charles' sons & daughters & a few aged friends of the family, & it was good fun.

... On Monday & Tuesday we expect to be at Borden Wood with the Lambs. I am glad to get Daddy away for a bit of holiday as he needs it, – & there is no peace at all to be got at home. By the way we bicycle from Liverpool St to Dolphin Square. The smashing up in the city round St Paul's is pretty awful & Daddy lost his way once! & we also lost it round Waterloo. What puzzles me is where people live most of the houses have their windows out, but there are still a lot of people about. When you look over the vast expanse of London from the balcony of Father's flat it <u>looks</u> unchanged except for one or two obvious gaps. It is only when you go close you see what a lot is empty walls ...

In her letter of 24th August Helen talked about Grandfather. She said:

... He told us principally about you, & of his talk w. Mr Dunbar & also of his visit to poor old Bertrand Russell and of his addressing a meeting in Virginia along with the Archduke Felix of Austria! who afterwards came to see him. ... Hitler certainly can perform some miracles, what w. Churchill shaking hands w Stalin & Father working in with a <u>Catholic</u> ex-emperor.

We are all well & happy (at least as happy as w can be during a war & in the absence of you & the babies). Joanna goes to a place near Berwick tomorrow to do a month's harvest work. Daddy made her read up Sir Walter Scott in the Encyclopedia first, so that she should have some knowledge of the places round there. Bassy is also going to a friend's in Lancashire for a week, until he has to come back here to register for military service. They will almost certainly let him finish his two years here, so he is very unlikely to be called up till next July ...

On 29th August Helen wrote:

Your birthday letter & parcel to me, dated June arrived a day or two ago!! It was ever so sweet of you to send me such lovely stockings & the little packet of tea, and also the school magazine which we were <u>very</u> pleased to have, & especially the photo with you in it. ... The stockings are beautiful & will do for when I want to be smart, as I haven't bought any for ages, – & don't expect to till the war is over. Even <u>I</u> have taken to going stockingless at home, though I cannot bring myself to going to Cambridge 'unclad' ...

Don't bother to send 'useful' things. What with customs etc they get so delayed; & besides the ships <u>ought</u> to be filling odd corners with important food & not taking private parcels of any size. If you want to send food etc. for Christmas the sort of things we can't get now are <u>curry powder</u> & other spices (except cocoa) chocolate, figs etc. ... The curry powder & spices will come in very useful when food is dull ...

On 22nd September Helen wrote:

Many happy returns of the day! I expect this will arrive about the right time. ... Dear old Chen, it is awful to think you are 16 & have been away more than a year. We miss you all terribly, but you are having a good time & apart from everything else it is a great thing to know another country besides your own, & the more English who know America & vice versa the better for after the war ...

Bassy had his interview last week & is to be allowed to stop up to take his Tripos next May.

Yes I <u>do</u> still give coffee at L.P. cttees etc. & invasion committees. I'm not going to let Hitler stop decent hospitality. In fact it is much more worth while in war time ... <u>I</u> can't say that giving coffee inconveniences us at all, we are really perfectly well off in this house, so don't bother about us ...

Helen wrote on 20th October:

... we still remain unbombed. The nearest we have had were some small ones a little while ago that managed to get the sewer, water main, electric light & telephone cables in the main road opposite what used to be Cousin Ida Darwin's house. Her fence was blown to bits & Mrs Roothams basement filled with paving stones, house fronts ripped off etc. – quite spectacular & no one hurt. All we knew of it at the time was that our lights went out ...

We are busy harvesting beans, wh. have been very good this year, & the army hut is full of boxes to be shelled!

On 4th November Helen said:

... Poor Grandfather had all his luggage and the manuscript of his new book sunk on the way over, – so it is just as well he came by clipper & not by that boat! ...

Helen's last letter of 1941, written on 10th December, was immediately after the Japanese attacked the United States Pacific fleet at Pearl Harbor in Hawaii. Helen asked Chenda to be discreet about the contents of this particular letter when talking with Americans:

I expect, as Daddy says, you have been going about these last 3 days with your eyes popping out of your head with excitement. Poor old Yanks, kicked into it from behind & by the Japs too! No chance of taking the 'high Maural Tone' & intervening when they felt like it at the right moment. Well if any Americans ever get 'fresh' with you, you remind them that you are English, & the British Empire is the only belligerent, who deliberately went into the war to keep their word & because somebody had got to stop Hitler and we went into it though the 'authorities' expected immediate devastating raids on London & 200,000 civilian casualties! We at least didn't wait to be kicked in, like every other country (except the poor old French). It was of course a beautiful instance (though deplorably belated!) of the English capacity for seeing their 'interest on the same side as their duty' (see Bernard Shaw, 'The Man of Destiny'). And jolly lucky for us too, or I suppose we should have waked up one morning to find the fleet sunk & London occupied. And I just wonder where the Yanks think they & the rest of the world would be if we hadn't held out last year! For that at least Heaven should forgive this country's many sins of omission & commission.

I don't think you had better read this letter to any American. You see we really can't help chortling at seeing them so unceremoniously booted in, bad as the outlook is for us in many ways. Thank goodness the Russian successes are a bright gleam in the darkness. May they keep it up ...

On the 10th December Josiah IV wrote to Helen saying Winston Churchill had offered him a baronetcy – he also talked about a substitute if he dropped out of his Labour position – either Josiah V or Helen herself might be suitable?

Helen wrote by return on 11th:

Well! well! well! ... Is it Winston's personal friendship, or to make the honours list look respectable? I wonder what Charles & Hugh will say? A title is rather an expensive adornment. Is it to be Lord Wedgwood of Wolstanton, or Moddershall? (see PCW where the news magnate writes out possible titles to see which looks best). Anyway it is splendid you have got some recognition at last, but there will be many who will wonder how they can possibly get on without Josh in the Commons.

I am writing to Fanny Deakin. I don't expect I have a dog's chance but we can't let Newcastle go to a party hack like Will Henderson by default! Personally I think if Jos won't take it (& I really don't see how his health would stand any more) that John Hamilton should take it. He has been on the Stoke Town Council & would like the job, & his war service would make him pretty safe in the post war election, which will matter a good deal. If those two won't, & if N'castle will have me, I will take it, though truly I do not at all like that kind of life, but I think it would be shirking not to offer.

Mike thinks so too, though it really would be a bit thick for him. He does hate me being away from home (I know you will make cynical remarks but it is true all the same) & if I got in, I should have to be away three or four nights a week. He would make a <u>much</u> better MP than me, but he must make the family living & there it is! However, with you to coach me in London & Mike to coach me here I ought to be an effective MP!

I had rather thought of having a last fling & having a shot at producing Joseph Winston (or possibly Josephine Sarah) & I certainly can't do both jobs. However, if N'castle turns me down perhaps I will console you by producing another grandchild instead. That also would be rather hard lines on Mike, it would be pure swank on my part – just to show I could. It certainly is the job I do best ...

Very very much love & congratulations

Your loving daughter Helen Pease

In 1942, despite Helen's aspirations to have a go at following in her father's footsteps as the MP for Newcastle-under-Lyme, this did not happen. She and Michael continued with their busy everyday life in Cambridge. Even now in the midst of a worldwide war, Helen's letters, although serious when writing about the war, still have that air of hope and optimism running through them. Her letters continued to give Chenda a picture of an almost normal life at Reynolds Close. Helen now hoped that some time during 1942 Chenda would be able to return home. However this did not happen until 1943.

Helen wrote to Chenda on 6th January, but did not post the letter until the 21st.

My last letter was about Dec 12; shocking, but I know Daddy has written twice & Joanna once since then. Your lovely box of spices arrived safely except for a slight spill of allspice, which fell out on to the little table in the dining room & scented the place so nicely that Miss Senser would not let Mrs Matthews dust it off. They will be most useful & precious, especially as spices etc. will now probably be quite unobtainable.

Daddy looks very smart in your stockings & they have washed beautifully so far. Aunt Camilla sent Jo & me knitted hoods + waistcoats so we are quite well set up. I am giving Jo a blueish skirt & blouses wh. will go well with your green jersey. What with coupons <u>and</u> the price clothes are now one really has to be careful. On the other hand one needn't mind going about shabby, as it now merely looks patriotic, which saves one a lot of bother.

Jan 21 I never sent this because Daddy said he had just posted one, – & here it is a fortnight later ...

Grandfather Wedgwood came last Sat. to speak in Cambridge & stopped the night with us. He is very wild because our Col. Blimps have never armed & trained the Chinese & Malayans to defend themselves (& us!). He is trying to get them to start a Home Guard in India. Pretty necessary too, with the Japs cavorting all over the place ...

The Russian successes are so cheering we feel good in spite of Malaya & Singapore. If the U.S.A. & our brass hats don't pull up their socks it is <u>Uncle Joe</u> who will dictate the peace terms in Europe while we are still busy with the Japs & won't Big Business be annoyed with the Red flag flying from Vladivostock to Cadiz!!

... I have been frantically busy these six weeks, & this week Mrs Matthews (who was very pleased to get your letter) scalded her arm badly & has not been to work. Did I mention that poor Mr Kearsey is very ill, & I have had to take on the Sec & Treasureship of the Divisional Party, on top of everything else, so I really have <u>some</u> excuse for being behindhand with things. Besides with the clothes shortage there is such a lot of patching & mending to do.

Did Daddy tell you the Bells sent us a lovely coloured

film of the babies? We went over to Impington Village
College where they have a projector the right size. ... It
was a bit jerky, but really good colours & perfectly sweet
of the babies who have grown a lot. I do think it was a
nice idea of Mrs Bells.

... You mustn't go having nightmares about us! But if
you can get a passage & if it isn't too dangerous I think
you must come home in the autumn. It will be too awful
here with Joanna & Bassy gone. But you will find it very
dull after Boston, I fear! You could live at home & coach
for a Newnham Scholarship. But you must do well in
your entrance exam to Radcliffe as that will get you into
Newnham. Besides it may not be possible to get home.
They say we are to be allowed to send a little money to
you & the babies – but it will only amount to about the
billetting allowance for evacuees here. Still that would be
something ...

Helen and Joanna went up to London to see their father introduced
into the House of Lords and in her letter of 4th February Helen gave a
vivid description of the whole ceremony. Jos was happy because now
in the House of Lords no one could stop him from talking as often as
he pleased.

Just got your letter of Dec 31 about Aunt Anna's death.
We are so very sorry & I feel rather awful because I was
just in the middle of a long letter to her which I ought to
have sent ages ago in reply to her charming one to me.
Poor old Chen, it must have been a dreadful shock to you.
I do wish I had known her, she sounded such a splendid
person & she has been so kind to you. There is something
so terribly final about death. One finds oneself thinking,
"I must tell so & so this. It will amuse them" or "I must
remember to do something for them", – & they are not
there & never will be again.

Old ladies too are so often so much more to one when
one is young than middle-aged ones. The one that counted
most with me was my grandmother. We used to have such
long talks together & things she said & did come back

to me so often. *Florence has just given Joanna for her 21st birthday an amethyst brooch grandmother wore nearly every day. I remember it so well holding the lace on her black dress when she read to us.*

Last week Joanna & I went up to see Grandfather "introduced" into the House of Lords. We had lunch with him first in the H of Lords dining room, – & in case your American or other friends think the aristocracy guzzles in war time, I may tell you that lunch was soup, liver & bacon with carrots & potatoes, & <u>stewed prunes</u> (without cream or custard) It is true there were alternatives, but of the same plain style. Also we <u>did</u> have sherry.

Two bishops sat at the table next us & the Lord Chancellor (once Sir John Simon ...) at another. I was feeling even more irreverent than usual, which embarrassed Joanna because I asked Father for a 'tip' on who is to be the new archbishop as I thought we might have a sweep on it in the village – the proceeds to go to the Aid for Russia. Also when he said "There is the Lord Chancellor, whose hand I am going to kiss" I said "<u>That</u> Man. If Bassy gets killed I am going to shoot him" (Simon was the chief wrecker of the League of Nations & responsible for letting the Japs go ahead in Manchuria ...")

Then we went up into the gallery with Fingwan's aunt & cousins, – Fingwan & your cousin Veronica Wedgwood went in below. The H of L meets now in a smallish room as the Commons meet in what used to be the Lords Chamber, so it wasn't so impressive. The Lord Chancellor, in wig, red robes & a 3 cornered hat sat on the red woolsack. Grandfather came in, walking between his sponsors, – Lord Quickswood (better known as Lord Hugh Cecil) his 3rd cousin & Lord Wardington (once Beaumont Pease), – Daddy's 3rd cousin & a very old friend of Father's, all 3 in lovely red robes. The king's "patent" conferring the barony was read & then Grandfather, kneeling, took it from the Ld Chancellor, & afterwards took the oath of allegiance – & that was all.

... However Grandfather says he expects to have the

time of his life in the H of L because nobody can stop him there from saying what he likes & talking as often as he pleases! And indeed our few Labour peers there seem to do very well. Grandfather spoke on India last night ...

The war news is not particularly cheerful, except for the Russians, God bless them! General MacArthur in the Phillipines is magnificent ...

In a postscript to this letter Helen said:

Do you realise I am now addressed as <u>The Hon</u>. Mrs P. J.P. CC! In fact on the County Council I am the <u>only</u> "honourable", – & one of the leading "Reds" ...

On 21st February Helen wrote:

... Poor Aunt Camilla. I expect they are getting in a stew in Australia. The curious thing is they don't seem really to have expected it, but many of us (I mean us thinking persons) rather assumed the Japs would swoop on Australia 18 months ago, – which was partly why we did not send you & the babies out there to her.

I think the Australians are a bit hard on us in this country. The fault does not lie in the last 18 months, & it is all very well to say we are too much afraid of invasion here. After all the Germans are only 30 miles off & nearly all round us, & we have no room to retreat or take up strategic positions or anything, so we must keep ourselves ready. And Tokyo is 4000 miles (is it?) away from Australia.

... We hope to God the Yanks are taking the war seriously. But it must be rather easy for them not to. I mean, look at us here! 18 months ago "nothing but the mercy of God & 50 Spitfires" (to parody the Cardinal in St Joan) "stood between us & Damnation", & <u>then</u> we had 8 months blitz & we <u>may</u> be invaded whenever Hitler thinks we are easier game than the Russians, and still we are not what I should call <u>really all out</u>. So one can hardly expect the Yanks who are thousands of miles

from the enemy & live in a huge country to be really "war consciousness".

You may have seen in the papers that the Cambridgeshires & Suffolks were in Singapore, so people are hard hit all round here. ... Ordinary people seem to me much angrier & more humiliated by Singapore than by Dunkirk (say). In the case of Dunkirk 1) they did not grasp the full disaster 2) we saved so many more than we expected 3) we were let down by all those wretched foreigners 4) we expect the Germans to be a match for us. Singapore is us alone being defeated & by the Japanese!! The first bad breach in the Empire. And of course the simultaneous spectacle of the Russians going ahead rubs it in that somehow we governing class have 'let the country down again'.

... Daddy has just been reading us a cheering (& very amusing) article from the Eugenics Review on the fall in the birthrate in England & Germany during the war. 8% was our biggest decline on the pre-war rate & that was not in babies conceived during the Blitz, they were only 6% less than prewar. But in Germany, on their own showing 30% less babies were born last year than before the war (& that can't take into account any possible effects of the Russian Campaign) ... rather a new angle for assessing 'morale' ...

Helen's letter of 9th March said:

... I hope your Fabian speech went off well. What Granpa did not tell you was that he gave up the Stock Exchange & the certainty of a comfortable income to become the 1st Sec. Of the Fabian Society at £200 a year, – wh was all he got from them till he retired.

We've been writing to Eric's father North Whitehead, (who is at the Foreign Office as liaison officer, w. the U.S.A.) about getting you home this autumn. It may not be possible but if you want to get a passage you had better act now. Mr Whitehead has written to Mr. Tollington, British Consulate General at Boston, to give you every help.

... Mr Whitehead says see Mr Tollington, & not Mr Ford, the Consul General, because the latter 'has an unholy fear of girls!' mention Mr Whitehead's name to Mr Tollington when you write or call. Enclosed is a letter from us to hand to Mr Tollington when you call, as they may require evidence that you have your parents permission to come home ...

It is thrilling to think that you may be home this autumn. We miss you terribly – especially Daddy. By the way, better not tell the babies you may be coming home; we thought at first if you could spend a holiday in Canada & come from there it would be nice. But better not. Though they are very happy & thriving there, they might feel hurt & that we 'did not want them' if they saw you leaving for home without them.

Helen wrote on 15th March:

... I am sorry you distressed yourself & the Dunbars by showing them my letter of Dec 6th. I suppose I ought to have been more careful what I wrote, & you must remember before you show letters that a remark like mine looks worse in writing, esp. as they don't know us. Besides Americans are apt to take that sort of chaff a lot more seriously than we mean it!

Of course they couldn't come in to the war until a majority of their people wanted it, – just as the majority of our people accepted Munich & all the rest of our disgraceful foreign policy, wh. was a lot worse than theirs. And people like us & the Dunbars were in the minority – & are now proved right. I bet the Chinese are chortling (to use the phrase in my letter) over Singapore, & at having to help us in Burma! Mrs Vellacott & the others in the village with boys in Singapore are in an awful state after the revelations of the Hong Kong atrocities, Oh God, what a world.

... Yes the Pearl Harbour report was pretty startling, – but the cheering thing about it, it was not the home Govt. that was to blame, (unlike Dunkirk) so one can

feel confident for the future. MacArthur too is simply splendid, about the only general on our side who seems to have thought things out beforehand & prepared for all contingencies ...

In her letter of 6th April Helen wrote:

... Yesterday as Mrs Leakey & I were looking at her goats & new kids & discussing kidding & milking in all its aspects (most technical & agricultural) two men visitors turned up for her. I went off home & next day one of the visitors turned up here just after breakfast. It was Mr Stopford, Quentin's [Keynes] boss from the British Embassy at Washington!! whom we used to know well as children, as Bobby Stopford. I hadn't seen him since he came out here 20 years ago, though I have written to him at various times (mostly about refugees as he was in Prague before the war). However we were quits because he hadn't recognised me either. He used to insist on being called an <u>Irishman</u>, & his sisters were involved in the old troubles in Ireland, but we don't rub that in too much, now he is respectable.

Anyway he said he was working Quentin hard at dull honest work wh. he thought was good for him! I bet it is too. So we got a bit of American news (as heard in Washington). He said he thought you would be able to get a sea passage all right & that at present anyhow it was not too dangerous.

Uncle Jos [Helen's brother Jos V] is to become a director of the Bank of England!! There's glory for you. This family is going up in the world. We expect it is Keynes' doing, as Jos certainly has no "financial interests" backing him. Anyway he is young (for such a job) & ought to liven them up a bit.

Yesterday Easter Sunday two striking omens occurred. First a <u>terrific</u> thunderclap quite unexpectedly out of a blue sky w. white clouds – quite what you would expect people to think the 'Voice of God', & half an hour later a perfectly lovely rainbow, – the complete half circle (see *your Bible on the rainbow as the arc of promise). So that ought to mean something good for this year oughtn't it? Unless of course the Germans had them too, which would be too bad.*

On 17th April Helen wrote:

... The House of Lords in this war is really perking up. Even without Grandfather there are some quite lively people in it, who don't mind hitting out. But I am feeling too sick about the war news altogether to talk about it all. There are a terrible lot of people from round here missing in Singapore ...

If only the news would improve too! Bless the Russians, how awful it would have been & be now but for them.

We get nice letters from Dora now, & even Fabs can write. They sound extraordinarily well & happy. They will find Girton very dull when they come home, – especially as Mrs Bell draws them such rosy pictures of England!!

... Daddy has been re-reading Paradise Lost, – to keep pace with you. I haven't been reading much, – except P.G. Wodehouse & a history of the Charity School movement in the 18th century, – very interesting, though it doesn't sound so. Picture Post has not yet brought out the article about Daddy's hens, – rather annoying as they might just as well have let him have more time to write it ...

The daffodils are all out & looking marvellous, & the apricot has been a mass of blossom. If much of it sets we shall have to thin the fruit. The spring has been so late that the plum blossom is not out yet & it looks as if plum, pear & apple will all be out together ...

On 6th May Helen said:

... Mr Dunbar wrote to us both, saying you won't be finished school for another year & urging us to let you stay on with them. They are good. If they really feel like that it seems a pity to interrupt your work again. But we are waiting for your letter before we answer. We do want

you home dreadfully, but if Mr & Mrs Dunbar really think it best you should remain with them, and you are happy & (reasonably) good it seems foolish not to accept their kindness. No more till we hear from you.

Last week Bassy had a big 'event'. He & Hugh Cornford (vice chairman & chairman) are running the very successful University Labour Club, – Bas has become very keen politically this last year. The admirable secretary button holed Morrison (the Home Secretary in case you are now too American to know who Herbert Morrison is!) & persuaded him to speak for the Labour Club in the Guildhall. Great excitement & anxiety on the part of the organisers. Nearly all the Bedalians Justin Brookes niece, & Horace Barlow (another Darwin cousin) were involved. Rumours rushing round that the Communists & the Boat Club were going to make a row. Stubbs & I were invited on the platform as we had both spoken to the club.

Well, the meeting was packed (Daddy who foolishly came lateish couldn't get in). Hugh Cornford in the chair with Morrison on one side & Bas on the other. A bunch of communists in the body of the hall & the Boat club packed on the orchestra seats, – prepared to barrack each other as well as Morrison. However, I told Hugh not to worry, I knew Morrison. And I was right, – he completely settled both parties & in the most good tempered & cheerful way. He spoke admirably, I don't think I've ever heard a speech more exactly right for the audience. He has a knack of giving a good fighting speech without oratory & with a sense of humour, but with a feeling of power & passion behind. I am sending you the report – it doesn't do Morrison justice, & it very carefully slides over the fighting things he said about socialism. I do wish you had been there.

He was very good at questions too. Of course the communists were all on about the continued suppression of the Daily Worker. I expect they were a bit sorry they drew Morrison on that! Because he read out the most <u>damning</u> quotations from that rag, & Jo said she heard *people saying as they left the room that they had no idea the D.W. had been as bad as that. (Personally I think Morrison might just as well let the paper start again now, but there is no doubt he wiped the floor with the communists).*

After the meeting Morrison came to coffee in Bas' rooms. – The Chief Constable of Cambridge had been meekly waiting in a doorway & followed them to Trinity to see the great man safely in!

... You may not have seen it in the American papers but there has been a great row because Morrison has just sacked the civil commissioner for London for writing abusively in the papers. Rather a long story, but Morrison came out top all right. As Morrison said cheerfully at the meeting "I wasn't going to have Sir Warren Fisher writing cheeky letters to the Home Secretary just because I'm a Labour man" In fact one in the eye for the old School Tie ... He spent the night with Sir Will Spens, the regional commissioner ...

I am so pleased with Morrison for making Bassy's first political venture such a thundering success that he is welcome to suppress the Daily Worker & the Mirror & the Times too so far as I am concerned!! & the Labour Club members appear to feel the same! ...

Helen's letter of 8th June complained about previous letters having been censored and also about the shortage of goods.

It is annoying to have a book shortage as well as other things. It is funny the things you can't get, for instance washing blue & black lead for stoves! one seems to notice the absence of these little daily things more than, say, no bananas.

Wed. Yesterday the University Labour Club had a garden party (7–12) in our garden, about 80 people. I provided the 'eats' but they arranged everything & cut up themselves. We did wish for you. They are such a nice crowd of young things. Alas, most of them 'go down' this week, mostly into the army or the women's services, or to the hospitals, if budding doctors. So it was in the nature of a farewell gathering. Father was to have come but an important debate in the H of Lords (over the row there has been about his last broadcast to America re Palestine) kept him away at the last moment. So the Sec. of the Fabian Research Dept. came instead & was very good on Coal ... And dancing on the lawn till nearly 12 o'clock ...

I spent four days at the Nat. Labour Party Conference, as delegate from the Cambs. Labour Party. Very interesting ... we made some of the sleepy old Transport House gang sit up, & the vote was so near they won't try making us support the Tory candidates any more! Anyway we all felt cheered up after that day & knew there was plenty of life in the Party. I met lots of old friends, & also went to the flicks with Grandfather ...

Poor Chenda – in Helen's letter of 26th June the first page is taken up with telling her she must study, must not be distracted and must:

concentrate on school work ... only the next year or two to pass your exams & get a start in life, so Go To It!" Helen continued: "Bas & Jo have just passed their Triposes, 2nd class honours in both cases ... We hoped Seb would get a first, for if he had he would almost certainly have been told to stop up another year & do research. As it is he is probably going to do "operational research" whatever that may be, – he says he thinks it means sitting inside a tank & seeing what happens to it when it rolls over a bank!

... Now they are both spending a week in London at the Fabian research office, then Joanna comes back here to take pharmacology in the Long Vac. Afterwards she proposes to take a month working in a factory as part of a medical experiment on factory conditions & fatigue.

John (Wedgwood) turned up last week looking very handsome. He is at Guy's hospital at present & doing well.

... I suppose if they censored Daddy's remarks about Singapore I had better not say what Grandfather & we say about Tobruk! We seem to have lost even our capacity for 'brilliant strategic withdrawals'. If Americans get nasty about it to you, you can at least say that we have nothing in all our military or naval history as bad as Pearl Harbour! But that is not much consolation. If only we coud get a move on! when one thinks of all those poor starving devils in Europe hoping & praying that we may come soon & save them.

I must stop & write to the babies. I do hope you get to Canada this summer. In any case it would be a good plan to do a job for a few weeks, on the land if possible. Most girls of your age are doing something of the sort here. Mr Dunbar thinks it might be too strenuous for you; but if it was, you could drop it. One feels much the better for having earned pay & 'held down' a job even for a short while. Aren't any of the school children from your school going into camps on the land for harvesting or fruit picking?

Chapter 41

CENSORED LETTERS – JOSIAH IV
LORD WEDGWOOD OF BARLASTON DIES

Richenda went to Nova Scotia in July 1942 to be with her brother and sister. Helen's letter to her on 16th July again talked of her getting some work to do:

> *If you can get a real job on the land while you are stopping with Mrs Bell, I think it would be a good thing. Nearly all girls of your age in England are doing some such work in the holidays & really to work & earn money, even for a few weeks gives one experience & confidence. It is pretty hard work & Mrs Bell may be afraid of the company you would keep being a bit rough, but that is part of the experience. If you do nothing but play round for 2 months you will feel a bit of a slacker. So do talk to her seriously about it & see if there isn't something you can do, – not just an hour or so when you feel like it, but a regular up in the morning eight hour day for some weeks.*

Helen's letter on 31st July was heavily censored on both pages one and two. On 3rd August she continued:

> *Daddy & I are at Limpsfield on our way home from a weekend at Bedales, – very jolly. Aunt Ros & Uncle Doge were there. ... On the way across to Limpsfield*

*we went over Leith Hill, having tea w. Harvey Vaughan
Williams (Ralph V.W. the musician's brother) one of the
Darwin – Wedgwood cousins & then stopping the night
w. a cousin of Bertie Russell's, an old Bedalian. So we've
picked up quite a lot of old friends & relations. Leith Hill
was looking lovely, the woods like the Ark, but finer, &
magnificent view to the S & E over Surrey ...*

On 14th September, when Richenda is now back in Boston,
Helen's letter does not mention whether Chenda went out to work or
not, she just said: '*I am so glad you had such a good time in Canada
...*' This letter is again censored when Helen wrote about a raid on the
village:

[censored] *in the parish!! By a suitable irony they
fell on the experimental farm, Dr Walton's side, he is
head air raid warden!! Two ponies killed & a certain
number of pigs 'missing believed killed' Of course the
ponies would be two mares being used for important
pregnancy tests, one called Topsy, did you know her?
Daddy's casualties were one hen with its leg broken.
Also a number of unexploded bombs (or possibly they
exploded too deep underground to be noticed) fell in a
field especially set aside for land drainage experiments
– result some years research work gone west. No one was
hurt, though various cottages, some quite a way off, had
bits through them. The feature of the night was a most
magnificent display of flares – lovely stars appearing in
the sky one after the other till there were several groups
drifting slowly downward leaving winding trails of white
smoke, while each star dropped a golden necklace of
smaller stars. It beat any fireworks I've ever seen. What
they were up to we can't think. On seeing the flares we
supposed a terrific blitz was beginning but that dump of
bombs were the only ones. Village opinion is divided.
Walton's staff say it was a deliberate attack on his
precious experiments & point out that it was his mares
that were killed. Daddy's staff say it was really meant
for his hens – as a result of the article in Picture Post!*

More unbiased villagers say the Germans were really trying for [censored] *or* [censored]. *There is also a small official view who say the bombs were dumped in a hurry because the plane was being chased & got too low. This however considered a deplorably unpatriotic idea* [next line censored].

... Did I tell you by the way, that when we went to tea w. Harvey Vaughan Williams at Leith Hill we saw the picture by Romney of Bessie Wedgwood (Harvey's great grandmother & your great-great-grandmother). During the blitz he pt it under the billiard table with mattresses on top (this was sfr than storing it in London) To his horror when he took it out it was mildewed!! So he sent it to be cleaned & restored & now he is having a great row with the restorer because he says the eyes are brown when he sent it but have come back blue. The restr. says that blue was the original colour & they had been brown'd since! So now we search the family letters for any mention of the 'beautiful Bessis's' eye colour!!

I remember your cousin Maud Darwin telling me how when a bride, fresh from being a belle of Boston, she was taken to Leigh Hill place to meet the terrifying elders of the Darwin-Wedgwood clan (Josiah Wedgwood III of Leith Hill married C. Darwin's sister Caroline) & how alarmed of them all she was. I asked her if she didn't secretly parody the saying about Boston, & murmur about the place 'where the Wedgwoods speak to the Darwins & the Darwins speak only to God'. She said she hadn't thought of it, but that did exactly describe it!! – & does still a bit!

We are all well & busy. Bas hasn't had any orders yet, so has been having a holiday in Yorkshire with the Barlows & at the Fabian summer school. Joanna gets home for weekends from her hospital at Epsom, where she seems to be enjoying herself very much ...

Richenda's birthday came round again and Helen wished her a happy birthday in her letter of 1st October. She continued:

What a pity the censor chewed up my letter!!

... Daddy & I are having a very pleasant holiday in Yorkshire – Wensleydale. Today we went up a hill at the head of the dale & had a magnificent view all round. It was a perfect day for views, windy and sunny w. great cloud shadows passing over. We could see over the lake district & as far as the sea at Morecambe Bay & over the Eden valley. We did wish you had been with us. The Yorkshire dales are lovely, but not so good as Ireland because the colours are not so good and there is no sea. On the way up we stopped w. Aunt Kate near Crewe ...

Do take great care of your bicycle! They are now worth "much fine gold" never leave it wet or in the sun & keep it well pumped up always. If I could get a film I would send you a picture of Mrs Stewart with her trailer attached. You know she is well over 70! She goes round collecting paper salvage on the trailer, & the other day she had both her grandchildren in it! I am going to get one made like it. One could carry at least half a cwt that way on the Cambridge Rds. Of course Daddy & I as we bicycle about our beautifully empty roads feel that the war has its compensations in the almost total absence of motor cars & are inclined to hope that the world's petrol supply will have been destroyed by the end of the war that there may be no more of them!! We found the tracks of tanks along the old Roman roads across the moors in Yorkshire, but that added to the romantic historical associations! ...

Helen wrote on 3rd November:

... You are a good girl to write so regularly, – esp. as your loving mother doesn't write as often as I ought & wish to do. Now that Mrs Matthews only comes for a couple of hours twice a week, and we have a paying guest, the days simply fly by in a round of cooking, cleaning & washing. Bas is still at home (thank goodness) so I have three large men to 'do' for. Well, the busier one is the quicker the time goes till I see you all again ...

If I can collect a spare copy I will enclose a report of last week's meeting at the Guildhall, with Bas in the chair! Arthur Greenwood was to have come, but failed in the last few days, so we had a hectic time getting a substitute. Bas sent off floods of telegrams of the most lively kind, – all of course signed 'Pease' and coming from here, & I only hope he hasn't hopelessly damaged Daddy's reputation w. the Labour Party, who are already sufficiently confused by the numbers of Peases writing lively letters from different parties & societies. Anyway John Parker of the Fabian Society nobly filled the breach & the meeting went off very well. Though of course it was not in the same class with Morrison's meeting last term ...

Late in 1942 Helen's father's autobiography *Memoirs of a Fighting Life* was published and he sent a copy to Helen in November. She wrote to him by return:

Thank you so much for your book. It is good reading – though I think doing so is a bit like sitting in a car beside a very fast & enthusiastic driver who calls on one to admire the scenery. This is exhilarating but I wonder how much of the scenery those who don't know it as well as I do, really take in? Would you please send an autographed copy to Chenda for Xmas? (N.B. your Xmas present, not mine!)

J R C Pease

c/o Chas Dunbar
58 Highland St
Cambridge Mass.

Churchill can say what he likes ab. the N.African business being Roosefeldt's idea. I bet it was mostly Churchill's! It has the Marlborough – Blenheim touch all over it! And he would have done the same thing in Gallipoli in the last war if he'd been allowed ... Mike has had flu ...

On 16th November Helen wrote to Richenda:

*I hope this will be in time to wish you a Happy Christmas. Your present **should** go off tomorrow, but books, like everything else, are difficult to get & we couldn't get hold of the ones we wanted ... I enclose the account of one of our bombers that was missing the night we lost 37, because Mrs Cobb's nephew is the Scots observer mentioned! Her sister has just the two sons, both flying men, so the poor woman must have an anxious time. The amazing escapes & adventures that one hears of almost every day in this war will provide material for "historical novelists" ... for years to come. But they need properly telling. Most of the time the BBC just drones them out & one thinks nothing of them ...*

I am writing Miss Strachey about the arrangements for you to enter Newnham if you pass first into Radcliffe. I expect it will be all right, because there will be several Cambridge girls in the same sort of position. Also, if you want to take medicine, I am enquiring what, if any, American exams will exempt you from 1st M.B ...

Bassy expects to go to his operational research job (under the Ministry of Aircraft production) at the end of this term. He thinks & hopes it means the middle east or Africa. We hear tonight on the news that Sir Stafford Cripps will be his topmost boss, which will please him ...

We are all well, but have had flu. The fuel shortage is a bit tiresome – we have the stuff at home, but as one is in honour bound to use as little as possible one never knows just how uncomfortable one ought to be! ...

Helen's last letter in 1942 to Richenda, written on 23rd and 26th December said:

... I sent the cutting about Bim [Josiah V son Ralph Josiah] on to Grandfather who was hugely tickled & wrote to the Editor for another copy. How like [Dr] John he looks! The American readers wd probably have been

much more impressed by the reality of our <u>financial</u> war effort if he had mentioned that his Father was a Director of the Bank of England! I wish I could draw a cartoon of Grandfather, in robes & coronet of course, grinding his teeth & writhing w. aristocratic fury at the thought of his grandson washing dishes! + Jos in tails & spats nobly saying "It is for my country!"

Bother the censor! Did he let through the newspaper cutting of the 'Event' on the Farm? Our one & only little bit of war glory"? No, I have not had any S.S. men round. After giving Herbert Morrison coffee, & writing a glowing account of his meeting here to Grandfather, wh. Grandfather promptly sent on to him, I feel I am "in good" with the right quarters & that 18B is not for me! Besides as I said, I never put in anything that hasn't already appeared in the newspapers. Really we are extremely careful. Bassy, for instance, is now doing hush-hush scientific work for the R.A.F. & Daddy & I are careful not even to ask him what it is about, for fear we might let something out. Anyway he is billeted w. a Vicar! & somewhat exercised as to whether he ought to go to church out of politeness! However we have pointed out that he has seven generations on unbaptised forefathers (on Daddy's side) & he must fall back on a conscientious objection! Luckily the Keynes & the Barlows are quite close, so he gets out of the difficulty by going to see them on Sundays.

Helen went on to tell Chenda of the guests they entertained to dinner on Christmas Eve.

So we had an elegant dinner in the dining-room. Mrs Matthews looking charming as ever came to help. If you don't think it will make the Americans think we aren't as 'austere' as we ought to be, I'll tell you what we had! soup. Roast duck (two w. stuffing), mashed potatoes, cabbage, & apple sauce. Plum pudding (Mrs Beeton + Lord Woolton, i.e. a good deal of carrot & beetroot in & your spices). Mince pies – pastry made w. some <u>white flour</u>

I found I had put away – traditional flour does not make good pastry I find; Birds custard, bottled plums, biscuits!! & cheese. Dessert pears, apples, meddlars – of wh. we have a <u>magnificent</u> crop this year, raisins & almonds (sent by Aunt Camilla last year) & our own hazel nuts. Wine was home made plum Bordeaux (pre-war vintage) coffee – (we seem to have plenty of this owing, I suppose to ships coming home empty from E Africa)

Mostly you will observe home grown, so I'm afraid most people did not fare as well; but still we do quite well enough to give Goebbels a bad head & tummy ache. Oh yes, & a huge Yule log from the elm that died last year. It all went off very well. ... All the same this is the first Xmas I have ever spent without either my younger brothers & sisters or my own children with me – (even the 1st Xmas after we were married, when I was in bed, I had Joanna newly arrived in the cradle beside me) and I hope it won't happen again. Next year you will be home we hope, – & who knows how many of the others?

The film taken of you & the babies arrived in time for us to see it at Impington on the 22nd, – very good though a bit dark, & you <u>won't</u> look at the camera. Mrs M. says 'What a really elegant young lady Chenda has grown' ...

We have sent off the form to the British Consulate authorising your return. I also asked Mr Whitehead if he comes to Boston to see his parents to call on the Dunbars & you; – only Eric only told me his father was going to America 2 days before he went, so my letter may have had to follow him there. Daddy will be writing to Charles Dunbar about paying for the passage this side, but the arrangements will have to be made on your side ...

Mama, by the way, sent the Dunbars Hesketh Pearson's 'Bernard Shaw', wh. I've just been reading as Bas gave it to Daddy. Very entertaining. Do you remember the Pageant in the Potteries when Shaw turned up (unannounced) & Daddy spotted him? And he made a very good speech, a tall thin straight grey bearded figure? That was just like good old Shaw to come & cheer up all the provincial people, when even our own local celebrities like Arnold Bennett wouldn't be bothered, & he went round everything & was as nice as possible, & everyone was so pleased ...

P.S. Grandfather was very pleased w. the pencil you sent him; he has written a sort of circular letter to his children & grandchildren, but, knowing our family, it may never reach you.

Everyone was catching the flu and Helen sat up in bed and darned and patched two dozen pairs of stockings. She asked her father on behalf of Bas (Sebastian) to persuade the Archbishop to come to Cambridge to address the Cambridge University Labour Club at a public meeting in the Guildhall:

This is in earnest. So just pile on to the A.Bp. what a good sort Bas is & in particular what an admirable set of young people the Camb.U.L. Club are ... Mike is sending out notices for a Cambs. Labour Federation meeting on China & his pen is squeaking appallingly.

Very much love & be careful of yourself.

Your loving daughter Helen Bowen Pease

Helen was aware that her father was no longer a young man. In 1943 he was in his seventy-first year and understandably he had begun to take life more slowly. He grew tired very easily and sometimes had to spend days in bed. That January, Helen wrote to him voicing her exasperation at the way the War Office continued giving duties to the Home Guard:

Talking of wasting people's energies, the damned War Office is being a bit silly about the Home Guard. What is the use of forcing middle aged men who are already working full time to parade about when they don't want to? We aren't going to be invaded now, & the important thing is to get on with our work. The men in this village have to give up all Sunday mornings to it, & one evening

*a week, & besides being tired out they have no time to do
their gardens – really rather important in wartime. Even
the young ones (e.g. Eric Whitehead) find it hard to do a
10 hour day six days a week & Sunday morning on Home
Guard for months on end without a break. We find a lot
of people who are not themselves affected, but employ
labour, agree that it is wearing people out unnecessarily,
but they seem to think it is just one of the usual stupidities
of war ...*

Helen's letters to Richenda continued and on 20th January she
wrote:

*... I am so glad you had such a jolly time at Thanksgiving. It
was celebrated here for the Americans, & they very kindly
gave the turkey they should have had to the hospitals.
The American troops also gave a lot of parties to school
children at Christmas. We haven't met any yet ourselves,
though we are on the list for hospitality of course, but
Girton is too far out & there are not enough Yanks to go
round the people in Cambridge who want them. (Also we
don't have drinks in our house! & the <u>average</u> American
certainly does like to put it away!)*
*... There goes the siren! The second we have had this
week after months of silence. You may have seen there
was a nasty little daylight raid on London yesterday
with a school hit & a lot of children killed. Dear Hitler
reminding us he is still around & able to be nasty. ...
Please would you thank Charles Dunbar very much for
his letter to Daddy, wh. he will answer as soon as he can.
– He was in bed for a few days w. flu last week, & as he
has a new course of lectures to give this term he is even
more rushed than usual.*
*I went to see Cousin Maud [Darwin] today & found
her ordered to bed for 3 days. Considering she is 81 she
is extraordinarily active & does far too much. I consoled
her by pointing out that Father who is ten years younger
often has to have days in bed. We had a nice chat. Luckily
I don't think she suffers from the war so much as many old*

people. Poor dears they mind air raids much more than the young, & all their ways of a lifetime are changed & so many little comforts gone. Cousin M said the Bedford College students billeted with her are a great help with the housework (you know what that big house is like!) & she likes the young company.

Did you get that book by Durbin I sent you? It is a bit of a gush in some ways, & it is a mistake to try to get in views on Socialism & psychology into so small a book! And I thought his remarks about English snobbery rather silly. Being an Oxford Don you notice he doesn't mind intellectual snobbery, but only the more old fashioned class kind. And it isn't the labourer touching his hat to the 'gentleman' that matters – it is just as reasonable, or unreasonable, to 'respect' a man because you think he comes of a better fed & better educated class as because he is Charles Darwin's grandson, – or has $50000 a year. In fact the two last seem to me more dangerous. The snobbery that really matters is when Mrs C won't know or work with Mrs D because Mr C is a teacher, or a skilled worker or merely has a higher salary than Mr D. I'm saying all this because I believe in America they think they are <u>not</u> snobs because they have no division of classes by right of birth; but they often have the snobbery of wealth – from the unskilled worker upwards, and don't you go getting the idea that that isn't just as bad or worse than the English variety. Not that you would get that idea from the Dunbars, but you may see it round you. You stick firmly to Grandfather's practice of treating <u>everyone,</u> from a negro waitress to the Prince of Wales or Rockefeller as a man & a brother. He really does carry this out, you know (– with the result that he has had some queer life histories poured out to him!)

On Sunday night I went to talk to the University Labour Club, room crowded, mostly sitting on the floor; just as well it was a crowd as there was no fire! However it went off very well. I was introduced as Bassy's Mother! Quite a pleasant change after being nearly all my life introduced as Father's daughter! ...

I must go & get supper, – & milk the darned cow – the wretched beast is only giving me 5 pints of milk a day, & she has heaps to eat. However 5 pints is more than we could get for our ration if we had to buy it, so it is worth extracting the last drop ...

Getting Richenda back home was uppermost in the minds of her parents. In her letter of 1st February Helen said:

... We sent off the form "authorising" your return to this country to the British Consul in Boston; I hope it reached all right ...

What a lot of excitement lately; Rooseveldt at Casablanca & today the final end of the German armies at Stalingrad. Poor devils, one can't help feeling sorry for them. And what a lark the way we bombed Berlin on Jan 30th! Well the Russians can say truly they are the <u>first</u> people fairly & squarely to smash a German army in the field in any war. We defeated them in the last, but never smashed up a whole army like that. I expect the Americans got excited over Rooseveldt in N. Africa – I wish we thought they <u>had</u> settled the N.African business. We also wish the Americans could understand that asking the Free French to "settle their political differences" & shake hands w Vichyites is like asking Geo Washington to shake hands w. Benedict Arnold only much more so, because Washington was never defeated, & hadn't had his friends tortured & shot by the traitors.

I don't want to be a killjoy, but don't go to too many dances & <u>shows</u> during school term! I know the others do, & it is done more in America than here. But you know you do get excited & harum scarum & you really must put your work first. Jennifer Turner is having to work very hard to get in to Girton College, & the girls who aren't working to get in to college are doing war jobs & working really hard at them. So do be a bit strict with yourself. The Dunbars are too kind to be as stern with you as your parents would be! so it's up to you. Though we do like to hear that you *are having a good time & enjoying yourself!*

Daddy is busy w. his chicken hatching (we had a letter from India the other day from an Indian who had seen the photos in Picture Post!!) & also with a new course of lectures he is giving. I am busy mostly cleaning, cooking & mending! though last week was mostly County-Councilling & Labour Party-ing ...

In her letter of 28th February Helen wrote:

... We are all well & feeling cheerful over 1) the continued Russian successes 2) the recovery of our ground in Tunisia 3) that Churchill is getting well all right 4) the lovely spring weather. ... We are hoping to have Joanna & Seb home for a few days next weekend, which will be lovely as we haven't seen either of them since the New Year. Nothing except the usual round has happened at home. Daddy is giving two lectures a week which keeps him busy, besides the chicken hatching. At the moment he is sending out notices of another of our Labour Party Conferences – this time James Griffiths on 'Beveridge & Beyond'. We expect a big crowd – & as usual I've got to do the tea ...

It is getting late my brain is half asleep & Daddy has gone to shut up the hens. They have started to lay quite well, but we suspect that a couple of very handsome magpies have looted some of the eggs! We have 2 magpies, two Jays & two woodpeckers in the garden now, very beautiful birds, but the 4 first not exactly desirable, especially in war time ...

On 17th March Helen wrote:

... Joanna & Bas have just been home ... Bas, in the intervals of playing round with his friends in Cambridge, successfully felled the dead elm at the beehive end of the army hut ...

Talking of American history we looked up in the Encyclopedia the origin of the word 'Gerrymandering', it is very amusing; you should look it up too. I don't <u>think</u> you will find the politics in England at all like in America. The whole historical background & constitution is so different. Of course we like to think we don't backbite so much! We probably don't feel so bitter for one thing because I understand in America people vote for the whole party "ticket" which means that when the party in power is changed a whole lot of people lose their jobs, & the adherents of the winning party get them. Here it is only the M.Ps who change; the civil servants etc. are unaffected. Also we are such a much smaller & older country, that we have none of the racial & geographical separations which make a united national life so complicated in America ...

I've written to Mr Stopford at the Embassy about your coming home; because we gather from our returned friends that most of the Consulates always do say "No room no room" & the only thing is to retort like Alice "There's <u>plenty</u> of room"! One reason why we think you ought if possible to get home this summer, is that if you stop till you are nearly 19, you will be conscripted into the services anyhow, whereas if we can get you home & you have a year's hard training at science <u>in Cambridge</u> you will be much more likely to get a really interesting job in the services, – or in some scientific civilian War work. It is no good hoping airily that the War will be over by then! Even if we have got Hitler down there will still be the Japs! Not to mention the probability of having to keep an army to police most of Europe for some time to come.

We have been having marvellous weather here – sitting & mealing out on the verandah. There is a carpet of violets out under the shrubs & the daffodils are just flowering. Now the papers are allowed to say that we have had the warmest winter known since records were kept – jolly lucky for the coal controller too, if the winter had been like last there would probably have been an awful row! As it is we have only had the kitchen fire on all day 6 times! I have not lit it till after tea; we just had the electric fire during breakfast & lunch. Most extraordinary. We are still a bit anxious about the possibility of a late & devastating frost. The other side of the picture too is that a hard winter wd. have been much better for the Russian advance, – & have depressed the Germans ...

Josiah IV's health deteriorated and early in April he and Florence went to stay at a seaside hotel in the South. Helen went there to see him. He really was very ill but was better before she left and was more aware of what was going on. The hotel was quiet with a good view over the sea. Most of it was occupied by naval officers convalescing. On returning to Cambridge Helen wrote to Chenda:

A week ago I wrote to you from a "south coast town" where I was stopping w. Grandfather.

The censor seemed to think my description of one of our onetime pleasure resorts in wartime was too zyzsy, & sent the letter back – rather good they didn't chop it about. So I'll repeat the rest of the letter.

... I am so glad about your exam results. How curious that Shelley's "Cloud" should be your favourite poem! It was mine too at your age & I can still repeat it by heart. I don't think I was ever so keen as you on Scott – for one thing they were read aloud to us & though we loved being read aloud to, Scott is too long for it. Oh yes, & I knew a lot of Shelley by heart ... As I can't sing, I used, especially when working alone on the land, to repeat poetry aloud – the only trouble is that people think it natural if they overhear you sing, but mad if you only recite! I shall never forget the surprised face of a soldier popping up from behind a hedge when I was doing some monotonous digging to the accompaniment of some impassioned Swinburne!

I have been down on the s. coast where Grandfather has been very ill. He was better before I left & able to sit up & take notice, but we were very alarmed at one time. I am afraid he really will have to lead a really quiet life in future, poor man. He is in a very nice quiet hotel, w. a big sitting room, & balcony right on the sea & we hope he will stop there for some time. The rest of the hotel is full of naval officers convalescing, such nice looking boys. It is weird to see these posh health resorts looking so battered. – Even in this country we hardly notice the almost daily B.B.C. report. A few aircraft came over in daylight & dropped bombs & machine-gunned a coast town. There were a few casualities, & I don't suppose in America it is noticed at all! And I must say the inhabitants (– what there are of them in the absence of all tourist & other guests) seem to take it very calmly, – & I think Father rather likes it! he has a sort of feeling that as long as there is a chance of being killed in a raid he won't die any other way! It was lovely sunny, windy weather when I was there, w. a gale blowing & the good old English Channel all flecked with sea horses. One felt a positive personal affection for that cold green water that has saved us from so much …

Some lovely photos of the babies arrived a week ago, brought over by a convoy signalman who had been in hospital in Nova Scotia.

P.S. John Wedgwood's forthcoming marriage to Peggy Mason is actually announced! We haven't met her yet … Anyway she is an almoner at a hospital, & her father is a Science teacher. I'm hoping John will bring her here for a weekend.

On 29th April Helen's father wrote to her:

My dearest Helen,
We are back at Dolphin Square & I pick up. But I hanker after your presence always – though your letters do greatly compensate for your absence.

So come when you can & when you can get a room in Dolphin Square as my guest – i.e. write to them, not me. Bring Mike too.

Je t'aime de tout mon coeur.

Yours W

In her letter to Chenda on 19th May, Helen again discussed ways and means of getting her home and now they are thinking of trying to get Cooks, the travel agents, to help.

... We don't know if they will be able to do it, even by special & very expensive way via Lisbon, but they might. Anyway if there is an odd berth anywhere they may be able to slip you in & will let you know. We've told them, of course, of the steps we've already taken. ... Cooks have a special arrangement w. the Govt. by wh. they bring so many that way, look after them in Lisbon till the air passage is arranged etc. It is now a frightful price but worth it if the passage can be arranged for you this summer or early autumn.

I think you would feel rather 'out of it' both now & later or if you stopped at college in America & missed the whole of the war here. We are writing to the Board of Education to see if they will let you have one of the Radio 'Bursaries' at college ... but I don't know what view they will take of American exams ...

The garden is looking lovely – masses of blossom. We have nice feathery rings of carrots in the round bed & potatoes by the Army Hut! The cow calved on May 1, so we are now swimming in milk after being very short since Xmas ...

In her letter of 24th May Helen is optimistic that Richenda will soon be home again. She writes:

Well, we must hope for the best with the Cunard line. We don't think things will get much easier, so you must take any chance you can ... John [Wedgwood] is coming here next Sunday w his fiancee Peggy Mason. Her Godfather lives at Toft ... they intend to get married, in church too!! – as soon as he qualifies in June, & have a fortnight together before he goes off first as a house surgeon & then into the Navy – so they won't have much married life, poor things.

Yesterday Daddy & I were photographed w. the other Managers of Impington Village College, by the British

Council. The picture, if it appears at all, will be in foreign & dominion papers only so look out in American magazines for an article on the Village Colleges!

We are all on tenterhooks wondering when 'the invasion' will begin! What a blessed contrast to 3 yrs ago when <u>we</u> were expecting to be invaded ourselves. It is rather awful now hearing the roar of our bombers going out nearly every night. When we were the underdog it used to be a great comfort to hear them, now that we are winning one perversely thinks of the ghastly damage that that terrible roaring portends. However it is well to remember that war is Hell (I forget <u>which</u> American general said that) – only it is a much worse Hell to be defeated. If only we can win this year before half Europe is starved to death & smashed to ruins ...

It is marvellous to think we <u>may</u> see you within the next few months. We never stop missing you all, & it gets worse & not better as time goes on.

On 25th May 1943, in one of Helen's last letters to her father she mentioned that John Wedgwood (cousin) and Peggy Mason were joining them for lunch the following Sunday.

Dearest Father,
How are you keeping now? I have just taken to writing letters in French to Dora (for her good & mine!) so I must rub up my affectionate phrases. 'Je t'aime tant' will do to start with for you, ... I made a most beautiful little speech in seconding Dr Ellis (you know the man who says he picked you up in Gallipoli) for the vice-chairman of the council. I referred to that episode, which pleased him vastly. I didn't say anything that was not true, & got a number of congratulations – some rather acid 'fancy you buttering Doc Ellis like that' to wh I reply that I said what I thought & that personally I believe in butter whenever possible. Anyway Ellis & the Chairman & the people who asked me to second him, were all pleased, & I continue to disagree with him on the best possible terms!

... We expect John and Peggy to lunch next Sunday as they will be stopping w her god-father. Myra Curtis, new Principal of Newnham, came to lunch on Sunday, also Madeline Symons & Noel Olivier (Mrs Richards). I don't know if you remember them. Myra full of beans as ever.

Do take care of yourself – & don't try partially following two or three doctors at once + your own intuition! I hope John did not get you that enema I heard you asking for; you will give yourself an ulcerated bowel if you keep on using those irritants, for which on your diet of milk & eggs there really is no need, unless the Doc specially says so.

Very much love. Your loving daughter Helen Bowen Pease

Josiah IV, Lord Wedgwood of Barlaston, died on 26th July 1943, aged seventy-one. On his tombstone are words written by the Right Honourable Winston Spencer Churchill MP, taken from a foreword he wrote in Josiah's *Memoirs*:

But the distressed of the whole world have learnt to look to him, and through him to Parliament, for a patient hearing and the redress of wrongs.

Chapter 42

ENDINGS AND BEGINNINGS

With the death of her father, Helen's letters to relatives became less frequent.

Richenda returned home in 1943 and prepared for Newnham. She went up in 1944. In her third year she became engaged to Cambridge physiologist Andrew Huxley, son of Leonard Huxley and grandson of 'Darwin's Bulldog', the biologist T H Huxley. They were married on 10th July 1947. After the wedding Helen wrote to her daughter:

> *...I am so glad you enjoyed it all – the guests seem to have done so also, anyhow various people have said so since & appear to have found it a cheerful & friendly occasion ... Anyway I hope you will always look back on it as a pleasant festivity to inaugurate your married life. On getting home & realising you had really gone, I did the conventional thing & shed tears, & had to be revived by Bassy [Sebastian] who made me drink nearly half a bottle of his wine, after which I felt better & was able to take my usual part in the evening's conversation. Mama & the other Peases & the Stevensons were here. Sunday we kept open house with a succession of friends & relations from 11 in the morning till 10.30 at night. Miraculously the food held out – & there was wedding cake for tea ...*

Richenda and Andrew made their home in Grantchester just outside Cambridge and over the years they had six children, five girls and one boy. During the first years of marriage, because Andrew's scientific work sometimes took him abroad, he and Richenda were away from home for short periods. Whenever that happened Helen took care of the children, or supervised whoever was in charge of the Huxley home.

Helen lived a full and rewarding life with Michael and her family. They were a team both in local government and in shared interests. All their lives they took an active part in the Labour movement.

The main interests of both of them were education and planning together concerning the preservation of rural England. In later years Michael was founder of the National Association of Parish Councils and chairman of the Cambridgeshire Association. He was also to have the role of president, treasurer, secretary and trustee of the Cambridgeshire Labour Party. They were both dedicated to their Labour beliefs.

In 1948, in the *Cambridge & County Labour Review* Helen wrote an article entitled 'In My Opinion' and this gives a very clear picture of the kind of person she was.

> *I have been asked why I joined the Labour Party and what do I think of things now – and to make my answers short. So I will write the truth, but it will not be the whole truth.*
>
> *I joined the Labour Party by way of the I.L.P. just after the 1918 election, the immediate reason being that I was a pacifist in the first war and the I.L.P. seemed the obvious party to join. The real reason was no doubt the good old English reason, that I was following my family tradition Wedgwoods have been non-conformists and reformers for centuries, in fact the first known Wedgwood followed Simon de-Montfort to war against the king. So my red tie was really only the old school tie. I married a man who was born in the Labour Party, his father being one of the original founders. So my fate was sealed and since 1922 I have been a member of the Executive Committee of the Cambridgeshire Labour Party, and have taken an active part in every election both general and local. My first job*

as president in 1940 was to warn local secretaries that, if the Germans invaded, they must at once burn all lists of names and addresses.

What do I think of things now? It is my considered opinion that this is the best Government this country ever had. I am certain that no other could have held the country steady through the many troubles of these post war years. We are all so used now to getting our rations, our social services, as a matter of course, to seeing the children well fed and to having work and wages for everyone that we do not realise what a great, what a unique achievement all this is. It isn't until one compares notes with foreigners, particularly with Americans, that one understands how much we owe to the Labour Government and the British good sense which backs it up.

The future – assuming that the Russians are not crazy enough to go to war with the British and Americans combined – seems full of hope. The only danger, I think, is that some people, particularly those who are too young to remember the bad old times of hunger and unemployment, imagine that a Labour government can give them something for nothing. They will not face the fact that no Government can 'deliver the goods' unless everyone 'gets on with the job' and that everyone who consumes goods and services without giving of their honest best in return is a swindler and a thief. We must never cease to preach and live up to the Socialist motto 'From each according to his ability, to each according to his need'.   H B Pease

Helen's daughter Joanna, now aged twenty-nine and a doctor, in 1949 went out to Tanganyika (now Tanzania) to work, where she remained until the summer of 1966. Her letters home to her family were informative and most interesting.

In conversation with Joanna in the Spring of 1994 she talked about her mother and father's activities in support of the Labour Party. One activity was to hold whist drives in their shed at Reynolds Close which were a 'howling success'. All profits went to the Labour Party.

Joanna talked some more about her memories of her mother:

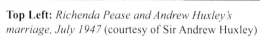

Top Left: *Richenda Pease and Andrew Huxley's marriage, July 1947* (courtesy of Sir Andrew Huxley)

Top Right: *Hon. Julia Wedgwood, 1980s* (author's collection)

Above: *Joanna Pease, Ruth Badertscher, Hon. Julia Wedgwood, Bern* (author's collection)

Right: *Michael and Helen Pease*

Below: *Hon. Helen Pease and family, Christmas 1973*

And, of course, we ran a little smallholding with hens and ducks to feed ... Dad experimented with hens and rabbits, so we had numerous hens and rabbits. The rabbits were skinned and Mother used to send the skins to be cured. She used to make our coats out of lovely white rabbit skins. She used to make lovely gloves too, with fur inside and outside which made all the difference to cycling. Your hands were really warm ... She used to say 'I think you need a new pair of gloves dear'

The children would place their hand on the table and Helen would draw around their fingers for size: '*Drawing out and putting on the fur, cutting out, you had to have some special fur needles, needles that are sharp on three sides.*' Joanna said that her mother used to make dresses for the girls too sometimes, '*but she wasn't very good ... I and my sisters used to grumble no end.*'[1]

Helen's sister Camilla left Australia to attend a UNESCO seminar in Paris in 1951, and took the opportunity of visiting her mother and sister Julia in Lucerne. This was the last time Camilla saw her mother, as Ethel died the following year.

Joanna recalled that while Michael was alive Helen did not like to travel very far from Cambridge. However when Ethel died in Switzerland in 1952, Helen accompanied other members of the family to Lucerne to be with Julia for the funeral.

Helen's brother Jos in Barlaston was always in contact with Helen. In March 1954 she was unwell and had to spend some time in hospital. Jos wrote:

For heaven's sake give up cow-keeping & buy your milk pasteurised. I don't believe in studio-potting & studio-farming except for Super tax purposes ... My health is moderate, and I certainly feel my advancing years; but I'm working pretty hard ...

In October that year, Jos wrote regarding their sister Camilla who had undergone an operation for a growth on the lung:

It is difficult to take it in. Do you think we should try to persuade her to come back to England where she could spend her remaining time among her family – or shall I go & visit her?

In a letter the following month:

I've written John to ask his view on isotope treatment for Cam. It's very recent, but a friend of a friend was cured of it via Westminster Hospital. ... So fate really points to my going out in January. If so, I'll be away three months i.e. mid January to mid April. It's a pity it will be Australian hot season – & probably devilish hot in Sydney; but I don't think I sh'd funk this one; tho' I'm almost certain, as you say, to take to my bed or bunk at some time or other! My nature requires work, woman, and rest – & too little of any of that trio makes me sick.

I refuse to despair of Cam; and I think we sh'd leave no stone unturned. Pester my son John, who is a dear on these things, & Michael's scientific pals. Cam has tons of faith & charity – & I think we sh'd give her Hope, not sympathy ...

Camilla, however, never recovered her health and died in Australia on 17th May 1955, aged fifty-four.

In 1955 Gloria, Helen's youngest sister, brought her family from abroad to visit Helen. On 8th August 1955, from his home in Stoke Grange, Jos wrote to Helen. He had been suffering from stress. Having said he was glad that Helen gave Gloria and her children a taste of English family life, he was sorry he did not invite them up to Stoke Grange but he still felt like a 'flat tyre' and he would have to go to London for X-rays on 17th to 19th August. He continued:

... there are still signs of a little bleeding, tho' there is virtually no pain, so long as I continue the life of a strict convalescent & lie up as much as possible.

He talks of probably having to go to America again to help Hensleigh Wedgwood in his troubles:

There is a bit of a slump in Pottery in the U.S.A. – the U.S. potters are running 20 per cent at least under normal – tho' pottery is the exception, along with some textiles, to the general U.S.A. boom of the last 10 months or so. I fear the existence of Japan cannot fail to create problems for potters and textile men.

Jolly good luck to Fabian. I somehow don't think he will dislike the R.A.F. as much as I (at the time) disliked the R.F.A. in 1918! In any case even I do not & never have regretted the experience – really more valuable than 10 years of Greek & Latin (which I have now entirely forgotten).

If one can read, & has enough experienced guidance to select one's reading, the rest of intellectual schooling is of small importance (apart from discipline).

Much much love to your whole large family. Jos Especial welcome & love to Joanna [Joanna had been home on leave that summer].

Helen passed her driving test in 1956 – she was very pleased and wrote to Richenda on 11th April to give her the good news. The tester had said she was a good careful driver and had no hesitation at all about passing her.

... Anyway, here I am a Free Woman (when Daddy hasn't got the car out!) Nice letter from Joanna, now moved to Nzega, Western Province – no electricity, so I suppose she won't be able to have a fridge. Funny how one is so used to electricity one hardly believes that medical practice can be carried on without it! Daddy seems very well ...

Helen was very happy with the reunion between herself and her two 'lost' sisters, Gloria and Julia. Julia had already visited Cambridge in 1953 and came over again in 1956 to meet more of her many relatives.

Gloria, who had grown up abroad with Julia, in 1937 married Paul Oppenheim, with whom she had one son. She left the marriage after a short time and in 1939 married Peter Michael. They had three children: two boys and a girl. In the 1960s in England, Gloria and

Peter were having marital problems. Helen, in a letter to Richenda in August 1960 remarked how complicated the marriage laws were in their case, i.e. three countries and the languages of two – Gloria's solicitors could not even read Peter's solicitors' letters, let alone answer them in German. Helen was supportive to Gloria, as she was with all her family, and was there for her whenever Gloria arrived on her doorstep in distress. Gloria made her home in Stevenage where she lived until her death in 1974, aged sixty-five.

In September 1961 Helen was talked into going to Austria on holiday with Michael and their daughter, Rosamund (Dors). She wrote at the top of her letter to Richenda, '*6,000 ft up above Zell an Zee*'. She said also:

> ... *we got involved in a fearful pass betw Innsbruck & Zell an Zee, wh looked OK on the map but turned out to be under repair, a shocking surface & gradients as bad, & much longer than the Simplon wh is quite easy by comparison. The car took it all right, but they only got me over by keeping my mind on <u>Fen drainage</u> & sewerage problems ... A most successful remedy for mountain sickness!*
>
> *We hope that Bas & Susan will join us tomorrow for 2 nights. Dora will prob go home with them. The Salzburg papers have a lot about the "Nuclear-Fusion Conference" unfortunately no person is recognisable in the picture they gave inside the Conference Hall, apparently all in English.*
>
> *Dora seems to be keeping very well, anyway she has done some good climbs without being too tired afterwards & has been <u>very</u> good company, & a very competent navigator ...*

At the end of December 1962 Charles Darwin, grandson of Emma Wedgwood and Charles Darwin, died. Charles and his wife Katherine lived at Newnham Grange in Cambridge, which had been the home of his father Sir George Darwin's family for many years. After his death the family decided to move from Cambridge and so leave Newnham Grange.

On 14th April 1963 Helen wrote to Richenda:

... The farewell party at the Darwins was pleasant, though the occasion was sad, but really K [Katherine] is quite right not to try to live in that house. The University is probably going to lease it as a club & small classrooms for non-collegiate people connected w. the University. Lots of people at the party, including John Ham & Diana, & a number of young Darwins & Barlows. Two of Erasmus Barlow's daughters have been 'Ban the Bombing' & got arrested, but not gaoled, last year. Eras. rather perturbed about it in talk w. Daddy. But Mrs Eras. & I agreed that the great thing was that they should care enough about something to get arrested. So I egged them on a bit, but exhorting them to "do time" & find out for themselves what the prisons were like! ...

What is now history is that the Darwin properties, Newnham Grange and the Old Granary, were acquired in 1964 by the University of Cambridge and, to the delight and approval of the family, became the nucleus of a new graduate college bearing the Darwin name.

During 1966, Michael Pease became seriously ill. Joanna returned home from Africa for good and cared for her father, who died at home in August of that year. On the 9th August Helen wrote to Richenda who was in the United States with her husband at that time:

My Darling Chenda, Thank you so much for your sweet letter & the ones you have written since. I am very glad you did go when you did. It had to be 'goodbye' sometime, & you had Andrew to comfort you as I had Daddy when my Father died, & shd have hated to think of you alone at Grantchester without him. There was nothing you could have done here that cannot be just as well done when you come back. The lawyers must settle about the value of the estate – ... the way the money has piled up these last six years! Joanna & I are kept busy, I am thankful to say, tidying up, keeping the garden going etc. J has told you a memorial service is Sat Oct 8. They want Bas to play. People seem glad it is not till Oct 8, nearly everyone, including the University will be back then ... Dora seemed much more serene this weekend, & has been most energetic in the garden.

You will like to see some of the many letters I have had – some very nice ones & from quite unexpected people. Please thank Andrew very much indeed for his. The thought of you two together & your happy family has always been such an abiding joy to Daddy & me. May you reach your golden wedding which we have not done ...

J. & I are waiting for the men to do 1) the water, 2) the sewerage, 3) the storage heaters. I wish they would buck up. We can't go away till it is all safely done. Possibly we shall fly out to Fabian after October 8. I am also writing to the Israelis who so pressed M & me to go there. Jo has friends too in Israel, so we should both like to see more of the country – so long as our promised V.I.P. treatment is not too overpowering!

Very much love my darling & kiss the babies for me.

Towards the end of Helen's life her grown up family were settled in their own lives – Joanna, a doctor, remained at Reynolds Close, as companion to her mother, after her father died. Following Helen's death Joanna made her home in Histon where she lived until her death in 1994, aged seventy-four.

Sebastian (Dr Sebastian Rendel FRS) a physicist and research director at Culham for the UK Atomic Energy Authority, was married, had two sons and three daughters. Sebastian died in 2004.

Richenda, Lady Huxley followed in her mother's footsteps and was a JP in Cambridge from 1956 to 1995. Her husband, now Sir Andrew Huxley, Nobel laureate, was Master of Trinity College, Cambridge from 1984 to 1989. Lady Huxley died in March 2003.

Dora (Rosamund Dorothy Benson Pease) lives in London with her partner, Timothy Nodder CB. They have one son. Dora worked for the Department of Health until she retired.

Fabian is married and lives in the United States. He is a professor of physics at the University of California at Stanford.

Helen had taken on the business of keeping records of the ever-widening circle of Wedgwood lives. Her 'Wheel' depicting 'The Decendants of Josiah Wedgwood F.R.S.', printed in May 1959, is a work of art. So many Wedgwoods had married cousins she found she could display it all on a wheel – a unique insight. Family letters, photographs, and political material from her father Josiah IV she gave to the Wedgwood Museum archives, all dated and boxed in a methodical manner. She also filled many albums with pictures of her family, past and present. Until her death in 1981, aged eighty-six, she was active both in her own interests and those of her children and grandchildren.

On the evening before she died she had spent her time happily and peacefully and appeared as usual. On that evening she had an enjoyable time discussing old times with a young colleague of her husband Michael. However, in the middle of the night she died as she had lived, surrounded by her family.

Chapter 43

THE HON. JULIA WEDGWOOD

Elizabeth Julia Wedgwood was born in London on 1st May 1907, the sixth child of Josiah and Ethel Wedgwood. Her childhood was happy and secure in the love of her mother and father and of her older siblings. When her sister Gloria arrived in 1909 they were 'babies' together.

When her parents separated in 1913, Julia was six. As one of the 'babies' she had a life of uncertainty – sometimes with her mother, sometimes at the Ark, sometimes with her Darwin relations in Cambridge. When she spoke of those years she remembered how she and her brothers and sisters used to pray that their parents would make it up and stay together. That did not happen.

When Ethel and Josiahs's divorce became final, Ethel went abroad taking Julia (then twelve) and Gloria (aged ten) with her. Julia's life abroad, until she returned to England in 1974, is something of a mystery, as little is known about those years. Ethel Bowen Wedgwood (as she signed herself for evermore) kept her two daughters under her strong and determined control, and communication over the years was negligible. Josiah IV had arranged financial support through banks, and trusts had been set up for the girls. Otherwise Ethel distanced herself from her English Wedgwood connections.

Dornach in Switzerland was Ethel's first new home abroad. She was occupied within the Anthroposophical Society translating and working at the Goetheanum (the movement's world centre). 'Julian' (as Julia was always known in Switzerland) and Gloria were educated at the Steiner Anthroposophical school at Dornach.

Jos missed his two youngest daughters and in one letter he wrote to Julia in 1921 his loneliness and frustration come through. It is not known whether he ever posted, or if she ever received this letter. He wrote:

Dear little girl,
This is to catch you and give you good wishes on your 14th birthday. I have not written to you for so long because I thought you disapproved of me, that for that reason you never replied to my letters; and I was too proud and you too young for any explanation. You are still too young to understand all, but when you grow up you will discover that neither I nor your mother have done anything that we are ashamed of or that need make you ashamed of me. Your parentage is good enough for any child to be proud of. In any case, whether you think hardly of me or not, I love you and I cannot go on for ever hearing nothing of or from you, and for ever wondering if I shall see again my two youngest children.

I wish I knew what you were doing. Do you talk German naturally yet? What are you keen on? Music? or drawing? or dancing? Do you read much? and what? Do you sulk, or explode? or are you contented and smiling? Are you a rebel or a cabbage? Have you acquired wisdom from Goethe's Faust or stuff to spout from Schiller's Glocke? Do you believe in God or merely in goodness? Do you find it easy or hard to tell the truth? What is the worst vice and what the greatest virtue?

As I lie in bed and write this I only think that, alas, I do not know you at all and cannot help ...

Later in the 1920s Ethel moved to Stuttgart, where the girls went to the Waldorschule.

The whole persona of Ethel Bowen Wedgwood, a divorcee living abroad, is an intriguing mystery now lost in the mists of time. It is known that she returned to England briefly in 1933 to give some Steiner lectures. A person who attended a lecture on Schiller described her as having a great strength and a strong core. 'She looked eternally young, beautiful ivory skin without any pink in it, intelligent face, very expressive eyes, very strong personality, also a very loving interest in everything and everyone and especially interest in her subject ... very magnetic ...'.

Ethel and the girls returned to Dornach in 1926, where Julia studied speech and drama under Rudolf Steiner's widow Marie. Steiner had died in 1925.

Julia concentrated on speech and drama and eurythmy; Marie Steiner said eurythmy meant singing as movement. 'It is song. It is not dance, it is not mime, it is singing.' One very dear friend from 1963 onwards was Ruth Badertscher, who also worked in eurythmy. Eventually they shared an apartment in Berne for ten years. Later when Ruth talked about Julia, she remembered that her health was delicate and she often had migraine attacks which confined her to bed.

Dr Pierre Grossheinz was a friend of Julia's from their early school days at Dornach. Pierre grew to love Julia and proposed to her. In 1998 in a discussion with Ruth in Berne, she said that when Pierre proposed Julia refused him because, although she loved him, she wasn't a housewife and was not used to practial work so she did not think she could be a good wife. He eventually married someone else and when he died in 1992, in reply to Ruth's letter telling her of his death, Julia wrote:

> *Many thanks for your lovely letter with the news of Pierre. In between times I have received a very nice letter from the daughter who is now living in Canada. His death affected me because I was very close to him. We were friends since I was 13 but then we did not have contact for several years because he spent many years in England and America and me in Switzerland and Italy.*
>
> *All the same I thank you very much that you have written to me in this connection ...*

Ethel was in Dornach at the outbreak of World War Two, but in the 1940s she took the girls to Italy and lived there for about ten years.

While in Italy, in 1947 Julia became a Roman Catholic and also persuaded her mother to convert. Julia remained a Catholic until she died. In 1951 they lived in Lucerne. Camilla went to visit them in Switzerland and Ethel died the following year. She was eighty-two years old.

Julia had friends both in Switzerland and Germany. In 1957 she moved from Lucerne to Stuttgart – she said it was much cheaper and much more amusing.

After Richenda's father, Michael Pease died, Julia wrote to her on 2nd August 1966:

> *I wish to send you my affectionate sympathy at the loss of your father. Will you please give my love and sympathy to Dora & your brothers and quite especially to Joanna. I am very glad she was able to return and look after your father at the end & also be near your dear mother. Your mother writes that Joanna has returned to England for good now & that they are keeping on the house. It seems to me that this would be as your father would wish it and I am thankful for your mother's sake. How wonderfully upright, truthful and kind your father was! I shall not forget him & am so glad I was able to get to know him towards the end of his life. The artistic trait in him I enjoyed so much. Mozart, Bach and Brahms were, I think, his favourite composers, & I am glad there will be a Memorial Service – all music – at Impington College ...*

Again on 2nd January 1967 Julia wrote to Richenda:

> *I shall be thinking of you all very much at Christmas time and hope that your mother is picking up. I'm afraid she will find the long winter in the house without your father hard to bear. Her lively interest in the world at large will, no doubt, be a help to her to pull through. I hope that Joanna, too, feels better & enjoyed her stay in California ... I am very much looking forward to seeing you and the children again next summer or perhaps even after Easter ...*

That year Julia went to England in midsummer and again in the summer of 1973 she stayed with her sister Helen and was welcomed by many relatives. It was obvious in later years when talking with Julia that she had always been loyal and supportive to her mother and that she had never criticised her for choosing her life away from her husband. However these feelings were not shared by Helen. Helen never forgot nor forgave her mother for her desertion of the family when Helen was eighteen years old.

Over the next few years Julia came back to Cambridge and stayed with Helen. Finally in 1974 she returned to England to be near her family in Cambridge. She was sixty-seven years old, had angina and was careful of her health. She settled down to her life in England, never losing touch with her friends in Germany and Switzerland and visiting them off and on over the next ten years. She enjoyed meeting so many relatives she had never known before.

Helen, widowed since 1966, welcomed her sister Julia into her family and was pleased to have her back. She had sold some land near her home in Girton to a firm which built Gretton Court, a retirement home, and accommodation had been arranged there for Julia in 1974, where she lived until 1984.

From Gretton Court, Julia wrote to Richenda on 27th February 1976:

> *... Your mother is keeping fine again. She comes over here & reads me Bernard Shaw's plays, which we both enjoy ... Your mother has framed for me the Christmas photo of you all of two years ago. It is incredible what she does with her arthritised fingers.*

Julia was an intellectual and could speak several languages – even at the time of her death aged eighty-six she was engaged in work on the translation of a book by a Russian friend of hers, Eugenia Gorvitch, on the Russian prophet Vladimir Soloviev. She lived a quiet spiritual life, reading, writing to her many friends and meeting with people of similar interests.

Writing to her niece Richenda from Gretton Court on 13th March 1977, she said:

> *I'm extremely sorry I could not come yesterday evening especially as I have not seen you since Christmas & have had only indirect news of yourselves. I am generally booked on Saturday afternoon & evening, also on Friday. A brilliant student versed in the English language &*

literature helps me with some very difficult translations.
He is absolutely wonderful but he can only come on
Saturdays. I just have to get on with the translations as
I am very much behindhand & was getting thoroughly
entangled in the long German sentences ...

In 1981 Julia's sister Helen, to whom she was deeply attached, died.

In March 1984 Julia decided to leave Cambridge and live in a residential convent in Dawlish in Devon, where she hoped she could live quietly. The convent was situated in its own beautiful grounds. But after two years she realised it was too far away from everyone she knew, especially her family. So she returned to Cambridge in the spring of 1986 and went to live with Joanna – her niece and Helen's oldest daughter – and sister of Richenda, Lady Huxley.

Joanna was at that time sixty-six years old; she had never married, became a doctor first in England and then worked in Africa from 1949 to 1966. Eventually she bought a house in Histon, on the outskirts of Cambridge. She worked as a GP in Histon from 1967 to 1981. Like her mother and grandfather Josiah IV, she was a staunch Labour supporter and was active in both local politics and charity work.

Joanna welcomed Julia into her home. She laughingly used to say, 'Here I am looking after Julia – I'm nearly as old as her myself.' They were so different from each other in appearance and background, although politics did not come into it as Julia was indifferent to politics. Joanna was lean and quick in her movements, while Julia, because of her weak heart, moved slowly and was about average weight for her age. Joanna was practical and efficient in everything she did. Julia was sensible, but from choice or perhaps circumstances, not very worldly. Joanna was generous to a fault, made all Julia's friends welcome when they came to visit and cared for Julia in every way until Julia's death in 1993.

In conversation with Joanna in the spring of 1994, Joanna spoke briefly about her grandmothe Ethel, and for her neglect of Gloria's and Julia's education. Joanna said

My grandmother had no excuse she knew all about the
environment, she knew all classes of persons, she was
born into an aristocratic society, she was well educated

and she had no excuse for ignoring, or rather not educating, her daughters properly. No excuse. She just didn't care, she was selfish ...[1]

However, from Julia's point of view she felt the way her life had progressed was all right with her; she knew no other and in retrospect, apart from missing growing up with her brothers and sisters, she had no regrets. In a letter to a friend in July 1991, she wrote:

I left England, following my mother, at the end of 1919 & did not return until after my mother's death in 1952 (except for a few weeks in the summer of 1928 & '33 when I was involved in the eurythmy & speech chorus of the Goetheanum). My mother and I had no contact with England whatsoever after we left in 1919. This owing to family tragedy & difficulties. I can't say that I missed England as it was a fascinating & interesting life on the Continent ...

Julia found her weak heart very frustrating – her mind was active and forever seeking knowledge and she enjoyed being with friends; having to be quiet and 'staying put' was sometimes unbearable. She wrote in March 1991:

I'm afraid I am not getting any better. The heart is damaged. However, if they manage to keep the pain away with their numerous pills it will prolong life, which is a sort of half-life always feeling strained & tired ...

She regretted in her later years not being able to travel to the Speech School at Rudolf Steiner House in London to attend lectures. One dear friend of Julia's was Andrew Welburn, whom she met while he was studying at Cambridge – she attended his graduation and followed his career to adulthood. While still able to travel to London she shared with students the work she had been doing on the book *Rezitation und Deklamation* by Rudolf and Marie Steiner. Then when she was forced to lead a more sedentary life, in collaboration with Andrew, they completed the translation of this book, printed under the title of *Poetry and the Art of Speech*.

Andrew, now Dr Andrew J Welburn, is British Academy Fellow in Romantic Studies at New College, Oxford. He is the author of a book on Shelley (1986) and *The Truth of Imagination* (1989) plus articles in various journals on literature and on Gnosticism.

Julia lived to the age of eighty-six. She died suddenly in the afternoon of Wednesday 14th April 1993 and one of her many good friends, Olga Holbek, was with her when she died. At her cremation in Cambridge, many members of the Wedgwood family came to pay their respects to the last member of the family of Josiah Clement, Lord Wedgwood of Barlaston.

Her obituary, written by Dr Andrew Welburn is reproduced here, in part, by kind permission of the Anthroposophical Society of Gt Britain.

> *Despite her frail health in later years she was a tireless worker for the spiritual life, especially in the arts of speech and eurythmy. ... With her knowledge of poetry in German, English and Italian (Dante was perhaps her greatest passion) she was strikingly cosmopolitan but never formidable, and always anxious to share her treasures with anyone who showed interest ... With her strong sense of individual destiny, she was both moved and perplexed by the experience of being welcomed back into an extensive family life in Cambridge on her retirement there ... she will remain for all who knew her the quietly supportive presence which she was in life, and a much loved companion.* [2]

Joanna died the following year and a private memorial booklet about her life was produced by her brother, Dr Sebastian Pease. This booklet tells the story of her life in loving detail.

Chapter 44

A WEDGWOOD IS A WEDGWOOD

This has been a long journey from the Potteries of the mid-1700s to Cambridge at the end of the 20th century. Studying these families through time has been a fascinating exercise. This book has been primarily an attempt to look at them in their individual environments and to find how and if they influenced their partners, also their similarities and differences despite, or perhaps because of, the social structures of their everyday lives.

One characteristic that is clearly obvious about these Wedgwood women is their personal strength and confidence in what they were doing. Their belief in the freedom of the individual runs through all their lives and this trait was personified in Helen. Like her father, she fought for this freedom all her life. Helen's mother Ethel Bowen Wedgwood, wife of Josiah IV, embraced this belief absolutely when in 1913 she made a decision to change her life and the lives of people in her family. She felt justified in leaving her husband because she had stopped loving him.

Where Sarah was concerned, individual freedom was difficult to define. In the 1700s there were certain standards of behaviour she would have had to observe, and because it was the norm she would not have thought of changing it. Sarah remained within an environment she knew and had a comfortable life. She gave birth to eight children and had one miscarriage. It would not have occurred to her to resent having so many children – at that time there was no alternative, and she did not have a choice.

Emma's most important individual freedom was her freedom to live her life in accordance with her beliefs.

Apart from Julia Wedgwood – who never married – all these women came from a comfortable well-to-do background, married for love and, except for Helen, married a Wedgwood relative.

Sarah's husband, Josiah, was exceptional: a potter, born and bred, who had the brains and foresight to look towards the future and recognize the path he wished to follow. Sarah, a distant cousin, was an ideal partner: with her intelligence and background she would have found it easy to be attracted to such a man. Apart from loving Sarah her dowry was also an extra bonus, which he used wisely.

Their granddaughter Emma was born into a comfortable home, the youngest of nine children. Charles Darwin was her first cousin and was a frequent visitor at Maer Hall whilst they were both growing up. When he began to think of marriage he shrewdly weighed the pros and cons of such a choice. He chose Emma, his cousin, whom he had known most of his life. She was gentle and caring and he was confident they would suit each other. In their marriage he was always loving towards her and their family and appreciative of her vigilance regarding his uncertain health.

Whilst Emma had been brought up to believe in God, as time went on Charles became less and less interested in Christianity. After the death of their ten-year-old daughter, Anne, he renounced all interest in Christian beliefs.

Like all mothers, these women knew heartbreak when a child died or left home for whatever reason. For example Sarah's son Tom was never well and was forever travelling, seeking respite from his continuing bad health. He was thirty-four when he died. Two of Sarah's other children died: Richard aged one and Mary Ann, eight. Emma lost three children: Anne at ten, Mary who was three weeks old and Charles aged two. Ethel, in a way, lost five of her children but that was from choice – she left them. Helen lost one child – Rachel aged six – but also during the Second World War three of her children were evacuated overseas and she was without them for three years – that was a heartbreaking time for herself and her husband.

Apart from Ethel Bowen Wedgwood, any differences that existed between these Wedgwood women were inevitable because societies change and develop at different points in time. Sarah in the Potteries married into a life already familiar to her. She and Josiah were more than happy when their sons married well and moved up the social ladder: this was not an issue with either Emma, Ethel or Helen. Emma married an intellectual, left the Potteries, and moved into a very different environment where, instead of being surrounded by pots she was surrounded by books. Emma's role as a wife was more demanding than Sarah's because of Charles Darwin's scientific work and his poor health, but like Sarah she too was often his amanuensis and sometimes his eyes.

Ethel married her first cousin Josiah Wedgwood IV, with whom she had a lot in common. Unlike Sarah, Emma and Helen, Ethel did not always live in a permanent home with her children, but had governesses and servants to look after them while she shared her husband's everyday political life in London. In later years in conversation with her daughter Julia, she said her mother was before her time in her attitude to life.

Helen, born almost at the beginning of the 20th century, was different because she had the freedom to choose how to live her life. She was voluble in her role as a pacifist during the First World War and passionate in her criticism of Nazism in the Second World War. She became a politician and worked in local government together with her husband most of her adult life. One very important choice Helen made – which had been denied her ancestors – was the decision about if and when to have children. This gave herself and her husband a certain freedom regarding plans for their future.

It is apparent that there was what could be considered an odd one out, namely Julia Wedgwood. Julia in her own way was steadfast in her concern for others. In her personal beliefs she had no doubts or regrets. Her destiny was inseparable from her mother's until Ethel died in 1952, when Julia returned from the Continent to England and her extended family. She accepted and was accepted by her relatives, but with everyone concerned there was an awareness of difficulty in communicating with Julia, and also a recognition of *why* Julia looked at life differently. This was mainly because of her anthroposophical upbringing and the fact that she had lived on the Continent most of her life.

Julia, in her formative years, had no freedom of choice. Her mother took her abroad, cutting all ties with her Wedgwood family. Julia studied the works of Rudolf Steiner and she, like her mother, became an anthroposophist. She never, ever regretted this. No doubt if she had stayed within the Wedgwood fold in England she would have been a completely different person, but that was not to be. She was different in her attitudes, but recognised and embraced her English family's way of life and endeavoured to understand *their* attitudes.

Did Sarah, Emma, Ethel or Helen influence their husbands? Look at it another way: would Josiah I, Charles, Josiah IV and Michael have been different, lived different lives, if they had been married to anyone else? Sarah and Emma married blood relatives, so there was a certain familiarity from the start. Sarah was Josiah's best friend, his helpmate and support. Charles Darwin was lucky to get a wife who was such a good nurse. Emma was patient and uncomplaining, and without her one wonders how he would have researched and completed as much work as he did. One could almost criticise Emma because she was *too* kind, *too* sympathic and *too* willing to nurse and look after other people.

Ethel up to 1913 certainly helped her husband in his political career, by her loyalty and by devoting most of her time to helping him in his work as an MP. Also socially she supported Jos whenever the need arose. By leaving him, yes she did influence him. What was once a complete family was now broken up; where there had been permanence there was now doubt and uncertainty; where there had been a loving, familiar wife there was now someone her husband did not understand. She influenced his future outlook on life and because he continued to love her he remained unhappy for quite a long time.

Helen, in marrying Michael Pease, in a way broke new ground. She recognised Michael as her soul-mate the first time she saw him. They complemented each other, and her political beliefs were in tune with his.

Josiah IV Lord Wedgwood, wrote in *Wedgwood Pedigree* that '*although Wedgwoods always have money and enough*' it was not enough to mix with the aristocracy or for daughters to be presented at Court. They were generous to the poor and always gave to charity:

> *They inherited wealth & lived in the country like the gentry with horses, dogs & flowers. From their country houses at Maer or Barlaston they rode to their works at Etruria. Thus they were of neither sort.*

References

PART I

Main material used is abbreviated as follows:
By courtesy of The Trustees of the Wedgwood Museum, Barlaston
Accumulation held on loan at Keele University: **WMSS**
   Century of Family Letters: H.E.Litchfield: **CFL**
   Charles Darwin Personal Correspondence: **CD**

CHAPTER 1: **Relative Values**

1.   WMSS E25—18055
2.   WMSS E25—18056

CHAPTER 2: **New Life – Lunar Group**

1.   WMSS E25—18070
2.   Eliza Meteyard *Vol.1 The Life of Josiah Wedgwood 1865*

CHAPTER 3: **Children – New Factory Site – Tragedy of a Brother
      and Son**

1.   WMSS E25—18059
2.   WMSS E25—18058
3.   WMSS E25—18139
4.   WMSS E25—18139
5.   WMSS E25—18127
6.   WMSS E25—18183
7.   Eliza Meteyard *Vol.1 The Life of Josiah Wedgwood* 1865
8.   WMSS E25—18199
9.   Eliza Meteyard *Vol.2 The Life of Josiah Wedgwood* 1865
10. WMSS W/M 2

Chapter 4: Etruria – New Factory – New Home

1. E J D Warrillow *History of Etruria*
2. WMSS E25—18269
3. WMSS E25—18268
4. E J Warrwillow
5. Eleanor Winyard. *The Building of Etruria Hall.* Document commissioned by the National Garden Festival, Stoke, Staff. 1983. Manuscript courtesy of Trustees/Wedgwood Museum.

Chapter 5: Sarah's Illness

1. WMSS E25—18273
2. Eliza Meteyard Vol.2
3. WMSS W/M 1441
4. WMSS E25—18360
5. WMSS E25—18634
6. WMSS E25—18378
7. WMSS E25—18392
8. WMSS E25—18399
9. WMSS E25—18402
10. WMSS E25—18415
11. WMSS E25—18418
12. WMSS E25—18429
13. WMSS E25—18430
14. WMSS E25—18431

Chapter 6: Family Affairs

1. WMSS E25—18435
2. WMSS E25—18561
3. WMSS E25—18570
4. WMSS L95–17651A

Chapter 7: Children's Education – Mary Ann Ill

1. WMSS E25—18620
2. WMSS E25—18848
3. WMSS E25—18845
4. WMSS E26—18936
5. WMSS E26—18939
6. WMSS E26—18939

CHAPTER 8: Etruscan School

1. WMSS E26—18928
2. WMSS E26—18929
3. WMSS E26—18939

CHAPTER 9: George Stubbs – Death of Thomas Bentley

1. WMSS W/M 1441
2. WMSS W/M 1441
3. WMSS E25—18833
4. L Jewitt *Life of Josiah Wedgwood*
5. L Jewitt *Life of Josiah Wedgwood*

CHAPTER 10: Friendships

1. Eliza Meteyard Vol. 2
2. WMSS W/M 19
3. Eliza Meteyard *A Group of English Gentlemen* 1871
4. WMSS E3—2490

CHAPTER 11: Joy and Sorrow – Josiah Dies

1. WMSS W/M 1460
2. Not catalogued
3. WMSS L121–29021
4. L Jewitt

CHAPTER 12: Susan Marries Robert Darwin – Sarah Leaves Etruria Hall

1. WMSS W/M 61
2. WMSS W/M 60
3. WMSS W/M 21
4. E J D Warrillow

CHAPTER 13: Cote House – Coleridge Connection

1. R B Litchfield *Tom Wedgwood* 1903
2. Unpublished letters of Samuel Coleridge 1932
3. "   "   "   "
4. WMSS W/M 81
5. R B Litchfield
6. R B Litchfield
7. R B Litchfield

8. R B Litchfield
9. WMSS W/M 86

Chapter 14: End of an Era – New Horizons

1. WMSS W/M 21
2. WMSS W/M 39
3. Rt.Hon. Josiah Clement W & D J G E Wedgwood *Wedgwood Pedigree*. Kendal 1925
4. WMSS W/M 65
5. L121—29021

Chapter 15: Maer Hall – Josiah II and Family

1. CFL (Vol.1)
2. CFL
3. CFL
4. CFL
5. CFL
6. CFL
7. CD
8. CFL
9. CFL

Chapter 16: Charles Darwin – Emma Wedgwood

1. CFL
2. CD (Charles Darwin His life in a selected series of his published Letters edited by his son Francis Darwin)
3. CFL Vol.1
4. CD
5. CD
6. CFL
7. CFL
8. CFL
9. WMSS W/M 198

Chapter 17: Love Letters – London – House Hunting

1. CFL
2. CD
3. CD
4. CD

5. CD
6. CD
7. CD

Chapter 18: Wedding Plans – New Home

1. CFL
2. CD
3. CD
4. CD
5. CD
6. CFL
7. CFL
8. WMSS W/M 158
9. CFL

Chapter 19: Married Life in London

1. CFL
2. CFL
3. CFL

Chapter 20: First Child – Family Letters

1. CD
2. CD
3. CFL
4. CFL
5. CD
6. CFL
7. Maria Edgeworth Published Letters
8. CFL
9. CFL
10. CFL
11. CFL
12. CFL

Chapter 21: Down House

1. CD
2. CFL
3. CFL
4. Francis Darwin

5.   CFL
6.   CFL
7.   CFL
8.   CFL
9.   CFL
10. CFL
11. CFL
12. CFL
13. CFL
14. CFL
15. CFL
16. CFL

CHAPTER 22: **The Potteries – Upper House – Darwin Children – Annie's Death**

1.   J & G E Wedgwood: *Wedgwood Pedigree* 1925
2.   CFL
3.   CFL
4.   CFL
5.   CFL
6.   CFL
7.   WMSS W/M 310
8.   CFL
9.   CD (ed. F. Darwin)

CHAPTER 23: **The Great Exhibition – The Origin of Species**

1.   CFL
2.   CD
3.   CD (ed. F Darwin)
4.   CFL
5.   CFL
6.   CFL
7.   CFL

CHAPTER 24: **Achievements – Loss**

1.   CFL
2.   CFL
3.   CFL
4.   CD (ed. F Darwin)

5. CD
6. CFL
7. CFL
8. CFL
9. CFL

Chapter 25: Charles Darwin's Illness and Death

1. CFL
2. CD (ed. F Darwin)
3. CD
4. CFL
5. CFL
6. CFL
7. CFL
8. CFL
9. CFL
10. CFL
11. CFL

Chapter 26: Cambridge – Second Home for Emma

1. *Sir J D Hooker* by Leonard Huxley. *Life and Letters* based on Materials collected and arranged by Lady Hooker. London 1918.
2. CFL
3. CFL
4. Gwen Raverat: *Period Piece* 1954
5. CFL
6. CFL
7. CFL

Chapter 27: Emma's Last Days – Relatives in the North

All letters from Century of Family Letters

PART II

All correspondence regarding Josiah IV and his family from the Wedgwood Accumulation at Keele University.

CHAPTER 28: The Potteries

CHAPTER 29: Ethel's Diaries

Ethel Wedgwood's 1906 diary, lent personally to the author.

CHAPTER 30: Josiah IV and Ethel – Life's Uncertainties

CHAPTER 31: Political Friendships

CHAPTER 32: Josiah's Family – Helen Wedgwood

1. Rudolph Steiner: Cosmic Memory introduced by Paul Marshall Allen 1981.

CHAPTER 33: A QUESTION OF CUSTODY

1. Personal interview with Joanna Pease 1994

CHAPTER 34: Pacifism and War

CHAPTER 35: The Fight Goes On …

1. Hon. Helen Pease interview with Ms Margaret A Brooks, Imperial War Museum London Sound Archive, 000821/20 Reel 08 1976.
2. Ibid Reel 18 1976

Chapter 36: The End of a Marriage.

1. J.C. Wedgwood: *Memoirs of a Fighting Man* 1940
2. Newspaper ref. *The Daily News* July 1919

Chapter 37: Cambridge – Helen Marries

1. Personal interview with Joanna Pease 1994.

Chapter 38: Children Evacuated – Letters

Richenda, Lady Huxley gave permission for her mother's letters to her to be included.

Chapter 39: The War – Life in Cambridge

1. Helen's letters to Richenda.

Chapter 40: Letters – Baronetcy for Josiah IV

Letters

Chapter 41: Censored Letters – Josiah IV Lord Wedgwood of Barlaston Dies

Censored letters

Chapter 42: Endings and Beginnings

1. Personal interview with Joanna Pease 1994

Chapter 43: The Hon. Julia Wedgwood

Some personal letters loaned by Richenda, Lady Huxley
1. Personal interview with Joanna Pease
2. Anthroposophical Society of Gt Britain

Chapter 44: A Wedgwood is a Wedgwood

SELECTED BIBLIOGRAPHY

Annan, Noel "The Intellectual Aristocracy" in J H Plumb ed. *Studies in Social History Presented to G.M. Trevelyan.* 1995.

Atkins, Sir Hedley J.B. *Down; the home of the Darwins; the story of a house and the people who lived there.* Royal College of Surgeons of England, 1974.

Blackstone, Sir William *Commentaries on the Laws of England.* Joseph Butterworth & Son Ltd, 1819 (29th chapter 'Of Title by Succession, etc.').

Bowlby John *Charles Darwin.* Hutchinson, 1990.

Bryant, Arthur *English Saga (1840–1940).* Collins, 1947.

Burton, Anthony *Josiah Wedgwood.* Andre Deutsch, 1976.

Church, Sir Arthur H *Josiah Wedgwood.* London, 1903.

Coleridge, Samuel Taylor *Unpublished Letters of Samuel Taylor Coleridge Vol 1.* Ed. Earl Leslie Griggs. Constable & Co Ltd, 1932.

Colp, R Jnr *To Be an Invalid. The Illness of Charles Darwin.* University of Chicago Press, 1977.

Cottle, Joseph *Reminiscences of Samuel Taylor Coleridge and Robert Southey.* London, 1847.

Cunningham, Sir Henry Stewart *Lord Bowen.* John Murray, London 1897.

Curle, Richard (ed.) *Robert Browning and Julia Wedgwood; a broken friendship as revealed in their letters.* London, 1937.

Darwin, Charles "Personal Letters".

Darwin, Charles *On the Origin of Species by Means of Natural Selection, or the Preservation of Favoured Races in the Struggle for Life.* 1859.

Darwin, Charles *Life & Letters.* Ed. Francis Darwin. (Plus two volumes of *More Letters* edited by Francis and by A C Seward.)

Darwin, Charles *The autobiography of Charles Darwin 1809–1882.* 1958 ed. Nora Barlow (latest edition with Appendix by his granddaughter), 1958.

Darwin, Erasmus *The Essential Writings of Erasmus Darwin.* Ed. Desmond King-Hele. MacGibbon & Kee, 1968.

Edgeworth, Maria *Chosen Letters.* With an introduction by F V Barry. London, 1931.

Edgeworth, Maria & Richard Edgeworth *Memoirs of Richard Lovell Edgeworth.* 2 vols. London, 1820.

Fabian Society *100 Years of Fabian Socialism 1884–1984.* Ed. Deirdre Terrins & Philip Whitehead. Fabian Society.

Farrar, K E (ed.) *Letters of Josiah Wedgwood.* 3 vols. Women's Printing Society Ltd, London, 1903–6.

Gater, Sharon and David Vincent *The Factory in a Garden.* Keele Life Histories Centre, University of Keele, 1988.

George, Henry *Progress and Poverty.* Hogarth Press, 1881.

George, Henry *The Life of Henry George.* Wm Reeves, 1900.

Hooker, S J *Life & Letters of Sir J D Hooker.* based on materials collected and arranged by Lady Hooker. 2 vols. London, 1918.

Huxley, T H (ed.) *Charles Darwin 1809–1882.* With an introduction by Gavin de Beer. Oxford University Press, 1974.

Jewitt, L *Life of Josiah Wedgwood with Notices of his Works and their Productions, Memoirs of the Wedgwood and Other Families and a history of the early potteries of Staffordshire.* Virtue Brothers & Co, 1865.

Keynes, Margaret E *A House by the River Newnham Grange to Darwin College.* Privately Printed, Cambridge 1984.

Librefure, M *S T Coleridge: A Bondage of Opium.* Gollancz, 1986.

Litchfield, H E (ed.) *Emma Darwin wife of Charles Darwin: A Century of Family Letters 1792–1896.* 2 vols. London, 1915.

Litchfield, R B *Tom Wedgwood, the first photographer: an account of his life, his discovery and his friendship with S T Coleridge.* London, 1903.

Maisky, Ivan *Journey into the Past.* Hutchinson of London, 1962.

Martineau, Harriet *Letters to Fanny Wedgwood* Ed. Elizabeth Sanders Arbuckle. Stanford University Press, 1983.

Meteyard, Eliza *The Life of Josiah Wedgwood from his private correspondence and family papers.* 2 vols. 1865–1866.

Meteyard, Eliza *A Group of English Gentlemen (1795–1815) being records of the Young Wedgwoods and their friends.* London, 1871.

Paine, Tom *The Rights of Man: being an answer to Mr Burke's attack on the French Revolution (Pts I & II).* London, 1791–1792.

Paul, C Kegan *William Godwin, His Friends and Contemporaries.* 2 vols. Henry S King & Co, 1876.

Pearson, H *Dr Darwin.* Dent, London, 1930.

Raverat, Gwen *Period Piece. A Cambridge Childhood.* Faber & Faber, 1954.

Reilly, Robin *Biography of Josiah Wedgwood.* 1992, Macmillan, London.

Rendel *The Personal Papers of Lord Rendel.* Ernest Benn Ltd, London, 1931.

Royle, J & F W Headland *A Manual of Materia Medica and Therapeutics.* 4th edn. John Churchill & Sons, London 1865.

Sandford, Margaret E *Thomas Poole & His Friends.* 2 vols. 1888.

Sayers, Dorothy *Clouds of Witness.* Harcourt Brace & Company,

New York, 1926.

Seward, Anna *The Swan of Lichfield: being a selection from the correspondence of A Seward.* Ed. with short biography and preface by H. Pearson. London, 1936.

Shaw, C *When I was a child, by An Old Potter.* (With introduction R.S. Watson.) (Reprinted with a new introduction by R Haggar.) East Ardsley, Yorks, 1969.

Shaw, Simeon *History of the Staffordshire Potteries.* Hanley, 1829.

Smiles, Samuel *Josiah Wedgwood.* John Murray, 1894.

Smiles, Samuel *Lives of the Engineers.* 5 vols. London, 1904.

Smiles, Samuel *Self Help.* 1812–1904.

Smith, Adam *The Wealth of Nations: An inquiry into the nature and causes of the Wealth of Nations.* 2 vols. London, 1776.

Stein, Joshua B *Our Great Solicitor.* Selensgrove: Susquehanna University Press 1992.

Steiner, Rudolf *A Man Before Others. Rudolf Steiner remembered. A collection of personal memories from the pages of The Golden Blade and other sources.* Rudolf Steiner Press 1993.

Thompson, Francis Michael Longstreth *English Landed Society in the 19th century.* London, 1963.

Vincent-Kemp, Ruth *George Stubbs and the Wedgwood Connection.* R. Vincent-Kemp, London, 1986.

Warrillow, E J D *History of Etruria Staffordshire England 1760–1951.* Etruscan Publications, 1952.

Wedgwood, Henry Allen *People of the Potteries.* Adams & Dart, 1970.

Wedgwood, Barbara & Hensleigh Wedgwood *The Wedgwood Circle 1730–1897 Four Generations of a Family and Their Friends.* Studio Vista, 1980.

Wedgwood, Julia *Personal Life of Josiah Wedgwood The Potter.* Revised and edited by C H Herford. London, 1915.

Wedgwood, J C *Staffordshire Pottery and Its History.* Sampson Low, Marston & Co, 1913.

Wedgwood, J C *A History of the Wedgwood Family.* The St Catherine Press Ltd, 1908.

Wedgwood, Rt Hon. Josiah Clement W & J G E Wedgwood *Wedgwood Pedigree being an account of the complete family reconstructed from contemporary records.* Kendal, 1925.

Wedgwood, Rt Hon. Josiah C *Memoirs of a Fighting Life.* Hutchinson & Co. Ltd, London and Melbourne 1940.

Wedgwood, C V *The Last of the Radicals Josiah Wedgwood M.P.* Jonathan Cape, Thirty Bedford Square, London, 1951.

Wetherell, D and C Carr-Gregg *Camilla Wedgwood A Life 1901–1955.* New South Wales University Press, NSW Australia, 1990.

Wollstonecraft, Mary *A Vindication of the Rights of Women.* Ed. C H Poston. New York, 1975.

INDEX